CONCEIVING AGENCY

CONCEIVING AGENCY

Reproductive Authority among Haredi Women

—ιιι—

MICHAL S. RAUCHER

INDIANA UNIVERSITY PRESS

This book is a publication of

Indiana University Press
Office of Scholarly Publishing
Herman B Wells Library 350
1320 East 10th Street
Bloomington, Indiana 47405 USA

iupress.indiana.edu

Manufactured in the United States of America

Cataloging information is available from the Library of Congress.
ISBN 978-0-253-05001-4 (hardback)
ISBN 978-0-253-05002-1 (paperback)
ISBN 978-0-253-05003-8 (ebook)

1 2 3 4 5   25 24 23 22 21 20

Pregnant existence entails, finally, a unique temporality of process and growth in which the woman can experience herself as split between past and future.

IRIS YOUNG

To my parents, Gail and Steve
To my spouse, Yoni
To my children, Naftali, Nessa, and Hadas
You are each my past, my present, and my future.

CONTENTS

ACKNOWLEDGMENTS

IT IS SAID THAT WRITING a book is a solitary activity, and while I have spent many hours alone in a room with my computer, I owe a great deal of gratitude to all the people who made that possible. At the most challenging moments, it has meant everything to know that on the other side of that door were many people who wanted me to succeed and who would help me finish this book.

An ethnography requires, first and foremost, people who are willing to be vulnerable with a researcher. I am fortunate to have learned from many individuals over two years in Jerusalem. I am thankful for the Haredi women who courageously shared intimate details about their lives with me. They took time out of their busy schedules to welcome me into their homes and share their innermost thoughts and experiences. I feel grateful that they trusted me to share their stories. I hope that I have done so with integrity and respect. I also appreciate the doctors, nurses, doulas, and teachers who I interviewed for this book and who allowed me to shadow them at work. The staff at the EFRAT organization allowed me to observe their internal operations. Although I entered all of their lives for only a short period of time, these research participants and interlocutors have had a lasting impression on me as I have become a scholar and a mother.

I have been researching and writing this book for over ten years, but the intellectual journey that began this book can be traced back to my earliest educational experiences. I owe a debt of gratitude to all of my teachers—both formal and informal—who, over the years, instilled in me a love of learning and a desire to keep digging until I could answer my questions. They also modeled for me a life of scholarship and teaching that I continually try to emulate. Notably, Paul Wolpe and Vardit Ravitsky, who were at the University of Pennsylvania when I was a master's student, inspired me to take a social sciences approach to bioethics and to focus my studies on Israel. Paul introduced me to Laurie Zoloth, who was my primary graduate advisor and continues to be a mentor, colleague, and friend as well as a brilliant scholar whose work reminds me of my commitments to the vulnerable Other. Laurie saw something in me before I did, and she has helped me become the kind of thinker and teacher I am today.

In addition to Laurie, many professors and colleagues from Northwestern University helped me develop this project in its early stages. Cristina Traina read my work carefully and asked me questions that pushed me to interrogate my own assumptions. It is because of Cristie that I learned about Christian ethics and entered into conversation with many inspiring colleagues in that field. Helen Schwartzman taught me how to be an ethnographer and to think like an anthropologist. She helped me figure out where my interests fit in with anthropological scholarship and pushed me to engage with larger theoretical analysis. I am so fortunate to have benefited from the mentorship of three brilliant female advisors who modeled successful professional and family lives. Barry Wimpfheimer and Robert Orsi also provided intellectual and professional support over the years.

Colleagues from Northwestern who have become trusted friends have provided me with immense encouragement and critical advice. I especially want to mention Alyssa Henning, my bioethics buddy, who has shared many hotel rooms and meals with me when we were the only students at the Society of Jewish Ethics conferences. We are often mistaken for each other, and I certainly do not mind. She is an insightful thinker who challenges me to clarify my arguments and defend them against my staunchest critics. Amanda Baugh, Tina Howe, and Kate Dugan have provided invaluable support as my dissertation developed into this book, commiserating when necessary and pushing me to improve. Our writing group, the "Brilliant Lady Scholars," is one of my favorite things about writing. They have a keen ability to help me figure out what I am saying and then make it better. Thank you all for your friendship.

Colleagues at many institutions turned me from graduate student to professor. At the Jewish Theological Seminary, Shuly Schwartz gave me my first academic job and taught me how to be a professional academic. She protected my time to write, encouraged me, and welcomed a new schedule when I had a baby. Burt Visotzky, Stephen Garfinkel, and Alan Cooper appreciated my somewhat alternative approach to studying Jews and Judaism and demonstrated confidence in me. Julia Andleman and Alisa Braun taught me how to translate my scholarship for a broader audience. I hope that the work within these pages will be read and understood by nonspecialists as well, and if I have done the job correctly, then it is because of them. At the University of Cincinnati, the faculty in the Department of Judaic Studies offered encouragement, support, and friendship. Thank you for creating an academic home for me. I appreciate the mentorship of Erynn Masi De Cassanova, Littisha Bates, and Ethan Katz, and colleagues in the Women's, Gender, and Sexuality Studies Department, in particular Deb Meem. I especially want to acknowledge the feminist writing group that read drafts of these chapters: Ashley Currier, Michelle McGowan, Carolette Norwood, Valerie Weinstein, Gergana Ivanova, and Sunnie Rucker-Chang. This group provided me with critical reading and robust discussions about my work. Currently, at Rutgers University, I am grateful for my colleagues in the Jewish Studies Department, who have supported me as I ushered this project to completion.

Many individuals and institutions made my research possible. Jessica Fain was a wonderful research assistant in Israel, and the archivists at the Knesset Archives were supportive and helpful. Librarians at many academic institutions have helped me find sources, held books for me, and offered an encouraging smile when I was in over my head. Many individuals found citations or sent me news articles over the years. Although I cannot name all of them here, I am appreciative of their help.

I received generous funding for this project as well. The Religious Studies Department at Northwestern supported me for the first five years of my PhD and helped me attend conferences all over North America. A Fulbright Fellowship supported my first year of research in Israel, and the Wenner Gren Foundation financed my second year of research. The Memorial Foundation for Jewish Culture also contributed to my research funds. The Center for Jewish Studies at Northwestern provided funding for my last year of dissertation writing with a Crown Family Fellowship. Finally, the Charles Phelps Taft Research Fellowship at the University of Cincinnati gave me the gift of time to work on this book. Thank you to my colleagues at Taft, especially Adrian Parr, for that opportunity. All of these institutions have truly invested in my success, and for that, I am thankful.

I have also benefited from a wider intellectual community not tethered to any one academic institution, one whose members have helped me develop the ideas contained within this book. A few individuals have read this manuscript in its entirety and offered critical advice in these last stages. Thanks to Liz Bucar, Mara Benjamin, Ayala Fader, and Cristie Traina. Liz raised important questions about audience and focus, helping me amplify my contribution to scholarship on women in religion. Mara believes in this work's contribution to the field of Jewish ethics, and she helped me articulate that. Ayala offered a close reading with the intention of making sure this book clearly reflects the current debates and conversations in the anthropology of Judaism. Her mentorship, as well as that of Orit Avishai and other members of the New York Working Group on Jewish Orthodoxies, has provided me with encouragement during the last year of writing. Alison Joseph, Lynn Davidman, Rebecca Steinfeld, Aana Vigen, Rebecca Levi, and Emily Cook read chapters in various stages and offered critical comments. Kate Ott and Toddie Peters have been interested in my work and invited me to be their intellectual colleague in so many different venues. They are models of generosity in academe, and their commitment to religious ethics in all its diversity and challenges is an inspiration. Kate and Toddie introduced me to the nonprofit organization Feminist Studies in Religion, which is very much an academic home for me. I presented versions of this work at many conferences, and colleagues in the audience offered critical feedback. I am thankful for attendees at the American Academy of Religion, the Association for Jewish Studies, the Societies of Jewish, Christian, and Muslim Ethics, and the American Society for Bioethics and Humanities for their guidance. Finally, my academic community extends to Facebook, where my JAMmies have offered encouragement, laughs, and critical help with book titles. This broad intellectual community has improved my work in many ways.

Thank you to everyone at Indiana University Press who helped convert this manuscript into a book. I am thankful for the anonymous readers and my editors, Dee Mortensen and Ashante Thomas. Dee's partnership has ensured that this book is in the best shape possible and will be read by many. Leigh McLennon and the copyeditor helped finish this book. Leigh answered my questions quickly and thoroughly. Although she is not affiliated with the press, Ilse Lazaroms organized my notes and citations at a critical time in production. Any errors that remain in this book are entirely my own.

My friendships over the years have sustained me as this project developed, and they deserve recognition. Rachel Saks (Einhorn), Aimee Brookhart, and Elly Cohen have known me for so long and have accepted me for who I am without any judgment. Rachel has fed my body and soul in ways that have kept me afloat through this journey. Elly Cohen is my thought partner and a great friend. I am thrilled to have her as a colleague as well. Dahlia Kronish just *gets* me and asks essential questions about my work and my life. Alison Joseph and Jennie Grubs are trusted friends and colleagues.

I have lived in many cities while working on this book, and I am thankful for the Jewish communities that supported me in Chicago, Jerusalem, Riverdale, Cincinnati, and Teaneck. I am thankful for friends from Chicago like Nicole and Ken Cox, Leah Kahn, Darrell Cohn, Ravit Greenberg, Gabe Axler, Jess and Dov Robinson, and, of course, our landlords, Denise and Stuart Sprague. Nicole and Leah continue to be good friends who have inspired my intellectual journey and my writing. In Israel, Carmit Rokah and Omri Caspi opened up their lives for the new Americans on the block. Our late-night dog walks were restorative and enjoyable. Roee Rahamim and his family took us in for holidays and welcomed us into his family. I shared many late nights and delicious meals with Hillary Menkowitz, Jonathan Madoff, Arie Hasit, Sarah Cyrtyn, Gabi Mitchell, Elana Kieffer, Ari Lucas, Ari Saks, and Rachel Einhorn while we were in Israel; Kara Robarts, Davina Bookbinder, Dahlia Kronish, and Josh Maudlin in Riverdale; and Shena and Brian Jaffee, Ari and Jenn Finkelstein, Matt Kraus and Sissy Coran, Tamar and Elliot Smith, Oren and Reena Pollak, Cathy Bowers and Hillel Gray, and Arna Poupko and Bobby Fisher in Cincinnati. For the last two years, we have been blessed with a large community of friends and colleagues in Teaneck who will be eager to read this book and offer me important critique. I am grateful for all of their encouragement, and I know that they are excited to see this project come to completion.

On a personal level, I want to acknowledge the village that spans multiple states, continents, and time zones, often operating behind the scenes. My spouse, Yoni Shear, has offered daily support, in things great and small, from such a deep, genuine, and honest place. He makes it possible for me to dream and to realize those dreams. Yoni has always believed in me and helps me relax enough so that I can think and write clearly. Yoni, thank you for all the cups of coffee, the Swedish fish, and the many ways you sustain me. I love you. To say that my parents are supportive is an understatement. Gail and Steve Raucher take every opportunity to celebrate my accomplishments. They have also provided shelter and material support at critical times. My mom is always interested in my research and asks me important questions about my findings. She knows just the kind of encouragement I need at any given moment and is happy to help. My dad was my first editor, and he is the closest I will ever come to having an academic agent, sharing my work with friends and colleagues. He has also helped me navigate the academic world. They have both gladly taken care of my children and sent me off to write. One of the great things about marrying Yoni was gaining his parents. Susie and Kenny Shear have been staunch supporters in many ways. I never had to ask twice for Susie to come to our house to care for the kids, cook, clean, or sew. I know this book will hold a prominent place on Kenny's overflowing bookshelves. My siblings, Ari Raucher, Carly Sorscher, Noam Raucher, Aviva and Matthugh Bennett, and Adena and Andrew Sternthal, have reminded me—some since I was born—never to take myself or my work too seriously. They add lightness to my life and bring me back down to earth when I need it. I am grateful for their children, my nieces and nephews, who make me laugh and force me to step away from my work for quality family time. Extended family members have always been available with love and laughter over the years. Thank you to Aunt Adele and Uncle Don Zwerling and Cousin Marty for your encouragement. A few loved ones did not live to see this project to completion, but I know they would be kvelling. I wish I could share this moment with my grandparents Anna and Julius Simon and Florence Raucher. I want to also thank all the teachers and babysitters who have embraced and protected my children, allowing me to write while knowing that my kids were being loved and kept safe. Special thanks go to Inna Furman and Jessie Paley, who came into my home to take care of my babies. I wrote a great deal of this book on my living room couch, or in my home office, with a puppy sleeping at my feet. Shoko kept me company and got me outside occasionally, and for that, I am grateful.

Last and certainly not least, I owe a huge debt of gratitude to my children. If someone ever makes a critical edition of this book, they will note the layers that developed with each of my pregnancies and births. My children taught me more about reproductive agency than anyone. I wrote so much of this with a baby curled up on my chest or snuggled into my side. Thank you for being good sleepers and greeting me—sometimes very early in the morning—as I wrote during the #5amchallenge. Naftali, Nessa, and Hadas, you remind me on a daily basis why I write. Thank you for the joy and fun you have brought to my life, for the deep love I am privileged to feel for you, and for the perspective you brought when things got rough. You are growing up with an *eema* who schleps her computer to birthday parties and schleps you on research trips. I hope you know that while my work is always on my mind, you three are always in my heart.

CONCEIVING AGENCY

INTRODUCTION

A FEW MONTHS AFTER I settled in Jerusalem, I received an email from a woman named Dina. Dina had heard about my research from a friend of hers. At that time, I was only planning to interview women with three or fewer children because I wrongfully assumed that only these women would not yet be weary of or cynical about the experience of pregnancy. Dina was pregnant with her fifth child and offended at my assumption. She wrote me an email saying, "I assume that you were *never* pregnant in your life because believe me it doesn't matter what number pregnancy I am in, pregnancy becomes *the only* focus of my life" (emphasis in the original). She continued, "My entire life revolves around my pregnancy and impending birth and after. . . . I think it is a mistake to say you will only interview women who have less than three children. We who have had more pregnancies may be even more beneficial to you because we come with more experience and knowledge." Dina apologized for her rudeness and said I should call her to find a time when we can meet.

I was nervous about calling Dina, but she was happy to hear from me and invited me to her apartment the following week. Dina is a petite Haredi (ultra-Orthodox) woman whose husband studies in a yeshiva in Jerusalem. She has not worked outside the home in a few years because she has had four children in six years. The youngest, about eighteen months, was cranky when I showed up at Dina's apartment on a Tuesday morning. Dina nursed him for most of our interview, which she said helped with the nausea. Although she was only about six weeks into her fifth pregnancy and not sharing the news with most people, she told me and allowed me into her life for the next year.

As Dina told me about her pregnancies and labors, I realized she was right about women with more children having more experience and, therefore, more knowledge. Her pregnancies start with a fair amount of nausea and vomiting until the fifteenth week. Aside from her first pregnancy, Dina has never even needed a pregnancy test because she knows that she is pregnant when the nausea starts. If she is not nauseous one day, she tells her husband to pray until the nausea returns. That embodied experience is how she knows she is pregnant before any ultrasound or blood test confirms it. Dina's multiple pregnancy experiences also help her predict whether she is carrying a male or female fetus. With her second pregnancy, she knew she was having a girl, partially because it felt so different from the first (a boy) and also because she was so "emotional." Dina explained, "If something happened, then my stomach hurt. She's a sensitive child, and my stomach would clench, and I could feel that she was tense." The experience of multiple pregnancies gave Dina more knowledge about pregnancy itself as well as about the fetuses inside her.

As she became more of a pregnancy expert, Dina also came to challenge the doctors and rabbis surrounding her. Dina told me about each pregnancy chronologically. She told me that for each pregnancy, the doctors were concerned about fetal growth. They wanted her to come in for multiple scans, get more blood tests, track her nutrition, and have early C-sections. She passively put them off each time, switching doctors or just telling them not to worry because she and her husband are both rather small people. When she was pregnant for the fourth time, however, Dina could no longer remain polite. During an ultrasound scan in the twenty-fourth week, the technician made a mistake and wrote down the wrong date of conception, making it seem like she was two weeks further along than she really was. Dina had not gone in for an earlier ultrasound that would have dated the pregnancy accurately because she knew when she got pregnant. Dina tried to tell her doctor at each appointment, but he ignored her corrections. By the time she reached the ultrasound in the thirty-sixth week, Dina's doctor was very nervous about what he thought was a fetus that had stopped growing. He wanted to send her for more testing and induce labor. At this point, Dina got upset. She yelled at the doctor, "This is ridiculous. You obviously never listen to me. You never care what I say!" Dina stormed out of his office and did not return to the hospital until she was in labor at forty weeks. The baby was small but healthy when he was born. By her fourth pregnancy, Dina had gained sufficient embodied knowledge and reproductive authority to challenge the medical establishment.

Additionally, Dina, a devout Haredi woman who grew up Haredi, married a Haredi man, and is committed to the Haredi life, does not think her Haredi rabbi has anything to teach her about what is permissible or forbidden during pregnancy. This is striking because rabbinic oversight has expanded in the last few decades as rabbis have increased their involvement in matters that were previously considered beyond their purview. Haredi rabbis have come to provide oversight in the medical field in particular, which means that Haredi men and women often do not pursue medical treatment without the involvement of their rabbis.[1] During our conversations, however, Dina struggled to think of a question she might ask her rabbi. Although she ultimately said that she would ask her rabbi about getting an abortion after receiving a poor fetal diagnosis, a phenomenon I discuss in chapter 5, Dina introduced me to the entanglement she sees between doctors and rabbis. She told me, "Rabbis will just say, 'Do whatever the doctor wants,' so it's important to find a good doctor." She also told me of friends who asked multiple rabbis about aborting a fetus until they got the answer they wanted. Her frustrations with doctors were tied to what she saw as the limitations of the rabbis. Rabbis have never been pregnant, and just as Dina assumed I knew nothing because I had never been pregnant, she accused rabbis of the same ignorance.

This book analyzes the ways Haredi Jewish women like Dina make ethical decisions about their reproductive lives while subverting their normative religious tradition and the leaders who interpret it. Although they are faced with patriarchal religious and medical authorities, Haredi women find space for—and insist on—their autonomy from these authorities when they make decisions regarding the use of contraceptives, prenatal testing, fetal ultrasounds, and other reproductive practices. This autonomy, however, should not be read as freedom from religious life or the actions of an individual without any constraints. Instead, when Haredi women assert that they are in a better position to make reproductive decisions, they draw on their embodied experiences of pregnancy, cultural norms of reproduction, and theological beliefs in their relationship to divine activity during reproduction. Viewed in this way, Haredi women express agency as a result of their participation in the gendered norms of Haredi Judaism.

PREGNANCY IS "WHAT A JEWISH WOMAN DOES"

The matrix of control surrounding a Haredi woman's prenatal care might give one the impression that Haredi women are restricted in their decision-making capacity and are limited in their authority over pregnancy. This was not what I found during my research with Haredi women, however. They recognize this context and yet simultaneously talk about pregnancy as *their* space. When they are pregnant, they make decisions *without* their rabbis, husbands, or doctors, a fact that contradicted all my expectations. Thus, as my research progressed,

I embarked on my interviews and observations with the following questions: What knowledge system do women draw on to make decisions during pregnancy? Within the medical and rabbinic matrix of control, how do Haredi women exercise agency? What is a Haredi woman's reproductive ethic if it is created in contrast to the normative rabbinic ethic? And finally, if her reproductive ethic is not informed by Jewish sources, what does inform a Haredi woman's ethic of reproduction?

I found that the embodied experience of pregnancy shapes a woman's ability to make decisions without male authorities and to develop a sense of authority over pregnancy-related decisions. Haredi Jews understand pregnancy to be, as one of my informants described, "what a Jewish woman does." Put another way, pregnancy is a "way of life" for Haredi women.[2] These statements point to the ownership and authority that Haredi women express while pregnant. They also indicate that Haredi women construct their identities through pregnancy because this is a significant experience that distinguishes them from Haredi men.[3] In fact, it is women's embodied experiences like pregnancy and menstruation that are understood within the Haredi authority structure to keep women from attaining traditional rabbinic authority. And yet, because women believe pregnancy and birth to be ordained by God and entrusted to them as women, divine authority empowers their embodied authority. This sense of authority gives Haredi women the ability to override the influence of the rabbis. This is especially contradictory given the fact that Haredi life is predicated on the interpretation of God's laws by rabbis, but Haredi women see rabbis (all male) as those who have never and will never experience divine authority granted through pregnancy, a fact that leaves men at a disadvantage when making reproductive decisions. By drawing on her bodily experience of pregnancy and the cultural norms that dictate her role as biological reproducer, a Haredi woman can exert authority over her reproductive life. Throughout this book I argue that, paradoxically, the sources of a Haredi woman's oppression are also the sources of her agency.

Furthermore, in this book I show that the way Haredi women make decisions about reproduction reflects a religious ethic distinct from the way Jewish bioethics frames its discourse. This gap between normative religious ethics and the strategies of religious participants necessitates a rethinking of the discourse of religious ethics. Scholarly discussions of ethics should account for the embodied, cultural, religious, and contextual experiences of individuals. I maintain that a Haredi woman's agency over reproductive decisions is her reproductive ethic. Agency—built on bodily experience, bolstered by cultural and theological norms, and informed by socioeconomic context—shapes

Haredi women's reproductive autonomy. This is in contrast to those who see religious ethics as coming solely from sacred texts or rabbinic interpretations and legal applications. My findings speak to the relevance of normative religious and ethical doctrine in the lives of moral agents and the capacity of individuals to respond as moral agents to their situations. Ethics—and religious ethics in particular—must be viewed from the perspectives of embodied moral agents so that ethical discourse can better reflect the lived realities of ethics.

THEORETICAL CONTRIBUTIONS

This book grew from a set of questions about women, reproduction, and religious ethics. I wanted to understand how Haredi women make reproductive decisions—when they decide to use birth control, have an abortion, receive prenatal testing, or view the fetus on an ultrasound. Knowing that the norms of Haredi Judaism require the involvement of rabbinic authorities in most life decisions, I wanted to know if this applies to pregnant women as well and, if not, how Haredi women make these decisions. Cultural norms often imprint themselves on reproductive processes, and when they do not, the discord is noteworthy. Although there has been increased attention to reproduction in Israel and the ways that religion influences state and medical authorities, we have heard very little from religious individuals struggling to resolve tensions and make decisions in this complex system.[4] This book enters the conversation to fill this gap in scholarship and, more importantly, to turn our attention to the women who navigate this system as they manage their reproductive lives.

Israel, Reproduction, and Religion

For Haredi women, pregnancy is constant and normative.[5] Haredi women have the highest fertility rate in Israel, between 5 and 8 children per family since the 1990s. In 2011, the Israeli Central Bureau of Statistics released figures that revealed that the birth rate among Haredi women in 2005 was 7.5, while in 2010 the birth rate was 6.5.[6] Since completing this research, the Israeli Haredi fertility rate has continued to drop slowly, to below 6.[7] Despite this decrease, the fertility rate of Haredi women is still significantly higher than their secular and non-Haredi peers.[8] Furthermore, their engagement with the technocratic reproductive medical system in Israel presents the greatest tensions and conflicts due to their religious commitments in enclave communities.[9] Despite the strong norms and detailed religious laws governing the ultra-Orthodox population in Israel, Haredi women's reproductive experiences provide them with opportunities to eschew rabbinic guidance and medical instruction in favor of a reproductive ethic guided by their embodied experiences and theological commitments.

Reproduction in Israel has garnered sustained attention from political scientists, historians, sociologists, demographers, and anthropologists due to the high birth rates and a strong pronatalism linked to demographic conflict in the country. Israel's birth rate across religious and ethnic identities is higher than that of the rest of the developed world. In Israel the birth rate is about 2.9 children per family, whereas in the United States and other Westernized, developed, and democratic countries, the birth rate is around 1.2; it is even lower in certain European countries. This was not always the case, though. Lilach Rosenberg-Friedman demonstrates that Jewish birth rates in Palestine under British rule steadily declined among most ethnic groups. Because abortion was the contraceptive method most women used, Rosenberg-Friedman shows how Zionist efforts to increase the Jewish birth rate manifested in opposition to abortion.[10] Others, however, find support for childbearing in medical manuals for Jewish women from Palestine in the 1920s;[11] in David Ben Gurion's cash prize to every woman who gave birth to her tenth child;[12] in the 1949 Defense Service Law;[13] or in maternity grants from the National Insurance Law—tax-free monthly grants for each child under the age of fourteen in a family with four or more children.[14] The fact that Israel has the highest per capita rate of infertility therapy in the world serves as more proof of Israel's pronatalism.[15] Furthermore, the National Health Insurance Law includes within the basic basket of health services unlimited fertility treatments for a couple or an individual woman up to the birth of two live children.[16]

Scholars claim that the Israeli government had two primary reasons for pronatalist policies, which, all agree, were directed specifically at increasing the birth rate of Israeli Jews, as opposed to the minority populations in Israel.[17] One body of scholarship focuses on the Zionist argument that because the Jewish people in Israel are in a demographic war with the Arab population, increasing the Jewish birth rate would ensure the survival of Israel as a Jewish state.[18] Jacqueline Portugese writes that the need to "maintain a Jewish majority vis-à-vis the Arab Palestinians, and the desire to replenish the Jewish people following the destruction of the Holocaust" originated from Zionist concerns.[19] Those who criticize these policies for encouraging Jewish women to reproduce while restricting the reproductive freedom of Muslim women also maintain that Zionism is driving pronatalism in Israel.[20]

Others argue that Jewish religious values contributed to the pronatalist policies, but these claims often lack deep engagement with either Jewish texts or Jewish individuals. As Carmel Shalev and Sigal Goldin argue that

infertility is socially constructed as a disease, they explain, "In Jewish tradition, procreation is seen as a positive duty (mitzvah) and a sign of prosperity,
while barrenness is viewed as a curse. The biblical commandment to 'be fruitful
and multiply' (Gen 1:28), the mythological suffering of the barren woman, and
theological interpretive discourses . . . are all part of a Jewish cultural code of
in/fertility. This code is part of the contextual ground upon which 'barrenness'
is made into a concrete and meaningful experience for many people in the Jewish state."[21] Shalev and Goldin do not show how these textual sources inform
the public, nor do they draw on data to suggest that the Jewish tradition is
driving the high use of assisted reproductive technologies. Similarly, Portugese
claims that Jewish religious ideas about the importance of childbearing and *halakhic* (Jewish legal) attitudes toward birth control and abortion shaped Israel's
fertility policies. Portugese argues, "Halachic interpretations of abortion and
contraception are significant to the study of Israeli fertility policy because of
Orthodoxy's influence, via infiltration of the state and manipulation of the
parliamentary process, on the decision-making process in Israel."[22] Portugese
and others do not support this claim with a close reading of the Jewish legal
positions or demonstrate how they influenced Israeli law or policies. Instead,
these scholars rely on generic claims about Judaism's support of reproduction.
In fact, as I have shown elsewhere, we can find just as much support for contraception in Jewish sources.[23]

To be sure, ethnographies of assisted reproductive technologies (ARTs)
from around the world have shown that religious beliefs or legal texts are
often implicated in fertility, either in religious understandings for the causes
of infertility or religious oversight for its treatment.[24] A notable exception to
these incomplete references to religious influences in Israel is Susan Martha
Kahn's classic work *Reproducing Jews*. Israel has embraced various reproductive
technologies through the proliferation of these technologies and the National
Health Insurance coverage of fertility treatments.[25] Kahn considers how the
prominence of reproductive technologies encouraged rabbis to create religious
laws that would accommodate their use.[26] As rabbis interact with medical professionals to sanctify the spread of reproductive technologies, sometimes this
overlap leads to conflict.[27] Some rabbis advocate for the use of medical treatments to rectify a problem created by adherence to Jewish law, while doctors
claim that it would be much easier and safer to change Jewish law.[28]

The cooperation and conflict between religion and medicine is often seen
against the backdrop of the technocratic process of reproduction in Israel. In
her comparative study of pregnancy in Israel and Japan, Tsipy Ivry claims this
technocratic model is prominent throughout Israeli medical care and especially

through geneticism.[29] Ivry defines *geneticism* as "a fatalistic theory that explains fetal health through genes and chromosomes that are independent of the pregnant woman's willpower."[30] Ivry concludes that biomedicine still reigns supreme as the most authoritative source of information for Israeli women. Geneticism and a reproductive process laden with technological intervention can also facilitate women subverting Israeli norms.[31] Elly Teman's investigation of surrogacy offers an example of women manipulating cultural norms of motherhood so that their act of surrogacy is not construed as unnatural.[32] Israeli surrogates, Teman found, distinguish the "strong emotional attachment they felt for their own children prenatally to their emotional distance from the surrogate child."[33] They draw on the use of technology in the surrogate pregnancy to "undo the natural tendencies" that would otherwise occur with a pregnancy.[34]

This focus in anthropological studies of reproduction in Israel mirrors the evolution of anthropological research about reproduction globally. Early analyses of reproduction in the United States consisted of feminist, anti-technology arguments.[35] As reproductive technologies such as in vitro fertilization, preimplantation genetic diagnosis, and amniocentesis became more routine, anthropologists broadened the scope of investigation and soon thereafter advanced arguments about the individual and cultural interaction with these technologies.[36] In particular, scholars demonstrated that religious, political, and national values affect the individual's use of ARTs.[37] Others, however, focused on the conflicts that arise between cultural values and a woman's embodied knowledge, an area of research that has strongly influenced the argument in this book.[38] These studies and others like them highlight, first, the potential for conflict between a woman's embodied knowledge and the authority of medical information and, second, the fact that women do not reject their embodied experience in the face of medical authorities.[39] As my ethnographic study reveals, drawing on one's embodied knowledge does not necessarily include the rejection of medicine, but it can result in a different prioritization of information. This study demonstrates how embodied knowledge takes precedence over medical and cultural authorities without erasing their influence.

This book enters the conversation to explore precisely how religious and medical influences shape reproductive decisions on the individual and communal levels. Even Kahn admits that her study lacks an investigation into the way men and women use reproductive technologies, emphasizing instead Israeli policies toward reproductive technologies and the rabbinic oversight of the clinics. Robert Tappan, for example, argues that Islamic bioethics is more than just following fatwas: "Instead, clinicians and bioethics consultation groups consider a range of justificatory sources, including civil laws, fatwas, reason, and bioethical cases from the West."[40] Similarly, the Haredi women who are the subject of this book are influenced by religious, financial, and embodied experiences that shape their reproductive decisions.

Additionally, I join Ivry in turning scholarly attention toward pregnancy as a distinct and analytically important state of the reproductive experience. Opposing scholarship on reproduction that focuses on the beginning and end of the reproductive process (use of ARTs to get pregnant or the medicalization of birth), Ivry argues, "Pregnancy is first and foremost a process of physical and social change and, as such, marked with fundamental uncertainties within any system of cultural categories. For this and other reasons, experiences of pregnancy might be very far removed from what the noneventual language that designates them as 'expecting' suggests."[41] In order to create an anthropology of pregnancy as a subset of the anthropology of reproduction, this book explores how pregnancy is not just a means to an end but instead is a significant event in women's lives.

Finally, critics of the pronatalist state adopt a classical Western feminist response to these policies, emphasizing women's lack of agency in reproduction. For example, Nitza Berkovitch argues that encouraging Jewish women to reproduce solidifies their role as wife-mother.[42] Similarly, Meira Weiss demonstrates that the Zionist ideals of masculinity, physical strength, and procreation have led to the definition of women by "traditional gender roles" that suggest they should procreate "for the glory of the state of Israel."[43] Although the maternal role has national significance, similar to that of serving in the armed forces, Susan Sered claims that in practice women hold great responsibility for their reproductive capability without real authority.[44] These feminist critiques maintain that Israel's pronatalist policies reduce women to their reproductive capacity and neglect to appreciate women as agents in their own right. This book, however, demonstrates that agency and authority can also be found through conformity to reproductive norms.

Reproductive Agency

Throughout this book, I develop the concept that I call reproductive agency. Reproductive agency refers to the ability to make decisions about the process of reproduction—contraception, abortion, prenatal testing, ultrasounds, and birth. In other words, reproductive agency is how I describe the authority that Haredi women have over reproductive decisions. It is important to note that when I refer to women's authority, I am not referring to women as religious

leaders, either formally or informally.[45] The Haredi women whose lives have
informed this book have no intention of being religious leaders, nor do they
serve as reproductive authorities for other Haredi women. Women's authority
means that they are not turning to their rabbis, husbands, or doctors for help
when making reproduction-related decisions. This is significant because turning to rabbis, husbands, and doctors is otherwise the norm for Haredi women.
While many other scholars depict the Haredi world as revolving around book
learning and attentiveness to rabbinic instruction, these analyses have overlooked Haredi women's distinct participation in Haredi life. Haredi women
primarily are seen as those who support their husbands' continued yeshiva
learning.[46] My analysis demonstrates that Haredi women lead religious lives
distinct from their husbands' and that their reproductive experiences shape
their theologies and their participation in the hierarchical structures of Haredi
Judaism. Women express their reproductive agency through their reproductive
authority.

Although it might seem that rejecting the hierarchical and patriarchal authority structure within Haredi Judaism is the essence of rejecting Haredi norms, a
woman's reproductive agency is not countercultural. Instead, her agency is predicated on the theological and cultural assertion that reproduction is a woman's
duty within the Haredi world. These women understand pregnancy to be essential for Haredi society and embedded in theological understandings of a woman's
role. As a result, Haredi women see themselves as imbued with the responsibility
to enact these values, and their agency is, therefore, rooted in Haredi cultural
norms and theological beliefs. They exert agency through their participation in
religious traditions, not through their rejection of religious norms. While these
cultural norms and theological beliefs inform reproductive agency, a woman's
reproductive agency also challenges other religious norms—namely, the expectation that she defer to her rabbi with all her reproductive decisions. In this way,
when a woman expresses reproductive agency, she is both conforming to and
subverting religious norms. However, although she is subverting norms about
rabbinic authority, she does so with the understanding that her religious tradition makes it possible for her to act independently. Paradoxically, women capital-
ize on their bodies—the sites of their gendered limitations in Haredi society—as
they draw on their bodies' ability to participate in the divine act of creation. As
they use pregnancy as a source of agency, Haredi women are simultaneously
following religious norms and subverting those norms.

There are a few boundaries built into the concept of reproductive agency.
Because women's embodied experiences of pregnancy are so central in their
development of reproductive agency, women relied on to their ability to

make decisions only after two or three successful pregnancies. Furthermore, reproductive agency is tied to a woman's capacity to carry a pregnancy, so after menopause, this agency is irrelevant. Last, reproductive agency does not allow a woman to have authority over every area of her life but, rather, only those decisions related to reproduction. Therefore, reproductive agency extends to questions of contraception between pregnancies, and it accounts for women making decisions about ultrasounds or where to give birth; however, it does not allow a woman to make decisions about her husband's business, for example. For those questions, she still feels obligated to turn to her rabbi.

It is important to note that my interlocutors would not describe their actions as demonstrating "agency" or having "autonomy." Although the Haredi women I spoke to discussed their knowledge (*yedah*) about pregnancy, their ability (*yecholet*) to make reproductive decisions, and their authority (*samchut*) over such decisions, they did not use the term *agency* or refer to themselves as autonomous. There are likely two reasons for this: One is that these terms have a popular understanding of acting independently, with freedom, outside the bounds of religious guidelines, but Haredi women do not see their actions as being in conflict with religious norms and have no desire to institute religious change.[47] Haredi women see themselves as uninteresting followers of a religious tradition, which leaves space for them to act in such a way that they end up challenging Haredi Judaism's authority structure. The other reason they would not use this term is that *agency*, in particular, is a term associated with Western feminism, which they reject in much the same way that Elizabeth Bucar's interlocutors rejected feminism. In her article "Dianomy: Understanding Religious Women's Moral Agency as Creative Conformity," Bucar shares an anecdote from her fieldwork with female politicians in Iran. Shahla Habibi, special adviser on women's affairs to former Iranian president Hashimi Rafsanjani, balks when Bucar refers to her as an "Islamic feminist." In Bucar's description, Habibi "slams her hands down on her desk cutting me off mid-sentence and declaims in an annoyed tone: 'I am not a feminist. Do not call me a feminist. I do not believe in your feminism.'"[48] As a feminist ethnographer, I intend to prioritize the voices of my interlocutors and to use their interpretive strategies to describe their actions. At the same time, I am engaged in a contemporary conversation among scholars who resist simplistic, critical understandings of women in conservative religious traditions.[49] Therefore, despite the fact that my interlocutors would not use the terms *agency* or *autonomy*, I have found these to be helpful concepts in describing the tensions, negotiations, actions, and understandings of the Haredi women who shared their reproductive narratives with me.

Researchers have historically rejected the possibility that women in conservative or fundamentalist religions exercised any agency in their participation in these religious traditions. Within the last twenty years, however, scholars have explored many different ways of understanding women's actions in conservative religious traditions, rejecting what Orit Avishai, Lynne Gerber, and Jennifer Randles refer to as "feminist orthodoxy."[50] My use of the term *agency* to describe Haredi women draws on recent scholarship that theorizes women's agency within the seeming contradiction of the patriarchal religious context that subordinates it. In *Politics of Piety*, Saba Mahmood demonstrates how women in fundamentalist religious traditions can simultaneously adhere to patriarchal norms and exercise agency. For many, this is counterintuitive because they understand these norms to be externally imposed constraints on the individual. Learning from Judith Butler, however, Mahmood argues that "social norms are the necessary ground through which the subject is realized and comes to enact her agency."[51] An individual's subjectivity is inseparable from these cultural and religious norms; therefore, one's agency, inasmuch as it is also an action of the subject, need not be a rejection of cultural norms. Instead, agency is the capacity for action even while drawing on those oftentimes subordinating norms. Importantly, Mahmood finds agency among Muslim women in Egypt to be not a rejection or resistance to domination "but as a capacity for action that specific relations of subordination create and enable."[52] Agency is, in Anna Korteweg's terminology, "embedded" in the religious context and the norms that shape the individual.[53]

Also wanting to distance herself from the impression that agency must, necessarily, mean the rejection of cultural norms of subordination, Bucar finds agency within what she calls "creative conformity." Creative conformity refers to actions by women who are operating within the structure that subordinates them. While operating within this system, women might subvert or reinforce that structure, but they do so in a way that reflects their negotiation of autonomy and heteronomy.[54] As Bucar understands it, autonomy refers to self-rule, seeing a "woman as the source of her freedom and innovation."[55] In conservative religious traditions, however, a woman's autonomy is challenged by heteronomy, or the system of external forces and norms. Bucar insists that this binary neglects women's experiences of these religious traditions. Instead, she proposes we see women's actions through the lens of dianomy. "Dianomy recognizes that both an individual and her community are important; that agency is shaped within specific conditions and yet can also point beyond them, and that there is a possibility of creative compliance that is not necessarily intentional resistance."[56] Dianomy adds to our understanding of women's agency by seeing the individual as someone who is interpreting, negotiating, and applying cultural norms and religious rules.

Some have suggested using the term *freedom* instead of *autonomy* to describe agency among women in conservative religions. In particular, Allison Weir argues that *freedom* captures a Sufi understanding of devotion to God wherein one's relationship with God facilitates freedom from everything else. In this case, it is through the submission to God that one can be free. Weir explains, "Freedom, then, is found in faith: in a life whose meaning is clear and unquestioned. And freedom is found in the connection with God."[57] Like Mahmood, Weir maintains that although these concepts may have a differ-ent meaning within Western feminist critiques of conservative religion, they are nonetheless present within and inherent to these traditions. Similarly, Lihi Ben Shitrit finds freedom and autonomy to be consistent with the way female members of the Islamic movement and ultra-Orthodox Jewish activ-ists describe their work.[58] In other words, these concepts are not necessarily external to the women themselves.

This book adds important spatial and temporal dimensions to conceptions of women's agency. Mahmood focuses on women's activity in mosques and engagement with religious texts and discourse. This focus raises questions about whether the "moral dispositions cultivated in the ritual sphere are con-sonant with the actual behavior of these pious Muslim women in other social fields."[59] My ethnography, however, extends beyond the ritual sphere and reveals that women do indeed embody religious agency in multiple spaces. In this way, we can see how agency is embedded in a religious context and an embodied religious experience but not necessarily in a religious space. Further-more, my focus on a distinct period of time highlights the temporal elements of women's agency as well. Following claims that agency comes from particular social, religious, and economic contexts, I add that agency shifts during one's lifetime. Whereas Haredi women experience their first and second pregnan-cies as surprising and overwhelming, turning to rabbis, doctors, and mothers throughout these reproductive processes, most expressed a shift for their third pregnancies. After two pregnancies, they see themselves as those with more knowledge of, and thus more authority over, pregnancy and reproduction than the rabbis, who are otherwise the community leaders.

Instead of searching for the "bad girls" of religion who reject these norms, or insisting that this rejection is not authentic religious expression, I join Mah-mood, Bucar, and many others in exploring the lives of women who exert agency through their negotiation of religious norms in oftentimes creative and subversive ways.[60] This ethnography of Haredi women's reproductive practices reveals that Haredi women are able to exercise their reproductive agency because of their participation in religious norms. Haredi women are expected to be pregnant soon after their marriage, and many feel pressure to get pregnant every two years. Although it may seem like a Haredi woman is sanctioning the gendered roles that lead to the regulation and supervision of her body by acquiescing to another pregnancy, Haredi women call on their bodily experiences to inform their agency. Women's application and interpretation of these norms translate into women's authority over reproductive decisions. In this way, Haredi women creatively construct reproductive agency that fits within the bounds of their religious tradition. As the reader will see in the rest of this book, by adhering to gender norms that separate them from their husbands, through their employment outside of the Haredi world, in their understanding of theological texts, and with their repeated participation in reproduction, Haredi women are conforming to the norms of Haredi life.

Embodiment and Agency

The multiple experiences of pregnancy that inform a Haredi woman's reproductive agency provide not just a history of experience but also a shift in identity that results from the embodiment of pregnancy. This finding—that agency results from particular embodied experiences during a woman's lifetime—adds an important dimension to the claim that agency is embedded in context. Until now, that context was considered to be external factors like cultural and religious norms that shape the individual. Here we see that it is also an individual's embodied experiences that shape her development of agency. These women do not simply assume their bodies are under rabbinic authority; rather, they emphasize that the embodiment of pregnancy is precisely what provides them with authority over their rabbis. Their rabbis, in other words, do not and will never have pregnant bodies. Having a pregnant body as a Haredi woman cultivates agency and provides them with authority.

Embodiment is often a key feature of the regulation of Haredi women's lives.[61] Social science research about Haredi women's bodies has focused on distinct periods of the life cycle in demonstrating the role of embodiment in self-formation and the interplay between bodily regulation as a social norm and the development of the individual. Orit Yafeh's work with Haredi kindergarteners demonstrates that even girls as young as five years old are taught that the clothes they wear, the style of their hair, and the sound of their voice can arouse a man and thus must be controlled. As a result, young girls become overly aware of their body's presence and the role it plays in religious affairs.[62] Ayala Fader's research with young Hasidic women demonstrates the way they use ritual to elevate their physical reality to cultivate a spiritual connection to God.[63] Dress codes continue to shape the religious identity of adults, as Lynn Davidman demonstrates in *Becoming Un-Orthodox*. Additionally, "repeated, daily bodily rituals continually work to establish and maintain their relationship with the Divine."[64] Davidman contrasts the importance of embodied rituals in Judaism to the statements of faith in Christianity. The body and the embodied experience are central components to one's identity and subjectivity as an Orthodox Jew.[65] This book joins a growing chorus of scholars looking specifically at the reproductive lives of Haredi women, now recognized as a distinct and important part of the life cycle.[66] More sustained attention should be paid to the embodied experiences among postmenopausal Haredi women.

Focusing on bodily practices, modesty in clothing and action, and the ritualization of the body draws our attention—importantly—to the role of the body in religious identification and communal affiliation. An individual's body is the site of her self-formation.[67] Her subjectivity is informed by her interaction with others and the world, interactions that occur through her bodily practices. Moreover, paying attention to the way the body shapes identity during key points in the life cycle reflects the fact that bodies are constantly changing and individuals constantly becoming. Identity is not fixed and unchanging. Agency is not something that someone does not have and then suddenly—overnight—possesses. Instead, subjectivity is always changing; agency is always emerging.[68]

My turn toward pregnancy as a unique embodied experience draws on Iris Young and Rosalind Diprose's ideas about pregnancy embodiment. Diprose writes, "The capacities of the body, its habits, gestures and style, make up what the self is in relation to the social and material world."[69] Cultural norms, therefore, affect the way one's body shapes one's identity. Pregnancy and birth are events that occur in particular cultural frames, as the anthropology of reproduction literature has demonstrated. Therefore, the way these events shape a woman's identity will uniquely result from her cultural and religious setting and how that context—both time and space—relates to pregnancy and reproduction.

Moreover, reproduction itself involves a series of bodily changes, and as such, it is a unique embodied experience. Diprose suggests, "Pregnancy . . . involves profound changes to bodily capacities, shape and texture with attendant shifts in the awareness of the body."[70] She continues, "If the social identity of the self cannot be distinguished from the lived body by which it is actualized and if one's self-image cannot be distinguished from the living body as a whole, then it should not be surprising if changes in the body effect changes in the structure and fabric of the self."[71] Iris Young adds that pregnancy changes the self to such a degree that the individual who began a pregnancy is not the same as the individual who completes it.[72] As the contours of a woman's body changes, so too does her interaction with the world around her. Young explains that as her body grows during pregnancy, she has to rediscover where her body ends and the world begins. Furthermore, as the fetus develops, Young argues, the pregnant woman experiences a "splitting" of the self whereby her body now contains something that is both of her and other. "Pregnancy challenges the integration of my body experience by rendering fluid the boundary between what is within, myself, and what is outside, separate. I experience my insides as the space of another, yet my own body."[73] The physical changes of pregnancy, then, lead to changes in subjectivity and relation to others.

Women's embodied experiences of pregnancy influence their subjectivity and as a result their own authority within Haredi society. Women who have carried multiple pregnancies draw on these experiences to bolster their own agency, expressed through an authority that is respected by other women and that allows Haredi women to operate outside of traditional authority structures. Pregnancy and birth afford a Haredi woman the opportunity to experience the interchange between self and other, and within the cultural and religious framework of Haredi Judaism, a pregnant body is also God-like in its creative capacity. This additional splitting provides Haredi women with authority that overrides that of the rabbis, providing them autonomy from their patriarchal religious system and agency over their reproductive decisions.[74] It is this unique embodied experience that significantly informs Haredi women's reproductive agency.

Ethnography and Ethics

The way that Haredi women make decisions about reproduction reflects a religious ethic distinct from the way Jewish bioethics frames its discourse. Overwhelmingly, scriptural sources, religious doctrine and law, and central forms of religious authority have determined what Jewish bioethicists consider to be normative religious ethics. Haredi women demonstrate, however, that cultural, economic, theological, and embodied factors contribute to their reproductive ethic. This gap between normative religious ethics and the strategies of religious participants requires a rethinking of the discourse of religious ethics. Scholarly discussions of ethics should account for the embodied, cultural, religious, and contextual experiences of individuals. Exploring the implications of my findings, I turn to Jewish ethics and suggest that ethnography must be incorporated as a corrective to the gap in normative ethics and practice. Ethics—and religious ethics in particular—must be viewed from the perspectives of embodied moral agents so that our ethical discourse can better reflect the lived realities of ethics.

In this book, I argue that Haredi women develop a reproductive ethic that results from their embodied experiences and authority within Haredi Judaism. The reproductive ethics I found among Haredi women—that is, the specific decisions they make regarding pregnancy and reproduction—vary from woman to woman and even from one pregnancy to the next. My point is not to articulate a universal reproductive ethic but rather to highlight the fact that women have developed a unique approach to making these decisions. Women reject rabbinic norms and patriarchal authorities in favor of an embodied authority situated in their understanding of cultural and religious ideologies that profess a woman's importance in reproduction. This is their reproductive ethic. Some may object to my referring to reproductive decision-making as reproductive ethics; however, because reproduction is an act laden with ethical scrutiny from outsiders, a woman's reproductive decisions can surely be considered reproductive ethics.[75]

As I discovered such a significant gap between the professed importance of norms in Haredi life and the lived experiences of Haredi women—and, furthermore, the importance of women's lived experiences in their reproductive ethic—I began to consider whether normative religious ethics could benefit from more engagement with the ethnographic reality of ethics and, if so, what this would look like. This requires a shift in religious ethics from thinking about what books, laws, and authorities say one should do to what obstacles and approaches individuals face in making ethical decisions. It is what Don Seeman refers to as moving from "ethical, religious, and reproductive *norms* . . . to a discourse of cultural, religious, and reproductive *strategies*."[76]

Some religious ethicists have been actively engaging with the tools of ethnography to make this cultural turn. For example, Leela Prasad's *Poetics of Conduct* explores normative and lived Hindu ethics in South India through ethnographic research and narrative analysis. In their anthology, *Ethnography as Christian Theology and Ethics*, Christian Scharen and Aana Vigen showcase Christian ethicists who collect ethnographic data and demonstrate the relevance of their findings for the wider discourse of Christian ethics. Scharen and Vigen, furthermore, argue that ethnography is both a more ethical and a more authentically Christian approach to Christian ethics. These works, and others, demonstrate an increase in what Richard Miller called an "ethics of ordinary life," which enables religious ethics to broaden its methodological and theoretical framework.[77] It is important to note that these religious ethicists have been motivated by the question of whether ethical norms reflect the lived reality. The anthropological study of morality, by contrast, is interested in how cultures produce and reproduce values and morals, both collectively and in the individual.[78] This book builds on the questions belonging to religious ethicists with the intention that Jewish ethics will also make the cultural turn.

Jewish ethics has been slow to adopt any ethnographic methods; instead, the field has been largely determined by various interpretations of Jewish law or readings from Jewish biblical texts.[79] David Ellenson refers to this reliance on the text to find precedents and principles for Jewish ethics as "*halakhic formalism*."[80] Users of this method presume that Jewish ethics are located in the legal texts because these texts carry the most authority in Judaism.[81] For example, in *Introduction to Jewish and Catholic Bioethics*, Aaron Mackler examines the ways various scholars of Jewish law rely on legal texts, showing that across denominations, scholars use the text differently but maintain its primacy. Mackler, among others, understands the legal texts as the sine qua non of Jewish ethics. He argues, "The very fact of the centrality of halakha to Jewish ethics over the millennia might be regarded as itself carrying normative weight. A halakhically centered approach simply is the Jewish way to do ethics."[82] Elliot Dorff claims that Judaism is framed in the "legal expression of its views and values."[83] Dorff adds, "Most rabbinic writers in all three movements are united in their assumption that identifiably *Jewish* moral positions can emerge only through interpreting and applying the *legal* precedents and statutes of the Jewish tradition."[84] This implies that only Jewish legal discussions will capture essentially Jewish bioethics. While this methodology might include a consideration of contemporary morality, socioeconomic considerations, and the particular context of the situation, Dorff insists that what is Jewish about Jewish bioethics is its use of legal texts.

There are some indications that Jewish ethics is beginning to make the turn toward ethnography. In *Health Care and the Ethics of Encounter*, Laurie Zoloth argues for an ethic of encounter in Jewish ethics. In particular, she claims, "Jewish ethics presumes public choices; it assumes community, human sociability, and embodied dailiness, that ordinary human acts have a weight and meaning that ought to be the subject of urgent discourse."[85] Although not incorporating ethnography per se, Zoloth draws on Emmanuel Levinas to emphasize the importance of listening to the marginalized: "The listening people must hear in the commanding God the voice of the other as well. The right act is right only if it is imbued with this call."[86] Zoloth's insightful reading of the Book of

Ruth demonstrates how listening to the marginalized in the texts is the ethical act. Rebecca Levi's more recent work on autonomy and heteronomy in Jewish ethics includes a brief discussion of Susan Sered's ethnography of the health of Israeli women.[87] Despite the importance of these projects for the broadening of the field of Jewish ethics, neither of these examples utilizes ethnography as a method of analysis or a guide for ethical discourse. Some new work, compiled in an anthology titled *Bioethics and Biopolitics in Israel,* explores how bioethics in Israel has a variety of political intersections, whether they are religious, ethnic, legal, or historical in nature. Ethnography is cited considerably in this book, and some authors undertook social science research methods as data for their chapters.[88] My book expands the methods of Jewish ethics by advocating for ethnography of the marginalized to serve as a source for the field. An ethnographic approach to ethics will yield an ethical response that appreciates context and individual circumstance.

Ethnography is both a more ethical approach for Jewish ethics and a historically accurate way of determining an ethical response in Jewish thought. Ethnography is more ethical not only because it appreciates context but also because it is attentive to feminist critiques of religious ethics.[89] Jewish ethicists Dena Davis and Ronit Irshai critique Jewish ethics for relying on rabbinic literature, which excludes women. They maintain that this void has an effect on moral deliberation and moral conclusions.[90] In *Fertility and Jewish Law,* Irshai critiques halakhic rulings on the topic of abortion for their focus on the status of the fetus. She claims this is not a sufficient line of questioning and argues that particularly with issues of reproduction, the rabbis of the Talmud missed the mark because they were all male. She asks, "Does a determination of the fetus's status provide the exclusive moral basis for such a decision? In other words, does the fetus question tell the entire story, including the female point of view?"[91]

In addition to using ethnography and in particular ethnography of women, this book demonstrates how an ethnography of the body contributes to ethical discourse. In *The Bodies of Women,* Rosalind Diprose argues that understanding ethics as moral principles overlooks embodied differences between individuals and therefore significantly "disqualifies women from ethical social exchange insofar as our bodies signify womanhood."[92] Although feminist Jewish ethicists have advocated for the inclusion of women's voices in Jewish ethical discourse, this generally means the inclusion of more female scholars interpreting Jewish law. As long as bodily experience is overlooked, our ethical discourse will continue to ignore the subjectivity of those involved in the conversation.

I suggest reframing the discourse of ethics to reflect the lived realities and subjectivities of ethical decision-making. This requires a robust incorporation of ethnography into our ethical discourse, such as what is seen in this book. But ethnography is not the only area where we should pay attention to the subjectivity of ethical agents. Normative ethics is not divorced from the embodied agents constructing moral codes.[93] Individuals, informed by their subjective and embodied experiences, have determined normative moral discourse. In Jewish ethics, choosing which voice is authoritative and decisive in multi-vocal dialogic rabbinic writing is ultimately a moral choice each reader makes.[94] In other words, contemporary bioethics scholars who claim to be using the rabbinic texts to inform their moral positions are actually relying on their moral positions first and searching for justification in the text second.[95] This realization should not negate the validity of their arguments or the Jewish character of their ethical claims. I argue that the reproductive ethics of Haredi women in Jerusalem is, in fact, a Jewish reproductive ethic, just as much as ethical positions derived from scholarly reading of Jewish texts represent Jewish ethics. The hermeneutic of "lived religion" is helpful here in establishing what I call "lived ethics."[96] The everyday experiences of religion cannot be separated from what is understood to be "official religion." Similarly, the everyday experiences of making ethical decisions cannot be separated from what we call "ethics." To construct this lived ethics, we must avail ourselves of a methodological tool not often used in ethics and especially not in Jewish ethics: ethnography.

FROM CONCEPTION TO BIRTH

This project began as ethnographic research into the pregnancy experiences of mainstream Orthodox Jewish women in Jerusalem. Calling on a few Hasidic women I knew from prior time I spent in Jerusalem,[97] I began investigating how Orthodox Jewish women engage the realities and challenges of their pregnancies. I centered my questions on a tension I saw in Jewish life: Judaism lacks rituals and laws for marking pregnancy as a significant life event for women, yet especially for an Orthodox Jewish woman, pregnancy is not only frequent but also formative in shaping her identity. Despite the lack of ritual as well as the fears and concomitant taboos, popular traditions abound for a pregnant woman. For example, it is common practice to not discuss one's pregnancy or purchase clothing, furniture, or other supplies for a new baby before the birth.[98] In this way, men and women believe they can prevent complications during pregnancy or malformations of the fetus. Many women will also visit the ritual bathhouse (*mikvah*) every day during their ninth month in the hope of protecting themselves and the fetus. How, I wondered, does an Orthodox Jewish woman understand her pregnancy when it is shrouded in secrecy, lacking formal ritual, and filled with tensions of hope and fear? Those initial questions and contacts connected me to the ultra-Orthodox Jewish women who are the subject of this book.

In the first three months of research, I interviewed four Haredi women who spoke to me about their recent pregnancy experiences.[99] They told me about discovering they were pregnant, taboos they avoided, traditions they continued, labor and delivery, reactions from their husbands, and contact with their rabbis (among other things). The taboos and folk practices, which women refer to as *segulot* (pl. of *segulah*), reflect women's religious practices that they used to root fears and concerns in a Jewish theological framework.[100] Throughout the book, I will use their word, *segulah*, to refer to a variety of charms, omens, apotropaic objects, protective rituals, and comforting talismans that they have adopted to elevate the significance of their embodied experience. Although the word *segulah* has a variety of definitions and applications across the Haredi world, one of my informants clarified, "anything can be a segulah if someone wants it to be a way of connecting with God." Indeed, these rituals help Haredi women connect their pregnant selves directly to God. This connection is central in their reproductive agency.

As I quickly discovered, the context in which Haredi women experience pregnancy also significantly affects their response to challenges (questions of prenatal testing, warnings from doctors, etc.) and the development of reproductive agency. This context includes rabbis and doctors who attempt to control women's reproductive choices and pregnancy books, doulas, and teachers who help guide women toward reproductive agency. All of these elements taken together—the segulot and the Haredi cultural and medical context—are part of women's authority over pregnancy and birth.

I conducted my research over a two-year period in Jerusalem using a traditional anthropological methodology of participant and nonparticipant observation and interviews. I obtained approval from the Institutional Review Board at Northwestern University and received the consent of all research participants. I recorded almost all of the interviews I conducted and then transcribed them. After each interview, I also took extensive notes, wherein I documented my description of the apartment, the general atmosphere for the interview, some nonverbal cues, and my own reactions to the interview. For all except two of the interviews I was able to do this within a week of the interview, ensuring the most accurate recall. I stored and organized my data using the NVivo software, and my conclusions in this book derive from this grounded research.

I interviewed twenty-three Haredi women multiple times over the two years. All of the women who shared their pregnancy narratives were put in contact

with me through snowball sampling. Although a few were pregnant at the time
of the first interview, many were not but had been pregnant within the year
prior to the interview. All had at least three children. Two women were older
and already had grandchildren at the time of the interview. All were Israeli, and
most of the interviews were conducted in Hebrew. I excluded from my analysis
two women who suffered from infertility because the condition significantly
shifted their attitudes toward medicine and their bodies.[101] I interviewed these
women to maintain positive relationships with the interviewees who referred
me to them, but as I listened to their accounts of pregnancy, which were so
tinged by their struggles with infertility, I realized they were not a good fit for
this study.[102] Despite the slight variations among my twenty-one other informants, I found common themes in their reproductive lives. When necessary
I account for these differences in background or reproductive histories in my
analysis to provide some perspective for the reader.

At the beginning of each interview, I explained that each woman's privacy
and involvement in the research was maintained locked and secured in a file on
my computer. Interestingly, however, I found that women were less concerned
with how I was going to protect their privacy than with how I was going to
respect their time. While some interviews lasted four hours, which generally
included a whole morning or afternoon spent talking to a woman about a variety of topics, many women were wary to commit to an interview that would
last longer than two hours. They had too much else to do, they explained, and
they could only meet for longer if I accompanied them to pick up their kids
from school or prepare dinner, which I often did. Others, however, could not
even begin an interview until after 9:00 p.m., because they worked all day and
then had to feed their kids and put them into bed in the evening. Their lack of
concern with privacy was due to the fact that they saw me as an outsider, writing
for an outsider audience. The women I spoke to did not want their information
shared in an Israeli newspaper, which could eventually reach someone in their
community, but they felt secure knowing that nobody they knew would read
my book. Many did not even care whether I changed their names. Nonetheless,
I have changed all identifying details of all the participants in this research,
except for the heads of antiabortion organizations and one doctor, since their
names are part of the public record.

As each interview progressed, I found that women thoroughly enjoyed sharing their personal experiences with me. Though their answers were initially
quite reserved, about thirty minutes into our discussion, women chatted with
me as if we were long-lost friends, and I often returned for follow-up interviews
as their pregnancies progressed, after they gave birth, or when they got pregnant

again. Many women also invited me to attend doctor appointments and view ultrasound scans with them. When they found themselves on a tangent from the original question, they would apologize and explain, as one woman said, "I'm sorry I just never have had a chance to discuss this before. . . . Nobody is ever interested in my pregnancy experience." The simple fact that I was asking them about their experience led many women to confess things to me that they had never shared with other people; despite the importance and seemingly universal experience of reproduction in the Haredi world, women do not have a lot of opportunities to talk about their pregnancies. In chapter 3 I expand on the taboos and cultural setting in which women are pregnant constantly yet shrouded by silence about reproduction. This resulted in women eager to talk about their reproductive experiences with me.

My research also included interviews with almost twenty-five medical professionals. I spoke to thirteen doctors and nurses who work with Haredi women. Nurses easily agreed to participate after I mentioned that I had received their names from Karin, a prominent nurse-midwife for the Haredi community whom I discuss in chapter 1. Most nurses viewed Karin as the expert—well connected and with a lot of experience—so mentioning her name (which she allowed me to do) helped me gain their trust. After I spoke to nurses, they reached out to doctors and recommended that they participate in my research. Doctors frequently referred me to other doctors, but they were not always willing to allow me to use their names to make the connection. I also interviewed eleven doulas (labor coaches) who cater to Haredi women. To receive a more individualized and perhaps a less medicated birthing experience, many women in Israel hire doulas.

Readers might notice that I did not interview any Haredi husbands or rabbis, and some might take issue with this exclusion. Although I tried to reach out to some Haredi rabbis, they refused to participate. Women, teachers, and even doctors confirmed that the rabbis would not meet with me. As a non-Haredi female researcher, doing so would violate all norms of modesty in the community. Husbands, furthermore, were never around when I was visiting a woman's home. Most women did not want their husbands to know that they were participating in the research, so reaching out to them would have violated the trust I had established with Haredi women. Moreover, though, rabbis and husbands were not the subject of my research. Other research in Jewish studies has looked at the religious lives of men and rabbis, and this was not my interest. Instead, I focused on the religious and reproductive lives of Haredi women.

During my two years in Jerusalem I also observed in a few medical settings. I observed ultrasound examinations with Haredi women at two prenatal clinics in Jerusalem. One was a prenatal clinic based in a Haredi neighborhood and catering to Haredi clients, while the other was an ultrasound clinic located in a large hospital in Jerusalem. Hadassah, a nurse-midwife, also invited me to observe a set of prenatal classes she teaches for Haredi women. These observations came early in my research, when I was still uncomfortable in my Haredi clothing, but I was far more uncomfortable in that room because I was not pregnant. Sitting in a room with thirty women in their eighth or ninth month of pregnancy made me, a nonpregnant woman, feel exceptionally small and insignificant.

I also explored other educational settings for Haredi women, such as weekly classes for Haredi women on a variety of topics. Rabbis' wives taught the classes, and a variety of women attended—young, old, unmarried, married with many children. They were frequently held late in the evening—from 8:30 to 10:00 p.m.—to accommodate work and family schedules. These classes allowed me to get a better idea of some of the practical philosophies behind Haredi thought, as taught by and for women.[103] My attempt to understand other educational influences in Haredi women's lives extended to the prenatal advice books that women in this study recommended to me. These books served a purpose similar to *What to Expect When You are Expecting* in the United States, but I found that women did not frequently reference them. My analysis of these books and how Haredi women use them can be found in chapter 2.

As I began to see repeating patterns in my research with Haredi women, I launched into an area of research that I did not expect to encounter. I explored abortion politics in Israel as they relate to Haredi women's reproductive ethics. My foray into antiabortion organizations was due entirely to Haredi women's repeated reference to a person they called Rav Eli Schussheim, who was actually a doctor and better known for his role as the director of EFRAT, the largest antiabortion organization based in Jerusalem. I conducted a year of participant-observation with EFRAT.[104] As a participant-observer, I was primarily a volunteer performing a few secretarial tasks. In return, the workers at EFRAT allowed me to gather data and interview them. I draw on these findings explicitly in chapter 5.

Ethics in Research Relationships

This book is an analysis of reproduction, agency, and ethics as seen through the relationships I developed with Haredi women and the wealth of other data I collected and interpreted. Despite the many sites for this research, what I have collected here does not comprehensively account for all reproductive experiences among Haredi women in Jerusalem. Although some might claim that my sample size is too small to make any generalizations, I actively pursued new research subjects and new areas of inquiry until I repeatedly found the same patterns and themes emerging. While there will always be outliers to any findings, this research represents a number of core themes and realities in the lives of Haredi women in Jerusalem.

The relationships I developed were a result of the unique interplay between myself (as both a researcher and an individual) and those who invited me into their worlds. A goal of this book is to amplify the identities, experiences, and voices of Haredi women and to discuss their cultural and religious context, but it would be disingenuous to overlook my own context as well. The relationships we developed because of who I was at the time of data collection resulted in the particular findings shared in this book, and the analysis I present here is a result of how my life and my perspective have changed during the course of writing this book.

My insider-outsider status as a Jewish woman significantly contributed to developing trust and comfort among the women I interviewed. Though they knew I was not Haredi, each woman was aware that I was religiously obser-vant and married. When we spoke over the phone to coordinate details, most women asked if I was *dati* (religious), a word that in Israel indicates a certain level of religious observance. I answered honestly in the affirmative. At the time of my research, I identified as a Jew who often followed Orthodox ritual, so when I showed up at their house wearing a head scarf (a common religious symbol in Jerusalem), they knew that I was married and followed a particular set of customs. Some, though, commented on my adoption of full Haredi garb (long, dark-colored skirt, long-sleeved top, high neckline, flat shoes) during our interview. They explained that I did not have to come into their house like that, but most seemed to appreciate my respect of their community. Because I tried to blend into the community as much as I could, women did not have to explain to their neighbors who this relatively secular woman was visiting them so late at night.

As a practicing Jew, my religious identity and knowledge also meant that my interlocutors could use religious language and not have to define every word or concept, though I often pressed them to be explicit with their meanings. The fact that I was already observant of Jewish laws and customs, however, limited my access to a different level of intimacy. In *Mystics, Mavericks, and Merry-makers*, Stephanie Levine explains that one of the reasons she was welcomed so fully into a group of Hasidic girls in Crown Heights was her completely secular Jewish identity. Levine explains, "My genuine respect for Hasidism was fertile ground for the well-honed Lubavitch flair for proselytizing among secular Jews."[105] I, on the other hand, was never recruited to become religious; perhaps, because I was already observant but not their kind of observant, they saw me as heretical and a lost cause.[106]

Though I tried to blend in as much as I could, I learned repeatedly that I could never actually pass as Haredi. Even when I donned a long, pleated black skirt, black tights, black flats that make no noise on the street, a plain-colored sweater or button-down shirt, and a satin scarf covering every wisp of hair, I still walked differently, talked differently, and held my head differently.[107] These are things that my secular and non-Haredi friends never seemed to notice; when they passed me on the street, most did not recognize me, but Haredi children and women always tended to stare. As a twenty-seven-year-old married woman without any children, observed clearly as I walked without a stroller, I was also, relatively, an old lady. Because even the Haredi-born women who do not have children by the time they are twenty-seven feel like outsiders in their own community, I was doubly Other. During my interviews with Haredi women, I often felt them gazing at me, gossiping, and criticizing me for not having children. Although some assumed that I was infertile, most probably thought I was choosing to avoid pregnancy, and this made me a rather strange religious Jew. As Fran Markowitz has advised, this dynamic then became part of the ethnographic relationship.[108] A common closing to a conversation or an interview was "b'karov etzlech" (soon by you) or "b'sha'ah tovah" (in a good time), indicating that they hoped that I, too, would soon be pregnant. Additionally, my aspirations of a profession in higher education distanced me from the women significantly, since this was a goal they could not completely comprehend and that they did not value. Instead of trying to blend in and experience life as a Haredi woman, I ultimately accepted my status as different from theirs, and I learned from our interactions.

One of the most foundational educational experiences in the field happened early in data collection, when I was not yet comfortable with the differences between myself and those who participated in the research. As I prepared to leave the apartment of one participant, Devorah, around 6:00 p.m., I asked her one last question, "Do you have any friends who might be interested in participating in this research?" "Yes, actually!" she responded. "I'll call her right now." I started packing up my things, making a mental list of the food I needed to pick up on the way home so that my husband and I could make dinner. We had been married for three years and enjoyed cooking elaborate meals together. When Devorah got off the phone with her friend, she said, "Miriam would love to talk to you about her pregnancies, but she can only do it right now. She's giving her children dinner and then putting them to bed. Maybe you can help her with that because her husband is at the kollel [full-time yeshiva for married men], and then you can talk." Excitedly, I agreed and prepared to leave. "But wait," Devorah interrupted. "Won't your husband get home soon from kollel and expect dinner?" Devorah knew I was married and that my husband studied in a yeshiva, a religious learning community, but assumed, and I never corrected her, that our life was much like hers. As a married Haredi woman, she supported her husband's continued learning by working outside the home and performing all the domestic responsibilities as well. In our home, we shared responsibilities, supported each other financially, and my husband's yeshiva was quite different from the one where Devorah's husband spent his time. Notably, my husband studied with women. I was nervous to tell Devorah that I had not yet prepared dinner, that I was not the type of person to think about what my spouse would eat before I left the house at night. So instead I told her, "Oh, it's OK. I thought I might be out late tonight, so I prepared something and left it for him in the refrigerator."[109]

I felt terrible for lying to Devorah, who had just shared with me the most intimate secrets about her reproductive history, secrets she had not shared with anybody else. And yet I could not even admit that I did not make dinner that night. The line between researcher and friend, even in those early months of ethnographic research, had already begun to blur. For instance, while I thought about the data I was going to collect by speaking to another research participant that night and observing Miriam in her home, Devorah and Miriam were thinking about how I could help them with childcare. I had to blur the lines to create the kind of relationship that would enable me to conduct feminist ethnography. Feminist ethnography requires the forming of "kin-like relationships," according to Nandini Ghosh, and I felt like I might damage that relationship if Devorah knew how different we were.[110] As we became friends, however, I experienced a sort of crisis of identity. Immersed in someone else's values about family, religion, career, and children, I began to question my own.[111]

This dissonance arose again surrounding my fertility (or seeming lack thereof).[112] Batya, a mother of eight children, handed me a small plastic bag with an ounce of red juice inside at the end of our interview. The bag had been in the freezer, along with many others. Batya explained that the juice came from pomegranates that hung in the sukkot (ritual booths) of seven prominent rabbis in the area. She drank an ounce before each time she got pregnant, a practice she attributed to a successful pregnancy, and she wanted me to have the same luck. Although we did not discuss my fertility at length, Batya must have assumed I was having difficulty getting pregnant. As a result, she gently offered her own form of assisted reproductive technology. I thanked her for the bag and put it in my freezer in my Jerusalem apartment. The bag stayed there for a year, until the night before I left Jerusalem to return to the United States with my spouse. We were not ready for kids but knew we would want them someday. I did not believe that pomegranate juice could help with fertility, and juice culled from pomegranates that hung in a special sukkah did not seem to increase the likelihood in my mind. I thought about throwing it out, but I was struck by how my own doubts about the effectiveness of this juice were quashed as a result of my relationship with Batya and my many other interlocutors. What if throwing out the juice would endanger my chances of becoming pregnant? I thought about drinking it instead but feared that it might "work," bypassing all forms of contraception. I was not ready to be pregnant. I found myself staring at this bag of red juice, wondering what power I was going to allow it to have over my understanding of fertility. I did not want to risk infertility, so I drank it, hoping it would not work immediately.

As a non-Haredi academic researcher, I also worried what drinking the juice would imply about my positionality. If I drank it with the hope of getting pregnant, would I have become less of an observer and more of a participant? Would others question my ability to objectively analyze these traditions within a particular cultural and religious framework if I seemed to believe in them? Clinging to the idea of an objective research stance, I did not tell anyone about drinking the juice, just like I did not tell anyone that I lied about having dinner prepared for my spouse. I did not want to be seen as "going native," but this false sense of objectivity belies the many ways my own subjectivity was part of the data I collected and the analysis I provide in this book.[113]

Acknowledging my own vulnerabilities, in addition to those of my research participants, moves me toward a more "full-bodied" ethnographic method. Full-bodied ethnography recognizes that as ethnographers we enter the field as embodied researchers, and our intersubjective and embodied interactions with our research participants "produce community and identity."[114] The ethnographer is not there, objectively and abstractly, to decipher social codes. Instead, our "in-the-flesh interactions" with our research participants are part of how relationships are developed and research gains meaning. Borrowing the concept from Karla Poewe, Fran Markowitz explains, "Full-bodied ethnography offers an equalizing but risky research strategy that demands sharing scrutiny and power."[115] Conducting a full-bodied ethnography is a step beyond acknowledging power differentials as many feminist ethnographers have done. In an embodied approach, the researcher shares that power with her research participants, allowing their observations of her to become part of the data. When I set out to conduct research with Haredi women, I knew my clothing choices were important, but I entered the field as an abstract ethnographer, privileging the mind and the books I had read over my own embodied positionality. I prepared by finding recent scholarship on Haredim, organizing prominent theories, and thinking about where my findings might fit.

In light of my research findings, this approach is ironic. Embodiment, I argue throughout this book, is not something to ignore or control but rather something to embrace. For Haredi women, it provides authority and agency and should be prioritized as a source of knowledge. The fact that I saw embodiment among Haredi women and not in myself is due to my own biases about the Haredi world. As Ayala Fader writes, "My position as a Jewish anthropologist puts me in the uncomfortable but necessary position of recognizing some of my own assumptions that are rooted in my liberal Jewish upbringing."[116] Scholarship about Haredim has focused on Haredi men, insisting that they operate within a world of book learning. Although so much of their book-learning is concerned with behavior—namely, what to do with their bodies—analyses of the Haredi world have overlooked men's own embodiment. Women, on the other hand, have been assumed to operate within the life tradition, a subset of the Haredi world that is less connected with the mind and more with daily, bodily practice. I understood from this that women's bodies were ultimately controlled by the books and hidden from view. In fact, they are largely hidden because the scholars in question (all men) do not have access to female research participants.

Despite my access to female research participants, I still prioritized book knowledge when I attempted to be a disembodied researcher. On a walk with a doula who was participating in my research, she predicted that I would be the type of person who would handle childbirth pain pretty well, for a while. She said I would take all the classes, learn all the positions that would ease pain, and practice them. This doula thought I would breeze through the first twenty-four hours of labor but that I might need some pain medications toward the end. Although she was clearly valorizing a birth without medical intervention, I told her about a medical condition I have that requires quite a bit of oversight during pregnancy and that I would not be able to give birth at home as she would like. The entire conversation was abstract, as I was not even pregnant at the time, but this doula would not give up her insistence that I could still give birth at home.

I felt attacked and vulnerable in a way I had not expected as the one conducting the research. I knew that my entry into the field would place my research subjects in a vulnerable position, and I did what I could to respect my interviewees and prevent any abuses. I found, however, that my research participants did not always feel the same obligation to me. Though not frequent, when they commented on my body (either the way I was dressed or the fact that I did not have any children), they did it without concern for my sensitivities.[117] As a feminist researcher, I was sensitive to the ways I held power over my research subjects, but I have since realized that to conduct a full-bodied ethnography, I needed to accept my own vulnerability and recognize that my interlocutors were seeing and judging me even as they were the subjects of my research. This vulnerability should not be read as weakness but rather, as Erinn Gilson explains, "as openness and affectivity, and such openness entails the inability to predict, control, and fully know that to which we are open and how it will affect us"[118] Although the risk of physical harm is one component of vulnerability, it is not the whole story. Individuals are vulnerable in many ways, including socially, politically, and legally. But moreover, vulnerability is simply a way of being in the world. Gilson maintains, "All are equally vulnerable—open to being affected and affecting—and differences are made by the ways we are affected and respond to this affection."[119] Not comfortable with this vulnerability at the time of my conversation with the doula, I quickly changed the topic and moved on, but her remarks stayed with me. I felt that she was wrong and that my pregnancies would never be like the pregnancies of the women in my study. I would rely on my doctors and not my body.

Years later, this changed. When I was twenty-four weeks pregnant with my third child, I told my nurse practitioner that I would be away for the summer. I asked if she wanted me to set up appointments with doctors in New York, where I would be conducting new research. "No," she said as she shrugged. "You've done this before. You will know if something's wrong. And if it is, just go to a doctor or the hospital there." I could not believe it. My last pregnancy had felt like the most carefully tracked pregnancy of all time, and this one was being entrusted to me alone. I laughed as I left her office and drove home. For the first time in a long time, I thought about Sarah, who did not even see a doctor during her third pregnancy until she was in her last month. And I was reminded of Tamar, who went to the doctor but ignored everything he said because, she claimed, he did not really know what was going on in her body. As I looked over my research notes, I realized so many women said similar things to what my nurse practitioner had told me: "I've done this before. I know when something is wrong." On a certain level, it seemed right at the time. I trusted their understanding of authority, and I believed that a woman could feel so confident in her own embodied experience. But because my reproductive context differed so much from that of my research participants, I never fully understood that sentiment. I thought it applied to Haredi women alone, because they are raised to have children, but I never imagined it would apply to me as well.

Since completing my research on reproductive ethics among Haredi women in Jerusalem, I have had three children and four pregnancies. Although at the time of my research I could not compare my own reproductive experiences to theirs, I have found myself doing that in the years that followed, as I have read research notes, listened to interviews, and analyzed and written about my findings. With each of my pregnancies I have lived what Lila Abu-Lughod calls "a double life" as an anthropologist. Abu-Lughod also found that her own pregnancies, which all occurred after leaving the field, were significantly shaped by her ethnographic network. She writes, "I moved between the world of 'home' in the United States, with my network of friends and family and the resources of feminist scholarship on reproduction to help me think about the facts of life, and 'the field' in Egypt, where I was surrounded by women who became pregnant, gave birth, lived with children, and talked to me and to each other about why things sometimes go wrong. I looked to both places for help in understanding what was happening to me."[120] Abu-Lughod is describing how the ethnographic data that we gather affects not only our scholarship and our understanding of those who allow us into their lives but also our understanding of self. We as researchers are vulnerable in the sense that we, too, are permeable to the ideas and beliefs of those we research. We can be transformed by the process of ethnography.[121] Just as I had found among the Haredi women in my study, my third pregnancy conferred authority based on experience. Not expecting to share this in common with the women I interviewed, I needed the doctor to remind me of this. But as soon as she did, I found myself turning back to the women in my study as my guides for exercising authority during pregnancy.

The data and analysis contained in these pages reflects the relationships I had with my interlocutors from 2009 to 2011 as well as how my understanding of their actions has changed as I have changed. In embracing my vulnerability, as well as that of my research participants, I do not intend to make their story about me. The focus of ethnography is not the ethnographer, but the ethnographer is the medium through which another's story is told, and in that way, it is vital to be honest about my own context and ability to relate to and understand—on various levels—my interlocutors. Moreover, vulnerability is necessary for ethics. Gilson argues, "If we are not vulnerable, we have no need for ethics, and it is precisely because we are vulnerable—can be affected and made to feel sorrow, concern, or empathy—that we feel any compulsion to respond ethically."[122] In other words, recognizing my own vulnerability will help me see the vulnerability in others and help me act ethically toward others. I invite my readers to join the conversation as embodied subjects themselves, to accept their vulnerabilities, and to allow themselves to be affected by the findings herein to cultivate an ethical response to the challenges faced by Haredi women as they navigate their reproductive lives.

WHAT TO EXPECT WHEN YOU ARE READING THIS BOOK

In this book, I analyze Haredi women's reproductive experiences through a careful examination of the relationship between doctors and rabbis in Jerusalem, the social and economic context in which women reproduce, and the theological ideologies of reproduction within Haredi Judaism. Through this analysis, readers will understand how women's reproductive agency is supported by their cultural context. Readers will journey through how women develop reproductive authority that challenges the hierarchical structure of Haredi life. Readers unfamiliar with the norms and practices of Haredi Judaism will learn as they go through each chapter. This book begins with an overview of the medical, rabbinic, and epistemological context surrounding Haredi women. This context overwhelmingly determines women's first and second pregnancies, and as a result it forms the first and second chapters. The second chapter includes a review of pregnancy advice books, which pave the way for women's reproductive agency, taken up in chapters 3 and 4. Beginning with their third pregnancy, women take advantage of the space left for them to make reproductive decisions without the incursion of male authorities. They draw on cultural norms and theological concepts regarding women's relationship to reproduction as they express their agency. Finally, readers will see how even abortion can be seen as consistent with the current Haredi cultural and economic context.

Chapter 1 establishes the medical context for Haredi women's reproductive agency. By concentrating on the complex and often self-serving relationship between medical and religious authorities in Israel, I argue that doctors and rabbis cultivate mistrust among their constituents as they blur the lines of authority between doctor and rabbi. The result is that Haredi women struggle to enter the conversation about their reproductive health care because doctors and rabbis do not prioritize women's own reproductive experiences and authority. This leaves a space for women to make decisions about their own medical care, but this can have dangerous repercussions for the health of women and babies.

Chapter 2 explores how Haredi women establish reproductive authority by prioritizing their embodied experiences. Through an analysis of how Haredi women performatively use pregnancy advice books, this chapter demonstrates that Haredi women recognize the importance of book culture while rejecting rabbinic authority over their reproductive decisions. In so doing, Haredi women allow pregnancy advice books and their own version of "book tradition" to pave the way for their autonomy from rabbis, husbands, and doctors.

Chapter 3 describes how a woman's reproductive agency develops as a result of her embodied experiences of pregnancy, in conjunction with her cultural and religious context. I demonstrate that Haredi life actually makes space for women to exert agency over their pregnancies. Through an analysis of women's private relationships with their husbands, the financial stressors of Haredi life, and the way the Haredi public effectively ignores pregnant women, Haredi women find space to make reproductive decisions without the incursion of their husbands or their rabbis. Furthermore, although their bodies are heavily regulated, Haredi women also see their pregnant bodies as sources of empowerment. This is because Haredi cultural norms dictate that a woman's role is to reproduce. Paradoxically, in their uniquely female participation in pregnancy, Haredi women facilitate their own entry into the male sphere of decision-making.

Chapter 4 explores the theological elements of Haredi women's reproductive agency. I show how women's understanding of particular Haredi theological concepts justifies their reproductive decisions. They frame pregnancy as the embodiment of divine authority and in so doing reject the rabbinic authorities who otherwise are seen as the intermediaries between God and women. Drawing on data from prenatal classes, Haredi teachers, doulas, and the way women use two key theological concepts, *hishtadlut* (efforts) and *bitachon* (faith), this chapter investigates how women understand their relationship to God and their accountability for pregnancy outcomes. Because women place so much weight on their contribution to pregnancy and the production of a healthy baby, I also look at women's language regarding the unavoidable reality of biological disasters as threats to a woman's control over pregnancy.

In chapter 5, I consider how a Haredi woman decides to terminate a pregnancy. Sometimes women make this decision because of a fetus's physiological developments or risks to their own health. More often, however, Haredi women terminate pregnancies because of financial need. When they need to terminate a pregnancy, they understand it within Haredi theological frameworks and socioeconomic contexts. This chapter draws on ethnographic research with EFRAT, which has a distinct relationship with the Haredi community in Jerusalem. EFRAT's methods of preventing abortion highlight the tension between the economic stability of Haredi families and their high birth rates. This tension is felt by Haredi women themselves and reflects broader discourses about pronatalism in Israel.

The concluding chapter argues that when women's experiences move to the forefront of scholarship, our understanding of Judaism, religious authority, and religious ethics changes. Women's experiences have been largely excluded from Jewish studies scholarship and in particular from scholarship on Haredi Jewry. A turn to women's expressions of reproductive ethics allows us to see how religious authority results from one's embodiment. This claim reaches beyond the experiences of Haredi women, as I call for renewed attention to ethnography of Jewish bodies and to the embodiment of religious authority. I add that when we take embodied experiences into account in the conversation of religious ethics, we see that official doctrine and the writings of religious leaders represent only a piece of religious ethics. Religious ethics have not accounted for the lived religious experiences of those who are marginalized and do not have access to the texts or authority that have shaped the discourse. Therefore, it is necessary to utilize the tools of ethnography to bring those vulnerable voices to the fore. Listening to these marginalized voices means taking into account the ways that their agency develops despite—or because of—their vulnerability in the community. This inclusion can change the entire discourse of religious ethics.

NOTES

1. See Kahn, *Reproducing Jews*, for a full discussion of this oversight. Ivry, "Kosher Medicine," terms this "Kosher medicine."
2. Teman and Ivry, "Pregnancy as a Way of Life."
3. This is similar to a position from Orit Avishai, who argued in "'Doing Religion' in a Secular World" that Orthodox Jews "do religion" in a way that constructs their identity "against the image of a secular Other" (428).
4. Lea Taragin-Zeller's work is an important recent exception. See, for example, Taragin-Zeller, "Conceiving God's Children"; and Gantz, "Childbirth and Women's Strength."
5. Teman and Ivry, "Pregnancy as a Way of Life."
6. Jeffay, "In Israel, Haredi and Muslim Women Are Having Fewer Children."
7. Central Bureau of Statistics, "Families, by Type of Family."
8. Weinreb, Chernichovsky, and Brill, "Israel's Exceptional Fertility."
9. Ivry, Teman, and Bernhardt, "Pregnancy as a Proclamation of Faith"; Ivry, Teman, and Frumkin, "God-Sent Ordeals and Their Discontents."
10. Rosenberg-Friedman, *Birthrate Politics in Zion*.
11. Stoler-Liss, "Mothers Birth the Nation."
12. Kahn, *Reproducing Jews*; Haelyon, "Longing for a Child"; Yishai, "Abortion in Israel"; Kanaaneh, *Birthing the Nation*. Kanaaneh notes that the government

ended this prize a couple of years after it discovered that Arab women received it more frequently. Kanaaneh's research demonstrates that pronatalism was intended for the Jewish population.

13. Berkovitch, "Motherhood as a National Mission."

14. Schiff, "Politics of Fertility Policy in Israel."

15. Shalev and Goldin, "Uses and Misuses of In Vitro Fertilization in Israel," 151.

16. All services, except surrogacy, are available to homosexual as well as heterosexual couples and to all citizens of Israel. However, as Rhoda Ann Kanaaneh has noted in *Birthing the Nation*, the placement of fertility clinics indicates that Israel is indeed encouraging Jews to use these technologies more than non-Jews. See Teman, *Birthing a Mother*, for more on surrogacy.

17. For more on fertility policies toward Israel's minority populations, specifically Palestinians and Arabs, see Kanaaneh, *Birthing the Nation*, and more recently Zu'bi, "Palestinian Fertility in the Israeli Sphere."

18. Portugese, *Fertility Policy in Israel*; Amir and Benjamin, "Defining Encounters"; Yuval-Davis, "National Reproduction."

19. Portugese, *Fertility Policy in Israel*, 32.

20. See, for instance, Kanaaneh, *Birthing the Nation*; Portugese, *Fertility Policy in Israel*.

21. Shalev and Goldin, "Uses and Misuses of In Vitro Fertilization in Israel," 152.

22. Portugese, *Fertility Policy in Israel*, 47.

23. Raucher, "Be Fruitful and Multiply . . . Except. . . ."

24. See, for example, Inhorn, *Local Babies, Global Science*; Roberts, *God's Laboratory*; Czarnecki, "Moral Women, Immoral Technologies"; Maffi, *Women, Health and the State in the Middle East*.

25. Kahn, *Reproducing Jews*. See also Remennick, "Childless in the Land of Imperative Motherhood"; Birenbaum-Carmeli, "Reproductive Policy in Context"; Haelyon, "Longing for a Child"; Goldin, "Technologies of Happiness."

26. Kahn, *Reproducing Jews*.

27. Ivry, "Kosher Medicine."

28. I will return to the relationship between doctors and rabbis in chap. 1.

29. Ivry, *Embodying Culture*.

30. Ibid., 11.

31. See, for example, Benjamin and Haelyon, "Rewriting Fertilization"; Haelyon, "Longing for a Child"; Teman, *Birthing a Mother*.

32. Teman, *Birthing a Mother*.

33. Ibid., 39.

34. Ibid., 42.

35. See, for example, Davis-Floyd, *Birth as an American Rite of Passage*; Lazarus, "What Do Women Want?"; Martin, *Woman in the Body*; Rothman, *Tentative Pregnancy* and *Recreating Motherhood*.

36. See, for example, Ginsburg and Rapp, *Conceiving the New World Order*; Franklin, "Postmodern Procreation."

37. See, for example, Browner and Press, "Normalization of Prenatal Diagnostic Screening"; Kahn, "Rabbis and Reproduction" and "Making Technology Familiar"; Morgan, "Magic and a Little Bit of Science"; Rapp, "Refusing Prenatal Diagnosis"; Sered, "Religious Rituals and Secular Rituals."

38. See, for example, Georges, "Fetal Ultrasound Imaging"; Harris et al., "Seeing the Baby"; Morgan, "Magic and a Little Bit of Science"; Traina et al., "Compatible Contradictions." In the realm of assisted reproductive technologies, Gay Becker, in *Elusive Embryo*, and Margarete Sandelowski, in "Compelled to Try," have made similar arguments.

39. Another example, of Norwegian women's narratives of ultrasound, is shown in Saetnan, "Thirteen Women's Narratives."

40. Tappan, "More Than Fatwas," 103.

41. Ivry, *Embodying Culture*, 5.

42. Berkovitch, "Motherhood as a National Mission."

43. M. Weiss, *Chosen Body*, 2.

44. Sered, *What Makes Women Sick?*

45. For more on women as formal religious authorities, see, for example, Agadjanian, "Women's Religious Authority in a Sub-Saharan Setting"; Zikmund, Lummis, and Chang, *Clergy Women*; Schneider and Schneider, *In Their Own Right*; Nadell, *Women Who Would Be Rabbis*; and Chaves, *Ordaining Women*. For more on women as informal religious leaders see Peshkova, "Leading against Odds"; van Doorn-Harder, *Women Shaping Islam*; Bano and Kalmach, *Women, Leadership, and Mosques*; and Schwartz, *Rabbi's Wife*.

46. See, for example, Baumel, *Sacred Speakers*; Bilu, "From Milah (Circumcision) to Milah (Word)"; Stadler, "Is Profane Work an Obstacle to Salvation?," "Playing with Sacred/Corporeal Identities," and *Yeshiva Fundamentalism*; Heilman and Friedman, "Religious Fundamentalism and Religious Jews"; Heilman, *Defenders of the Faith*; and M. Friedman, "Haredi [Ultra-Orthodox] Society" and "Life Tradition and Book Tradition."

47. Other scholars have done fascinating work on women who struggle with religious norms or attempt to change them through critical religious participation. See Avishai, "Doing Religion," and Rinaldo, "Pious and Critical."

48. Bucar, "Dianomy," 664.

49. Avishai, Gerber, and Randles, "Feminist Ethnographer's Dilemma."

50. Ibid.," 406.

51. Mahmood, *Politics of Piety*, 19.

52. Ibid., 18.

53. Korteweg, "Sharia Debate in Ontario."

54. Bucar, *Creative Conformity*.

55. Bucar, "Dianomy," 665.

56. Ibid., 666.

57. Weir, "Feminism and the Islamic Revival," 330.

58. Ben Shitrit, "Women, Freedom, and Agency in Religious Political Movements."

59. Bangstad, "Saba Mahmood and Anthropological Feminism after Virtue," 32.

60. R. Marie Griffith's work on evangelical women is also formative in this area of study. See Griffith, *God's Daughters*. See also Avishai, "Doing Religion"; Rinaldo, "Pious and Critical"; Neriya-Ben-Shahar, "Negotiating Agency."

61. This scholarship was preceded by others who turned their attention to Jews and Judaism as embodied subjects at different times and in different contexts. See, for example, Eilberg-Schwartz, *People of the Body*; D. Boyarin, *Carnal Israel*; and M. Weiss, *Chosen Body*. Markowitz, in "Blood, Soul, Race, and Suffering," thoroughly discusses these contributions.

62. Yafeh, "Time in the Body."

63. Fader, *Mitzvah Girls*.

64. Davidman, *Becoming Un-Orthodox*, 13.

65. Ibid., 14.

66. Teman and Ivry, "Pregnancy as a Way of Life"; Ivry, Teman, and Frumkin, "God-Sent Ordeals and Their Discontents"; Taragin-Zeller, "Towards an Anthropology of Doubt," "Between Modesty and Beauty," and "Have Six, Have Seven, Have Eight Children"; Birenbaum-Carmeli, "Your Faith or Mine."

67. Foucault, "Subject of Power."

68. Clare, "Agency, Signification, and Temporality."

69. Diprose, *Bodies of Women*, 104.

70. Ibid., 115.

71. Ibid., 117.

72. Young, "Pregnant Embodiment."

73. Ibid., 49.

74. It is important to note that when I use the word *autonomy*, I am not implying that women are making decisions independent of all others. Instead, this autonomy is, as the reader will see, relational and contextual. I am specifically referring to autonomy from the authority of doctors, rabbis, and husbands who would otherwise regulate reproductive decisions.

75. See Shaw, "Performing Breastfeeding: Embodiment, Ethics and the Maternal Subject." Like breastfeeding, which is constantly subject to public moral scrutiny, it is very easy to perform reproduction wrong or incorrectly.

76. Seeman, "Ethnography, Exegesis, and Jewish Ethical Reflections," 345, emphasis in the original.

77. Miller, "On Making a Cultural Turn in Religious Ethics," 3.

78. Robbins, "Between Reproduction and Freedom"; Mattingly and Throop, "Anthropology of Ethics and Morality"; Fassin, *Companion to Moral Anthropology*; Das, *Life and Words*.

79. For an extended discussion of Jewish ethics and ethnography, see Raucher, "Ethnography and Jewish Ethics" and "Whose Womb and Whose Ethics?"

80. Ellenson, "How to Draw Guidance from a Heritage," 130.

81. For examples of this type of methodology, see Jakobovits, *Jewish Medical Ethics*; Rosner and Bleich, *Jewish Bioethics*; Tendler, *Medical Ethics*; and Abraham, *Medical Halacha for Everyone*.

82. Mackler, *Introduction to Jewish and Catholic Bioethics*, 45.

83. Dorff, *Matters of Life and Death*, 401.

84. Ibid., 405, emphasis in the original.

85. Zoloth, "Reading Like a Girl," 120.

86. Ibid., 126.

87. Levi, "Polyvocal Body." See also Sered, *What Makes Women Sick?*

88. Boas et al., *Bioethics and Biopolitics in Israel*.

89. Not all would agree that ethnography is a feminist method. Ethnography can violate many principles of feminism—namely, in that it is intrusive and exploitative of those very individuals that we seek to give voice to. See Stacey, "Can There Be a Feminist Ethnography?"

90. See Davis, "Beyond Rabbi Hiyya's Wife" and "Abortion in Jewish Thought"; Irshai, *Fertility and Jewish Law*.

91. Irshai, *Fertility and Jewish Law*, 17. This is similar to Daniel H. Gordis's argument, in "Wanted," that despite the scholar's desire to use the texts to speak to a variety of contemporary ethical issues, often this reliance on the text leads to many scholars missing the salient ethical issues of the case at hand. The text simply does not speak directly to many contemporary questions.

92. Diprose, *Bodies of Women*, 18.

93. See Foucault, *Power/Knowledge* and "The Subject and Power," and Diprose, *Bodies of Women*, for more on social and ethical formation and embodiment.

94. For more on this claim, see Gordis, "Wanted"; Henning, "Jewish Bioethics"; Newman, "What Are We Doing When We Do Jewish Ethics?"; and Washofsky, "On the Absence of Method." Washofsky states, "It is not the conclusion of a formula that distinguishes correct from incorrect interpretations of the halakha. It is a *judgment*, a reasoned but not logically required (and therefore defeasible) choice between plausible alternatives based upon an evaluation of substantive fact" (266, emphasis in the original).

95. See also Sinclair, *Jewish Biomedical Law*; Davis, "Method in Jewish Bioethics."

96. Orsi, "Everyday Miracles." Richard Miller refers to something similar, the "ethics of ordinary life," when he suggests that religious ethics should be

attentive to "cultural practices and their relationship to character and conduct" ("On Making a Cultural Turn in Religious Ethics," 3). The term I employ suggests that there should not be a difference between normative ethics and the ethics of the everyday. Instead, lived ethics recognizes that the two cannot be distinguished.

97. *Hasidic* refers to one group of Orthodox Jews. Although some Hasidic Jews are Haredi, the ones I knew previously were more mainstream Orthodox Jews.

98. This is more common among Ashkenazi families than Sephardi, but it is a tradition that has spread among even secular Jews. See Gaster, *Customs and Folkways of Jewish Life*, for more on prenatal taboos, and Sered, "Religious Rituals and Secular Rituals," and Ivry, *Embodying Culture*, for more on contemporary customs.

99. *Haredi* is the most neutral term to use to describe the population of women with whom I researched. *Ultra-Orthodox* and *right wing* are laden with connotations about other forms of religious practice and belief. Instead, I am using the term that they use to describe themselves. For more on the characteristics of Haredi Judaism, see chap. 2.

100. For more on segulot, see Sered, "Healing and Resistance"; Rock-Singer, *Prophetess of the Body*; and Taylor-Guthartz, *Overlapping Worlds*. In some cases, the word *segulah* has a connotation of only bringing about positive effects, as opposed to protecting against negative. Among women in this study, what was significant about the segulah was its ability to connect them to God. In some cases this meant protecting them from a miscarriage, in another it meant facilitating an easy birth. Importantly, each positive has a negative flip side. Protecting from a miscarriage could also be seen as continuing the pregnancy. Some scholars see segulot as folk, and therefore unofficial, women's religion because they are not rooted in rabbinic texts (see Soloveitchik, "Rupture and Reconstruction"). I do not mean to imply that these segulot are any less part of religious life, belief, or practice. When women use the term, they intend it to refer to religious practices, and this is how it should be read. Like blessings over food that elevate the act of eating (see Fader, *Mitzvah Girls*), segulot elevate pregnancy, despite their not having textual origin.

101. See Sandelowski, "Compelled to Try"; Becker, *Elusive Embryo*; and Thompson, *Making Parents*, for more on the distinct attitudes toward medicine and reproductive technologies found among men and women struggling with infertility.

102. Other scholars have researched infertility in Israel, and I direct the reader to that scholarship. See, for example, Kahn, *Reproducing Jews*; Ivry, "Kosher Medicine"; and Teman, *Birthing a Mother*; Remennick, "Childless in the Land of Imperative Motherhood."

103. Tamar El-Or's *Educated and Ignorant*, which is based on her research of education among Gerer Hasidic women, is a good introduction to these types

of classes. Kimmy Caplan has also recorded content analysis of some of these classes, in "Internal Popular Discourse of Israeli Haredi Women," based on his listening to audio recordings of the classes.

104. I also conducted research at Bead Chaim, another antiabortion organization in Jerusalem. However, Bead Chaim is founded and operated by Messianic Jews and other Christians. Its clientele is not Haredi, so I have excluded it from my analysis here.

105. S. Levine, *Mystics, Mavericks and Merrymakers*, 6.

106. Other ethnographers of ultra-Orthodox Jews have discussed similar entry points into a community of interlocutors. In "Fieldwork among the Ultra-Orthodox," Lisa Kaul-Seidman finds that when women conduct ethnographic research in the Haredi community, Haredi women often label them as *ba'alot tshuvah*, or those who have "returned" to Judaism, meaning they are becoming more religious. Otherwise, Kaul-Seidman claims, the research participants could not understand why someone was so interested in their practices. Similarly, Janet Belcove-Shalin found that before she spoke of her interest to deepen her understanding of Judaism, her Hasidic informants demonstrated great disdain for her research and her presence in their community. See Belcove-Shalin, "Becoming More of an Eskimo."

107. William Mitchell, in "Goy in the Ghetto," remarks that as a non-Jewish ethnographer, his entry into American Jewish families involved quite a bit of language shifting and body-language adjustment. Although seemingly similar to his research participants, Mitchell had to change his behavior significantly in order to not be excluded from research due to poor rapport.

108. Markowitz, "Blood, Soul, Race, and Suffering."

109. Raucher, "Feminist Ethnography Inside and Outside the Field."

110. Ghosh, "Doing Feminist Ethnography: Exploring the Lives of Disabled Women," 21.

111. Fox, "Observations and Reflections of a Perpetual Fieldworker."

112. Brown and Casanova, "Mothers in the Field," and Kahn, *Reproducing Jews*, address the ways their insider/outsider status was determined by their identities as mothers or nonmothers.

113. Jonathan Boyarin, in "Waiting for a Jew," discusses the ways his religious affiliation overlapped and influenced his ethnographic research.

114. Markowitz, "Blood, Soul, Race, and Suffering," 42.

115. Ibid.

116. Fader, "Reflections on Queen Esther," 129.

117. Although I did not go as far as Hilla Nehushtan in cutting off ties with a research participant who challenged me, I did want to escape from many interviews due to uncomfortable interactions (Nehushtan, "Impurities of Experience").

118. Gilson, *Ethics of Vulnerability*, 127.

119. Ibid., 137.

120. Abu-Lughod, "Tale of Two Pregnancies," 340.

121. In "Truth, Subjectivity, and Ethnographic Research," Lynn Davidman describes how she was transformed through her ethnographic research on women whose mothers had died.

122. Gilson, *Ethics of Vulnerability*, 11.

ONE

—ᴍ—

MEDICINE AND RELIGION

Doctors and Rabbis in Israel

DR. MIRI LEVIN, AN OBSTETRICIAN who works at Bikur Cholim as well as some clinics around Jerusalem, told me about a Haredi woman who was in labor when the baby's heart rate dropped significantly. The doctor wanted to perform a cesarean section, but the woman's husband called their rabbi, who objected to the procedure. After multiple phone calls sent back and forth between the doctor and the rabbi, the rabbi refused to approve the operation, and as a result, the husband refused as well. Eventually the doctor called a judge, who mandated the C-section. "This is rather scary," I remarked to Dr. Levin as she told me the story. She agreed, and I continued, "Because a rabbi is not a doctor." Levin laughed and responded, "I'm glad you think that, but many Haredi women do not know the difference." This, Levin claims, is what makes it difficult for the doctor to contradict the rabbi. According to Dr. Levin, because women do not trust that their doctors are advising them based on their medical expertise, they may see the disagreement as evidence of a mere difference of opinion, instead of understanding that a doctor and a rabbi are speaking from within two different frames of reference and have distinct reasons for issuing their opinions.

When Dr. Levin told me this story, I was shocked and disappointed. I could not believe that a rabbi, over the phone, could make a medical recommendation and that people would think he has sufficient information and authority to challenge a doctor. I was also concerned about the laboring woman whose life and fetus were in danger and yet who seemed to lack any say about what should be done. This was apparent both in her husband's actions and in Dr. Levin's retelling. And although I was relieved that the judge eventually mandated the C-section, I was scared to think that this event might be commonplace. I was surprised that Dr. Levin blamed this Haredi woman for not knowing the difference between a rabbi and a doctor. Instead, it seemed that this woman's husband and rabbi did not respect the doctor's authority over medical decisions. This case of a rabbinic challenge to medical care, and Dr. Levin's retelling of it, which includes her characterization of a Haredi woman as ignorant, capture the relationship I will dissect in this chapter. Doctors and rabbis work together, sometimes reluctantly, to make decisions about Haredi women's reproductive health care. Each views the other as merely instrumental in achieving his or her own goals, while they overlook women's participation. While I did not hear of any other cases of this magnitude, my research with physicians and nurses in the field of reproductive medicine revealed that Haredi rabbis and the doctors who treat Haredi women exist in a relationship built on mutual benefit and mistrust. What makes this relationship particularly challenging is that at least in the field of reproductive medicine—though we will see that their relationship extends beyond this specialty—the lines of authority between doctor and rabbi are blurred because of how the two figures have come to work together. Haredi women struggle to enter the conversation about their reproductive health care because doctors and rabbis do not prioritize women's own reproductive experiences and authority.

This chapter establishes the medical context for Haredi women's reproductive agency. Although it might seem odd to begin a book about women's agency with a chapter about doctors and rabbis, this chapter is a necessary starting point because doctors and rabbis are also a woman's starting point in her journey toward reproductive agency. When pregnant, a Haredi woman faces a closed network of doctors and rabbis who benefit significantly from this relationship. Rabbis claim authority over reproductive decisions because what is at stake in reproductive medicine is nothing short of establishing kinship with the next generation. Rabbis want their authority to be a central part of the family structure. Doctors, for their part, cooperate with rabbis either because they have a financial interest in the Haredi clientele or because they see cooperating with rabbis as the only way of providing medical care to Haredi patients. Although sometimes women benefit from this holistic model of medical care, women often feel stifled when they are unable to escape rabbinic oversight in medical care. A description of the setting for Haredi women's reproductive care is crucial for understanding how these women create reproductive agency that is embedded in their cultural and theological contexts and their embodied experiences of pregnancy. Other scholars have demonstrated how women and doctors in Israel are engaged in a struggle for authority, and some have spoken about the "triadic relations among Israeli rabbis, doctors, and infertility patients."[1] I suggest that when rabbis and doctors are working together, pregnant Haredi women are overlooked.

Drawing on interviews with doctors and nurses who work extensively with Haredi patients and building on ethnographies from Susan Kahn and Tsipy Ivry, I analyze the contours of the relationship between doctors and rabbis in Haredi women's reproductive health care. This chapter thus lays out the structural setting for women's reproductive agency. First, I argue that the way doctors and rabbis compete for authority reflects larger epistemological struggles between medicine and religion or culture. Then, as I explore the ways rabbis exert control over the medical field, I argue that the process of "koshering" medicine is the result of long-standing concern about medicine contaminating Haredi life. Rabbinic oversight, furthermore, leads to suspicion toward medical professionals, suspicion that can be allayed only with more rabbinic oversight. The next section looks at how medical professionals respond to the "koshering" of their field by stereotyping Haredi women's reproductive needs. Although this can result in holistic health care, these assumptions also tend to silence women's individual experiences.

Finally, this chapter introduces the idea, to be further explored in the next few chapters, that although doctors and rabbis benefit from cooperation in the medical arena, they compete unsuccessfully for authority over Haredi women's medical decisions.[2] This is because women have internalized a mistrust of both doctors and rabbis and thus prioritize their own embodied experiences. Throughout this book, we will see that sometimes this results in women ignoring medical care altogether.

COMPETING FOR AUTHORITY

A relationship of conflict and cooperation exists in a context wherein doctors and rabbis each have something to gain from the relationship. Doctors work with rabbis so that they can effectively treat Haredi patients and gain even more Haredi patients through rabbinic referrals. Rabbis work with doctors so that they can extend their authority. Rabbis have inserted themselves into medical decisions as gatekeepers for their Haredi constituents because there is a historical concern about the contaminating influence of secular doctors on Haredi life. Haredi patients, as a result, are often reluctant to turn to doctors for medical care and advice, unless those doctors have been sanctioned by their rabbis. Many doctors have therefore established relationships with rabbinic authorities and become familiar with halakhic concerns in order to attract and keep Haredi patients. If doctors and rabbis work together, both groups can benefit from the cooperation.

This relationship, however, often blurs the boundaries between doctors and rabbis and the distinct spheres of authority they maintain. Medicine and religion exist in this context as two competing epistemologies. Writing specifically about how medical knowledge came to dominate birthing practices in the West, Brigitte Jordan explains as follows:

> Frequently, one kind of knowledge gains ascendance and legitimacy. A consequence of the legitimation of one kind of knowing as authoritative is the devaluation, often the dismissal, of all other kinds of knowing. Those who espouse alternative knowledge systems then tend to be seen as backward, ignorant, and naïve, or worse, simply as troublemakers. Whatever they might think they have to say about the issues up for negotiation is judged irrelevant, unfounded, and not to the point (Jordan 1989). The constitution of authoritative knowledge is an ongoing social process that both builds and reflects power relationships within a community of practice (Lave and Wenger 1991; Wenger 1990).[3]

The complicated relationship between doctors and rabbis that is described in this chapter reflects how one group judges another in an effort to devalue a different form of knowledge and thereby restore one's own authority. Recall Dr. Miri Levin from the opening vignette. Dr. Levin seemed most concerned that her patient did not respect a doctor's authority. Dr. Levin wants all patients to prioritize medical information. Instead of one group becoming dominant, however, the resulting framework is one of a blended medical-rabbinic reproductive health care in which doctors and rabbis compete for authority. As women reject this blended system in favor of their own reproductive authority, they are responding to the relations of power within the community.

Rabbinic Involvement in Contemporary Israeli Medicine

Rabbinic involvement in medical decisions is an example of *da'at Torah,* or the idea that rabbis have the intellectual ability and the authority to weigh in on all sorts of decisions. In the last few decades, Haredi rabbis have come to regulate every decision and action among their constituents, regardless of whether it is ostensibly a religious question. Instead of only fielding questions about holiday observance or the permissibility of certain food items, Haredi rabbis now influence business, political, and medical decisions as well. Making decisions that are far beyond the religious realm reflects the rabbinic fear of secular influences and authorities. Haredi rabbis regulate all means of access to the non-Haredi world—the internet,[4] cell phones,[5] the radio,[6] and other media,[7] for example. Haredi culture works hard to protect Haredi Jews from outside influences because "corrosive secular Israeli culture might contaminate the Haredi enclave."[8] In a similar vein, to calm their fears regarding the contamination of religious structure from secular doctors, who will introduce a different way of prioritizing medical information, rabbis involve themselves in the practice of medicine.

Rabbinic concerns about the influence of medicine are compounded by the fact that medicine and medical technology are hegemonic forces in Israeli culture. Since the 1960s and 1970s, medical care in Israel has become increasingly sophisticated and reliant on technology. Additionally, medical care is regulated by national health insurance and heavily subsidized by the government. Within the technologically advanced Israeli medical system, individuals are expected to prioritize scientific information and the use of medical technology.[9] Fearing the authority of medical hegemony in Israel, rabbis promote the idea that one cannot fully trust a doctor to provide the best care because many doctors are hostile to religious patients and their needs; therefore, patients need the rabbinic community to tell them which doctors to visit.

This section will explore this phenomenon in medicine more broadly and then turn to its manifestation in the specific field of fertility treatments and reproductive care. Rabbinic involvement in fertility treatments is an attempt to prevent the contamination of kinship lines while also ensuring that rabbis—and, more broadly, Judaism—remain part of the kinship structure for those relying on medical technology to conceive. In this sense, rabbis are not just competing for authority but for a place in the Jewish future. Religious authorities fear that patients or doctors might think religion is not needed in a technologically sophisticated, medically advanced Israel. Therefore, rabbis have inserted themselves into medical care by sowing doubt and fear among patients.

By attempting to institutionalize rabbinic involvement in medical decisions, Israeli rabbinic organizations draw on the underlying mistrust many Haredi individuals have for the medical establishment. Based on a study of general practice consultations in Israel, Michael Weingarten and Eliezer Kitai found that Haredi individuals were more likely to turn to their rabbis than were Israelis belonging to other religious affiliations. Although patients turned to particular rabbis "to strengthen their faith in their medical healer," Weingarten and Kitai explain that the rabbis "took it upon themselves to pass judgment on the quality of care the patients were receiving from their doctors, even to the point of recommending that they change to the care of some 'better' specialist."[10]

Ezra LeMarpeh (A Healing Aide) is one such organization that provides medical referrals to Jews around the world. While the organization performs many charitable services (such as loaning wheelchairs, importing rare medications, and providing additional ambulance services within Israel), its leaders encourage patients to rely on rabbinic guidance for their medical decisions while reinforcing a sense of mistrust in the medical establishment. On the organization's website, Rabbi Elimelech Firer, founder and director, writes, "People don't come to us to get a remedy for their illness or a prescription for a cure. Instead, they come to receive support and advice. People come to us to strengthen their feeling of security to continue their fight, to know if the path that was offered to them is the right one, or rather if they should be looking elsewhere, with a different doctor, a different center or a different course of treatment."[11] Firer acknowledges that Ezra LeMarpeh is not a medical organization, as it does not provide any medicines or treatments, but states that it does provide people with advice regarding how to navigate the medical establishment. However, Firer does not make clear how Ezra LeMarpeh comes to recommend one doctor over another or one course of treatment instead of another. In this way, Firer's statement suggests that the purpose of Ezra LeMarpeh is to destabilize a patient's reliance on doctors and replace it with faith in religious authorities. Note, however, that this process does not imply that religious authorities are doing the healing or that healing should be faith based and not science based. Instead, rabbis attempt to direct and control the medical process by speaking with patients about their medical treatments and persuading them to see doctors who have received the organization's approval.

I suggest we view rabbinic approval over medical care in Israel similar to the way Ayala Fader sees the blending of therapists and rabbis among ultra-Orthodox Jews in New York. Fader's research with people who left the ultra-Orthodox way of life, or who are living a "double life," revealed that rabbinic leaders understood these actions to be a crisis of interiority. Here, *interiority* refers to the religious doubt felt by those who are leaving the community; rabbis, educators, and therapists see the internet as the source of this religious doubt and attempt to "cure" it by working on an individual's interiority.[12] In this framework, therapists became entwined with rabbinic authorities under the auspices of a new "kosher" psychology. Fader explains, "Psychology could be 'kosher' if its perspectives could be reconciled with previously existing Jewish religious sources, which had their own theories of the workings of human psychology."[13] To reconcile these two fields, rabbis reinterpret psychology in religious language and frameworks. As a result, religious doubt has become medicalized and psychology kosherized. Additionally, Fader has found rabbis without any formal training or education in psychology doing religious therapy.[14] As the field of medicine has undergone a process of rabbinic oversight, it has become the norm for doctors to refer patients back to their rabbis for approval. Problems that are entirely medical are treated as issues that require rabbinic oversight.

A similar pattern has developed in the field of reproductive medicine among ultra-Orthodox Jews in Jerusalem. Rabbinic oversight is perhaps no more extensive than in the area of reproduction, where "medicalized and technological reproduction is the default mode."[15] This applies to pregnancies conceived naturally as well as those that require fertility enhancements. As fertility treatments proliferated in Israel, rabbis became experts in evaluating treatments for their conformity to Jewish law, and an organization similar to Firer's exists that is specifically for fertility treatments, offering not just referrals but a range of Jewish legal considerations for various treatment options. In this way, rabbis serve as intermediaries between doctors and patients, educating patients on the importance of Jewish legal concerns with fertility treatments. In many ways, then, rabbis serve as the gatekeepers to these fertility treatments. Given the way many Israeli women view infertility as a "curse," rabbis have come to play a significant role in gaining access to these treatments and, ultimately, in rescuing Jewish women from this curse.[16]

Hilla Haelyon found that Israeli women often confront infertility as a problem that significantly disrupts "an essential aspect of a woman's life," because a pronatalist ideology presents motherhood as a natural state of being for Israeli women, while infertility challenges women to think about motherhood as something they must work toward.[17] For many women, the range of fertility treatments coupled with the increased involvement of medical professionals makes them feel estranged from the process of reproduction and motherhood. Tsipy Ivry argues that this distance is heightened among religious patients who "seem to experience the tension as part of a broader sense of otherness in a nonreligious system."[18] Susan Martha Kahn's ethnography of assisted reproduction in Israel was the first to explore PUAH, which stands for Poriyoot ve'Refuah Alpi haHalakha (Fertility Treatment According to Jewish Law). PUAH is not an organization that caters to Haredi patients, but it can serve as an example of how religious authorities have attempted to protect their social boundaries through medical oversight. PUAH has two purposes: (1) to make the range of fertility treatments less overwhelming to religious patients and (2) to ensure that infertility is treated within the framework of Jewish law.[19] For religious women, PUAH offers a familiar, religious place wherein they can learn more about their fertility treatment options while framing them within religious structures and language. However, PUAH, like Ezra LeMarpeh, is not a medical organization. The rabbis in these organizations focus on laying out a patient's course of treatment but not on providing medical information.[20] This course of action often includes explaining the halakhic concerns with patients who know very little about the halakhic complexities of fertility treatments. PUAH, therefore, encourages religious couples to pursue fertility treatments but in a way that requires religious involvement and emphasizes Jewish legal concerns.

Rabbinic authorities in PUAH are not just trying to emphasize that patients should be aware of halakhic concerns in order to adhere to religious guidelines. These rabbis fear the contamination of kinship lines among Jewish Israelis as a result of mishandled fertility treatments, which Kahn refers to as "reproductive lawlessness."[21] The medical education of rabbinic authorities and the subsequent religious legal rulings about fertility treatments are intended to prevent potential violations of Jewish law, particularly those related to kinship structures.[22] For example, rabbis aim to ensure that genetic lines continue as intended, that women do not conceive while considered ritually impure, and that sperm is not "spilled" during the course of treatments. There are religious and cultural consequences for a child conceived while a woman is ritually impure, and the incorrect mixing of egg and sperm could result in a *mamzer*, a bastard child, which is also accompanied by religious and cultural consequences.

Similar to the way Ezra LeMarpeh reminds patients that they should question their course of treatment and receive rabbinic guidance in medical care, the expansion of rabbinic law surrounding fertility issues and the enactment of these laws through PUAH reveals that religious influences on reproductive technologies seek to preserve traditional familial kinship ties while ensuring a place for religious authorities in the kin network. Reproductive technologies have introduced new actors into the process of conception, pregnancy, and birth, such as laboratory technicians, medical specialists, gamete donors, sonographers, and surrogates. As each participates in the process of reproduction, there are consequences for the subsequent relationships.[23] In Kahn's research in a hospital's fertility laboratory, ultra-Orthodox Jewish women monitored the fertility procedures to ensure that whenever sperm and eggs were being processed, the correct pair was combined. Kahn quotes one woman as saying, "We make sure that Lichtenberg and Silberstein don't get mixed up."[24] In other words, these women, called *mashgichot*, oversee the lab technicians to confirm that a woman's egg is fertilized by her husband's sperm and not someone else's.[25] This would be religiously and ethically problematic as a woman might give birth to a child who is not genetically related to her husband, thus unintentionally skewing kinship, which is so closely related to genetics in the ultra-Orthodox community. Rabbis insist on this kind of oversight to protect relationships within the community and to remind the lab technicians of the required involvement of religion in medical care.[26]

The mashgichot and the lab workers, all women, developed close relationships, despite their social and religious differences. All share an interest in enabling successful pregnancies and births, even referring to the babies born of their fertility work as "our babies." Kahn refers to this relationship as a "fictive kin network" because conception occurs as a result of these relationships.[27] Yael Hashiloni-Dolev argues that reconstituting the Jewish-Israeli family is common in Israel, where the Israeli family "is not a stable concept; rather, it is a constantly shifting notion, changing along with the new technologies . . . the ideal of the family is defined in diverse ways to justify various medical procedures and new family formations."[28] And yet some maintain there are limits about who can be included in the Jewish-Israeli family; the mashgichot distinguish between the religious contribution to the creation of the baby and the medical contribution. Kahn explains that the mashgichot often spoke about the fact that the technology only works because God wants it to work. One *mashgicha* shared a famous Talmudic aphorism that there are three partners in creation: the father, the mother, and God. Kahn writes, "I jokingly added the names of the lab workers to her list, and she replied seriously: 'they are not partners, they are only envoys.'"[29] The mashgichot may also be envoys, but their work—the religious work—is seen as the work of God; therefore, they, unlike the medical technicians, are partners in the creation of a new life, as they see it. Tensions such as these—who matters in the creation of life—strike at the core of the relationship between religious and medical authorities in Israel.

To limit ritual contamination and any medical challenges to rabbinic authority, PUAH and Ezra LeMarpeh act as overseers for the medical needs of Orthodox and ultra-Orthodox Jews. Drawing on patients' fears that medical authorities are at odds with religious concerns, religious authorities emphasize the importance of consulting one of these organizations before beginning medical treatment. In so doing, they have changed the practice of medicine and established a kin structure that preserves rabbinic involvement.

Rabbinic involvement in reproductive medicine does not end, however, with fertility treatments. Prenatal clinics in areas heavily populated by Haredi Jews are often certified by Haredi rabbis. At one clinic, this certification, or *teudah*, is posted prominently in the clinic, surrounded by information about payments, how to make an appointment, and where to find a lactation specialist. It reads, "This clinic has been certified by Rabbi Meir Cohen, head rabbi of Har Nof." As proof of the rabbi's approval of this clinic, the teudah both attracts Haredi patients and serves to remind doctors of the ultimate rabbinic authority in medical decisions. This certification is precisely why Ivry terms this religious intervention into medical care, "kosher medicine," much like the way Fader refers to kosher psychology.[30] *Kosher* usually refers to the process in which food is observed, inspected, and certified by rabbis. The individual Haredi rabbinic approval for medical clinics represents an extension of the current practice for restaurants and supermarkets.[31] A restaurant can seek approval from a few different umbrella organizations, each of which is considered to uphold the laws of *kashrut* to a particular level of stringency. The specific certification hangs at the entrance to most restaurants so that a passerby knows who has given his approval and thus whether or not it is an establishment with appropriate supervision. For example, Haredim do not follow the approval of the government-sponsored rabbinic organization, the Israeli Chief Rabbinate; instead, they will look for Haredi rabbis' approvals to know that the restaurant meets the Haredi standards of kashrut. Particularly they are looking for signs that read "Kosher L'Mehadrin," which indicate that the establishment meets more stringent kashrut standards than those approved by the Rabbinate.[32]

By certifying that certain doctors, clinics, and hospitals are kosher, the Haredi leadership, *haEda haHaredit*, sends a public message to both doctors and patients. These certifications remind doctors that cooperation with the rabbis will bring more customers to their clinic. Therefore, doctors are encouraged to include rabbis in medical decisions and conform to community norms for prenatal testing and birth control usage, for instance. A doctor in one of these clinics might ask her patient who requests a fetal ultrasound, "Does your rabbi allow ultrasounds?" before performing the exam. These certifications are also intended for Haredi patients. When Haredi women enter a clinic that has been certified, they know that the medical staff has a relationship with rabbis in their community. The certification, therefore, warns patients against getting any tests or pursuing treatment that would violate rabbinic instruction. A woman who sees this certification knows that in some way her rabbi and the norms he upholds are watching over her medical decisions.

Many of the instances of rabbinic control were directed at female medical professionals. For instance, Dr. Hadar Segel, an Orthodox physician, moved to Israel from England, where she specialized in surgical gynecology and obstetrics. Initially she amassed a client base among Haredi women in Israel, but after one appointment, her patients would not return. A few of the women explained to her that the *askanim* recommended different doctors, claiming she was not the best in her field. When a Haredi individual needs to know which doctor to call to treat an ailment, he or she asks the askanim (male rabbinic assistants who often provide medical advice), and they recommend a particular doctor. When Segel contacted the askanim and asked why they were not recommending her even though she was the best in England, they told her they did not need her to do surgery because they already had specialists in gynecological and obstetrical surgery. Instead, they decided she would be best for providing hormones and fertility treatments to Haredi women. Segel understood that she either had to switch her specialty or forfeit the Haredi client base, so she is now a fertility specialist for the Haredi community.

It is not a coincidence that female physicians are targets of rabbinic control. Women's public presence and involvement in Haredi society threatens the gender norms that separate men and women. We can see a widely publicized example of this in the Israeli Health Ministry's awards ceremony in December 2011. The Israeli Health Ministry invited Channa Maayan, a professor of pediatrics in Israel, to the awards ceremony to receive a prize for her research on Jewish hereditary diseases. Because the acting health minister at the time was Haredi and Maayan knew that other religious Jews would be in the audience, Maayan dressed modestly for the occasion. When she arrived at the ceremony in her honor, she was shocked to discover that not only were men and women sitting separately but also the health minister did not allow her to accept her own award; instead, he asked her to designate a male colleague who would accept the award on her behalf because women were not allowed on stage.[33] According to Haredi standards of modesty, it would not have been appropriate for a woman to speak in front of a mixed crowd of men and women. Despite the facts that this was a state-sponsored event and that the state awarded the prize to Dr. Maayan, the health minister organized an event that conformed to Haredi standards. These standards included limiting Dr. Maayan's public voice and presence, as had been similarly done to Dr. Segel.[34]

Rabbinic authorities are suspicious of female medical professionals because these women are generally not Haredi themselves, and even if they do identify as such, they do not conform to all Haredi cultural standards for women. Rabbis suspect that when Haredi women visit secular female physicians, they might experience what Tamar El-Or calls a "normative anomaly that creates a paradox in the life of the community."[35] How can Haredi women rely on these secular, medical authorities for advice, guidance, and instruction? How can they accept advice that conflicts with their religious ideology? And importantly, how can Haredi women accept guidance about pregnancy, their most important contribution to Haredi society, from secular women? Rabbis know that an unregulated paradox "invites a breakdown and interpretation that shape a revised understanding of reality."[36] This revised understanding may, rabbis fear, lead to a crisis of faith, or a Haredi woman wanting to reject the authority of male rabbis and the doctors they have sanctioned. Ultra-Orthodox rabbis see Haredi women as particularly permeable to these outside influences.[37] To avoid this, rabbis exert influence over female physicians in particular.

Doctors Respond to Rabbinic Involvement

The medical community has a multifaceted response to rabbinic involvement in medical care. Many doctors I spoke to are wary of rabbinic oversight because it interferes with the care they are trying to provide, and so it prevents them from treating patients the way they deem appropriate. However, I also observed many doctors and hospitals accepting rabbinic involvement and catering to Haredi patients and their religious needs. Some do so out of rabbinic persuasion, some because of the business incentives, and some because of the potential to offer medical care to a population that is often difficult to reach. Doctors recognize that in order to provide medical care to and guarantee a steady stream of Haredi patients, they must work with the rabbis. Regardless of the reason, when doctors permit religious accommodations or succumb to rabbinic oversight, women realize that even their medical care is supervised by their rabbis. The only way to escape their rabbis' oversight, therefore, is to avoid medical care.

Conversations during my research revealed that medical professionals are suspicious about how Ezra LeMarpeh comes to recommend certain doctors over others, implying that these decisions are based on money and not medical expertise. To the doctors' credit, the organization does not disclose how it makes its determinations, so doctors are left to assume the worst. When I asked Dr. Avi Gabai, an obstetrician and gynecologist and department head of one of the hospitals in Jerusalem, what he knew about Rabbi Firer, Gabai revealed his skepticism by relaying to me a rabbinic saying he heard once: "In addition to money, *halakhic* decisions should be based on *halakha*." Gabai's impression is that money—not Jewish law or medical knowledge—guides the organization's decisions. He explained that Rabbi Firer and his "crew" of rabbis are known for snooping around hospitals and following doctors as if they are medically trained themselves. Aviva Cohen, a licensed midwife in Israel, expressed a similar disgust with this practice. "On what basis are you making a decision about where a patient should go? They have these guys like Firer who claim, 'Go here for this and go here for that.' . . . These rabbis are sitting and learning." Cohen meant that the rabbis study rabbinic texts all day and thus have no knowledge of the medical field. She continued, "I want to know who is feeding them this knowledge. I want to know where it's from." Cohen's statements, like Gabai's, also reflect the impression that Ezra LeMarpeh is corrupt and guided by nonmedical advice.

Others expressed frustration with how rabbinic involvement changes their doctor-patient relationship. Dr. Levin, the obstetrician from the opening vignette, says that sometimes being a doctor for Haredi women means just being the "hand of the rabbi." She explains, "A woman comes in and says, 'I want to do this, this, and this,' but really she received instruction from the rabbi. The first person who tracks the pregnancy is the rabbi. A woman who is not Haredi comes to the doctor because she wants to hear from the doctor what the possibilities are." She seemed bothered by this, so I asked Dr. Levin what she thought about it. "It upsets me because I became a doctor so that I could work with sick people in cooperation with them. But here there is no cooperation. I'm like a secretary. That's frustrating." I cannot confirm whether Gabai or Cohen are correct in their assessment of Ezra LeMarpeh, and because I did not interview the specific patients that Levin is referencing, I do not know whether they enter her office with instructions from the rabbi. What is important here, though, is that these doctors—and many others I spoke to—see these rabbinic authorities as inappropriately compromising a doctor's ability to provide medical care to their patients.

Many doctors participate in this relationship because they risk losing religious clientele and thus the associated financial benefits if they do not accommodate religious demands. A doctor who receives a patient through a recommendation from PUAH will work with those rabbis, even for negotiations that do not necessarily concern any halakhic issue.[38] This is because the doctor knows that cooperating with rabbis will guarantee more referrals and more patients. Dr. Tamar Azulai, an obstetrician and gynecologist who knows her colleagues cooperate with rabbis' unethical requests, told me this relationship is "horrible" and "very dangerous." Unfortunately, she also understands why doctors participate: "If you don't give it to her, someone else will give it to her, and then she'll be that person's patient." Although most physicians who work for the four *kupot holim* (sick funds) or health maintenance organizations (HMOs) receive a basic salary, they get paid extra for additional patients registered to them. Refusing to accommodate a rabbi's demands means losing a great deal of business from the Haredi community because of their high birth rates. This is a risk many doctors are not willing to take.

Karin, a nurse-midwife who has worked extensively in the Haredi community, agrees to many rabbinic demands because she wants this population of women to receive good medical care. Many of our conversations started with her expressing a concern about a Haredi woman not having adequate experience with the medical field. For instance, she once shared that she had seen a pregnant Haredi woman the morning before we met who had never had an internal gynecological exam. Karin was disturbed by this and felt terrible. This young woman was nervous about the exam, because she thought it might cause her to bleed and make her a *niddah*, or transmit menstrual impurity. Karin was sensitive and caring as she recounted the story to me. She also helps women navigate the complicated medical system in Israel. Because she is known for this, Karin often sees Haredi patients who have recently moved to Israel, and she teaches them how the different HMOs work and how they can get the most out of their health care. Karin has benefited from her cooperation with Haredi rabbis, as she is widely endorsed by the rabbinic leadership. Karin frequently receives phone calls from pregnant women whose rabbis told them to call her, and Haredi communities circulate her writings. Furthermore, the clinic where she works receives certifications from many Haredi rabbis, including a teudah posted prominently on the wall behind the receptionists.

Karin and other medical professionals are also aware of what is at stake if they refuse to comply with rabbinic demands. When I first met Karin, it was on the eve of her annual seminar on prenatal health for Haredi women. This three-hour event is an opportunity for her to spread her message about the importance of prenatal medical care and to sell her books. Vendors from around Jerusalem sell prenatal vitamins, distribute information about umbilical cord–blood banking, and provide women with techniques for breastfeeding. Each year, she expects about five hundred women to attend. For her seminar in 2010, Karin was looking forward to teaching about the proper timeline for prenatal tests, the importance of discussing things with one's doctor, prenatal nutrition, and postnatal contraception. She felt more confident than she had in the past, because this year she was releasing her new book about postpartum depression, which she knows affects Haredi women and yet is still a taboo topic for Haredi families to discuss and acknowledge.[39] Just two weeks before her event, Karin received a phone call from the Haredi rabbinic leadership threatening to excommunicate her if she did not promise to avoid certain topics at the seminar. In an effort to control the medical information Haredi women would receive, the Haredi leadership told Karin to avoid discussing contraception, prenatal testing, or postpartum depression. When she told me about the rabbis' demands, Karin was frustrated, exclaiming, "They're holding these women hostage!" She understood that by limiting the medical information women could receive, these rabbis were also tying the hands of the medical community.

Though she resented having to spend three hours talking solely about nutrition, wasting this prime opportunity to talk about what she felt were more pressing issues, Karin understood that excommunication meant that Haredi women would not be permitted to access her for information, support, or help. Her clinic's certifications would most likely be revoked. Karin was motivated both by her desire to provide medical care and the financial benefits she (and her clinic) receive, so she agreed to the restrictions and proceeded with the event as the rabbis requested. Karin changed the program for the evening and updated her slides to reflect the new topics. However, when she introduced herself and welcomed the hundreds of women who had come out on a week-day evening, Karin made a point of telling the audience that there had been some last-minute changes in the program. Although she did not say why these changes were implemented, the audience understood the subtext. During the break, dozens of women rushed to speak to Karin privately about the topics she was explicitly asked not to discuss. Karin then explained that although the Haredi leadership did not want her to discuss these topics publicly, women could come to her office to discuss them anytime. Subversively, Karin communicated her distaste for this rabbinic control and made sure women knew how to access the information they needed.

Although in many cases it seems as if rabbis are manipulating doctors and controlling the practice of medicine without physicians' approval, some medical arenas have adapted to Haredi cultural norms and use the rabbinic involvement in medicine to their advantage, as they seek to provide more tailored medical care to Haredi women. The medical community in Israel frequently provides care to particular ethnic minorities based on stereotypes about the community.[40] The ways in which hospitals and doctors have offered services for Haredi maternity patients seems to fall within this practice. Bikur Cholim, a hospital that sits on the outskirts of one of the large Haredi enclaves in Jerusalem, takes numerous steps to accommodate Haredi religious and cultural needs. In 2009, Rabbi Dov Fobersky, a journalist for the Haredi newspaper B'Hadrei Haredim, interviewed Dr. Rafael Pollack, the medical director of the hospital, as well as Dr. Ilan Gur, one of the doctors who treated Fobersky's son when he was born prematurely years earlier. In the interview, Fobersky applauded Bikur Cholim for making a number of adjustments recently to accommodate the Haredi community. Pollack stated that Bikur Cholim "is the hospital of the Haredi community. The Haredi community founded this hospital."[41] Pollack explained that his is the hospital of the Haredi community not only because it is located within a Haredi area of Jerusalem but also because the doctors there try to serve the needs of the Haredi community.[42] After Bikur Cholim updated its birthing rooms, B'Hadrei Haredim interviewed Dr. Pollack again. In this later interview, Pollack explained that though the entire population of Jerusalem is welcome in the hospital, "our birthing rooms could even be said to be Haredi (birthing) rooms" because of the amenities for Haredi women and the services the hospital provides them.[43] These statements reflect Pollack's interest in maintaining and increasing Haredi business to his hospital through accommodations to Haredi cultural norms.

For each hospital birth, the hospital receives a sum of money directly from the National Insurance Institute of Israel, referred to as the Hospitalization Grant, to cover the costs of the birth and a mother's hospitalization.[44] Thus, hospitals have an incentive to encourage women to give birth in their hospital. According to one doctor at Bikur Cholim, a few years prior, Shaarei Tzedek had the highest birth rate in the city—fifteen hundred births per month— compared to five hundred at Bikur Cholim and five hundred per month at the two Hadassah hospitals combined. When Bikur Cholim began offering free strollers and a voucher for a night in its postnatal hotel for women who gave birth there, its birth rate climbed, as did the benefits it received from the National Insurance Institute.[45]

The services a Haredi woman receives from her doctor and the hospital in which she decides to birth are many, and they range from linguistic harmonization to more functional adjustments to accommodate a woman's religious needs. The changes in the birthing rooms at Bikur Cholim include increased privacy for the modesty expected of Haredi women, and a special curtain that allows her husband to stand at her head and not see any part of her exposed body during the birth, among other things. Noa, a nurse who has worked in Bikur Cholim in the labor and delivery ward, said that religious language becomes part of a doctor's repertoire when speaking with Haredi patients. Noa often hears secular doctors responding to a woman's questions with "b'ezrat hashem" (with God's help). Though this is a common refrain among observant Jewish individuals, for a secular doctor to utter it indicates sensitivity to his or her patient. Noa also witnessed doctors making limited medical concessions for Haredi patients. During a postdate check-up during the holiday of Hanukkah, a Haredi woman asked her doctor if she could go home and light the candles of the hanukkiah before being induced. The doctor replied, "Yes, you live in Meah Shearim, so just come back to the hospital later tonight." This concession indicates the doctor's familiarity with religious customs and her willingness to oblige to the Haredi woman's request. Although these might seem like minor gestures, for a Haredi woman, they signify a doctor's willingness to meet her religious needs.

Many women told me about additional services they receive as part of their births. For instance, Bikur Cholim and another hospital frequented by

Figure 1.1. Brochure for Hadassah Baby Hotel (outside), reads "Do not disturb."
The hotel's slogan is "A moment to yourself, between birth and home."

Figure 1.2. Brochure for Hadassah Baby Hotel (inside), describing the benefits
of time spent by just mother and newborn in the maternity hotel associated
with Hadassah Hospital. Features include time to yourself, your own private
room, a special nursery, and gourmet food that is Kosher LeMehadrin.

Haredi women, Shaarei Tzedek, have copies of *Sefer Noam Elimelech*, a collection of writings by a Kabbalistic rabbi from the eighteenth century, for Haredi women. During labor, Haredi women customarily place this book under their pillows because they believe this serves a protective function during labor. Noa says that she has seen women draw on a variety of customs to help the labor progress. The hospital, she claims, willingly accommodates these women and the segulot they bring to the birth. A common practice is to recite the names of infertile women during labor. While many women will bring names with them to the hospital, some nurses, doctors, or ambulance drivers provide laboring women with a supplemental list. Other women bring challah dough with them to the hospital and perform the commandment of separating challah dough while in labor. This is considered a significant commandment to perform during labor. It relates to the rabbinic adage repeated during prayer, "For three transgressions do women die of childbirth: because they have not been heedful in regard to their menstruation, in the separation of the priest's share of the dough, and in kindling the lamp."[46] By providing women with names of infertile women to recite and allowing women to knead dough in the hospital room, the medical professionals show their support of Haredi women's religious needs.[47]

I witnessed other examples of this as I observed in a prenatal clinic located in a Haredi area of Jerusalem. In addition to basic prenatal services, such as ultrasound screening, prenatal testing, prenatal examinations with a doctor, and postdate care, this prenatal clinic caters specifically to the Haredi community in a variety of ways. On a table in the waiting room are a plethora of magazines, books, prayer books, and dozens of back issues of *Mishpacha* magazine (a magazine for Orthodox families).[48] Among the books are those that address both the biological process and the religious laws of pregnancy. Some of the prayer books contain collections of prayers and psalms specifically for women. They feature prayers a woman should say during each month of pregnancy or particular psalms to recite before a prenatal medical examination. Others are generic prayer books so that women can pray one of the three daily services while they wait for their appointments. All of these items make the clinic a friendlier place for Haredi women and reinforce the impression that their medical treatment should conform to religious laws and practices.

Some doctors cooperate with rabbis and provide religious accommodations because they have found that this helps them care for their Haredi patients. When they spoke to me about working with rabbis, they did not mention the financial benefits they might receive. Dr. Maayan Sameh, for instance, was in favor of doctors working more directly with rabbinic leaders. Sameh thinks that doctors should discuss medical information with a rabbi to guarantee that the correct information is shared. Sameh has found that when women or their husbands call their rabbi for medical advice they dilute the information so that they receive the answer that they want. If the doctor recommends a cesarean section, but his or her patient does not want one, a patient's husband may talk to the rabbi and say that the C-section is not medically necessary and she can continue laboring without surgery. This, Sameh claims, is extremely danger-ous, so she prefers to speak to the rabbi and explain the situation. "There are crazy rabbis, definitely, but many are not, and instead of having the informa-tion passed on in a way that dictates how the woman would like it to turn out, it is better for the rabbi to receive correct information." For Sameh, a rabbi is a resource to support the doctors.

Some Orthodox Jewish doctors seek to educate other medical professionals to perform certain religiously relevant medical examinations in order to help Haredi women navigate a thorny religious problem. When a Haredi woman menstruates, she remains in a state of niddah from the day her period begins until a week after it ends. During this time, she cannot engage in sexual inter-course (or any physical contact with her husband), and she must observe cer-tain stringencies in their relationship to prevent any form of sexual arousal, either on her part or her husband's. If a woman sees blood from her vagina but does not know if it is menstrual blood, she needs to seek out a doctor or nurse who can examine her and tell her the source of the bleeding. The source deter-mines the length of her separation from her husband. However, determining the source of the blood is difficult because most doctors, nurses, or midwives are not trained in doing this type of medical-halakhic examination. Dr. Rachel Eshkol, a fertility specialist and a gynecologist with many Haredi patients, found that if a woman is unsure of the source of her bleeding, she is more likely to assume that it is blood that renders her a niddah and thus prohibits any physi-cal contact with her husband for almost two weeks.[49] For some women, this separation could lead to what has been termed "halakhic infertility," meaning a woman who otherwise would have no problem conceiving misses her ovula-tion period because she cannot, in accordance with Jewish law, resume sexual activity with her husband. Because it is increasingly difficult to find a rabbi who will permit a woman's entrance into a mikvah (ritual bath that marks the end of niddah) before she is technically allowed, rabbis and doctors increasingly recommend the use of hormone treatments to delay ovulation.[50]

In a desire to avoid both the medical treatment of a Jewish legal issue or the alteration of Jewish law, Eshkol began training nurses and midwives to become an *achot bodeket* (a nurse who checks). In conjunction with Jewish legal experts, Eshkol compiled a booklet that begins with the basic anatomy of the female reproductive tract as a review for nurses and midwives, but she added a definition of *dam niddah* (menstrual blood) and where the blood has to originate in the tract to be considered such. In the traditional Talmudic sing-song voice, Eshkol described to me what she tells the nurses: "When the blood comes from here, this is niddah blood. When it comes from anything else, it's a *petzah* [wound]." Eshkol gives her trainees images of granulomas, cysts, endometriosis, and other things an achot bodeket might see when she examines a woman. After reviewing the Jewish laws of menstruation, Eshkol provides the nurses and midwives with form letters that they should write to a woman's rabbi, specifying the origin of the blood so that the rabbi can determine whether a woman is indeed a niddah or whether she has a wound that will heal on its own. She tells the nurses explicitly, "An achot bodeket is not a rabbi. Therefore, she does not give a *psak* [legal decision]. . . . Just write your findings; the rabbi will decide." Eshkol also tells them when they need to refer a woman to a doctor for further examination. In this case, Eshkol uses the relationship between medicine and religion to improve a woman's medical care and her observance of Jewish law.

Another example of this kind of care is found in the organization Bishvilaych. Founded in 2004 by Sara Siemiatycki, Bishvilaych, meaning "for you," is a medical organization that provides well-health services to women in the Haredi community: early detection, education, and empowerment. During women's reproductive years, Siemiatycki explained, Haredi women are "constantly using the [medical] system" because at least once a year they are going to fertility doctors or gynecologists when they are pregnant. This means that these women are in the system but are neglected for their nonreproductive health care needs. In other words, Haredi women are not avoiding doctors or opposed to seeking medical treatment, but outside of reproductive concerns, they either do not understand the importance of medical care or simply do not prioritize it because they are busy working and caring for others. This has resulted in the unfortunate reality that Haredi women are significantly more likely to be diagnosed with late-stage breast cancer.[51] Not only are Haredi women more likely to die of breast cancer because of this late diagnosis, but they are also not availing themselves of preventative screening at the same rate as their peers in other sectors of Judaism.[52] With the help of Dr. Diana Flescher, a specialist in women's health in Israel, Siemiatycki created Bishvilaych as a place that would provide comprehensive medical examinations, train doctors, and educate women. Bishvilaych has a staff of doctors, nurses, and social workers in its office in Jerusalem who provide cancer screening, routine examinations, and

The best medicine is the one you never have to take.
Our approach is simple- Stay healthy.

Our medical center focuses on maintaining your health through personalized, realistic, and effective care for your unique health needs.

Once a year.
Every year.

With the understanding gained from years of service to women in Israel, Bishvilaych has succeeded in developing an integrative medical examination, "The yearly check-up"- taking the minimum time for maximum results.

Bishvilaych's medical examination is equivalent to three different doctor's appointments, covering internal medicine, gynecology, and breast health, while focusing on your medical and emotional needs. We emphasize disease prevention, health promotion, and early detection with personalized advice to fit your lifestyle.

At Bishvilaych we listen and address your medical issues from fatigue and P.C.O.S. to menopause and more.

Our specially trained medical staff are all women, providing professional care with warmth and compassion, attending to your privacy and answering your questions.

Bishvilaych - Providing personalized care at every stage of your life cycle, from adolescence through the golden years, with understanding, sensitivity and professionalism.

♥ There is nothing more precious then your health ♥

Figure 1.3. Pamphlet from Bishvilaych for its English-speaking clientele, advertising the medical care that it offers.
Reproduced with permission of Sara Siemiatyck, founder and executive director of Bishvilaych.

counseling to women during a two-hour appointment. Bishvilaych also hosts educational seminars in the evening about menopause and the importance of breast and ovarian cancer screening.

The staff of Bishvilaych recognize that there are a number of obstacles preventing Haredi women from receiving the medical care they require—namely, large families and a culture of self-neglect. In a promotional video for Bishvilaych, the voiceover begins, "There is so much that we need to look after, so many that need our care.... As women, we are there for them, ... But when do we use that nature to take care of ourselves?" Siemiatycki asks on the video, "How can a mother of six schedule tests and appointments on different days, in different parts of the city, when she is working and trying to raise her family?"[53] Here Siemiatycki is referring to an added obstacle: due to the nature of medical care in Israel, a woman must attend three different doctors to receive the comprehensive examination she receives at Bishvilaych, which includes a risk assessment and a general health physical.

Rabbinic support has propelled Bishvilaych to prominence in the Haredi community. Multiple leading Haredi rabbis have approved of Bishvilaych's work and have publicly offered their support. In promotional material for the organization, they advertise the praise of Ovadya Yosef, once the chief Sephardi rabbi of Israel: "I was happy to hear about the special clinic for women, 'Bishvilaych.'... This special clinic for women is run according to modesty and purity... and with great medical care. This is for the times when the daughters of Israel avoid going to a doctor because of lack of modesty and especially for things that in women's health care if they were discovered earlier they could be treated, and therefore women who are at that age must go and get checked from time to time." Yosef applauds the all-female atmosphere for maintaining modesty and implores all women to attend the clinic. On this same material, another prominent rabbi, Shmuel Auerbach, cites both the Torah and Maimonides for the importance of taking care of oneself and protecting oneself from harm. Like Yosef, he praises the clinic for providing a modest medical office for women to go for examinations. Many rabbis also applaud Bishvilaych's attention to Haredi women's busy lives in their approval of this clinic. Bishvilaych sought out the support of rabbinic authorities and publicizes it widely to leverage rabbinic influence on the Haredi community to their benefit. This support has led many women to Bishvilaych and garnered the organization broad respect for the work that they do. The staff at Bishvilaych accepts the reality of treating Haredi women, and these rabbinic certifications reflect the importance of rabbinic approval in Haredi women's procurement of medical care.

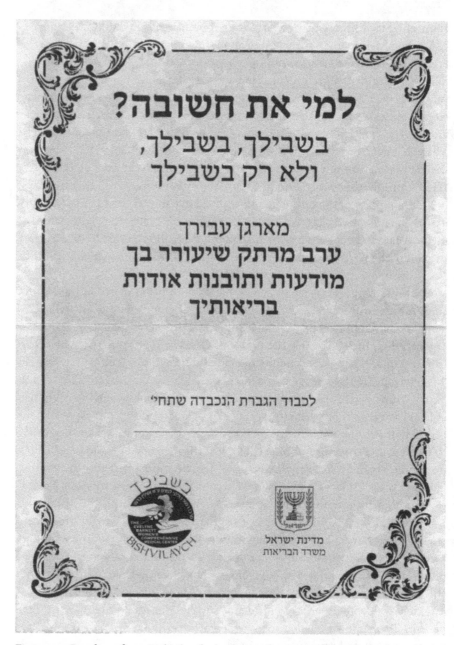

Figure 1.4. Brochure from Bishvilaych about an informational evening regarding women's health. Reproduced with permission of Sara Siemiatycki, founder and executive director of Bishvilaych.

הרבנים ממליצים...

הגאון ר' יצחק טובי' וייס שליט"א

"...הרבנית הגדולה מסדרת מרפאה לנשים על ידי נשים שחביב על צד היותר טוב הן בצדקי הרפואה והעזרה הנחוצה לנשים הן בצדקי הצניעות והקדושה כראוי ומובן לכל התועלת הגדולה מהמפעל חשוב כזה שפרט בעיר קדשתו ותפארתו המרובה באוכלוסין..."

הגאון ר' עובדי' יוסף שליט"א

"שמחתי לשמוע על המרפאה המיוחדת לנשים "בשבילך" שהקימה הרבנים החשובה...מרפאה מיוחדת לנשים אשר היא מנוהלת על דרכי הצניעות והטהרה כאשר נהגו בנות ישראל מקדמת דנא, ובמרבה רפואית מעולה, ופעמים שבבנות ישראל הכשרות נמנעות לילך לרופא מפני חוסר צניעות, ובפרט דברים שברפואה נשים שאם מגלים אותם מוקדם יש להם רפואה, ולכן חיבות הנשים שנמצאות בגיל המצוי להבדק מדי פעם, וטוב עשו שהקימו מרפאה מיוחדת לנשים כדי שלא יתבישו לילך להבדק, ויפה שעה אחת קודם."

הגאון ר' משה שטרנבוך שליט"א

"...הרבנית, אשת חיל, [הקימה] מרפאה מיוחדת בצניעות וברפואות מצוינות והנשים שם עוברות בדיקות וטיפולים מיוחדות. הדבר ברור בפיקוח נפש ומבי'א תועלת מרובה..."

הגאון ר' שמואל אוירבאך שליט"א

"כאשר נצטוינו בתורה הקדושה השמר לך ושמור נפשך. אשר זו מצות התורה להשמר ולהיזהר מכל חשש סכנת נפשות רח"ל, וכמפורש ברמב"ם הלכות רוצח ושמירת נפש פי"א ה"ד, וכלשונו הזהב, מצות עשה וכו' ולהזהר בדבר יפה יפה שנאמר השמר השמר וגו', וכפוסטות הגמ' ברכות לב', והדברים ידועים... הרבנית החשובה סעמיאטיצקי תחי' [הקימה] מרפאה על טהרת הצניעות לבדיקות ולטיפולים. והתועלת בזה עצומה עד למאוד"

הגאון ר' מאיר קסלר שליט"א

"הנני מכיר את פעילותיה המבורכת של הרבנית להביא בפני הנשים את הידיעות הנחוצות לבריאותן בכמה תחומים. בענין של המחלה הידועה אצל נשים שעל ידי בדיקה מוקדמת אפשר להנצל מסכנה ממש. ואין לחשש לענין הצניעות..."

הגאון ר' חיים פנחס שיינברג שליט"א

"הנני בזה להודיע בשער בת רבים להכיר ולהוקיר... את פועלה הנשגב של הרבנית החשובה מרת שרה סעמיאטיצקי תחי' למען נשים רבות אשר עקב טרדותיהן המרובות וכו' הזניחו את עצמן ומצב בריאותן, והגיעו לידי מחלות המסוכמות לנשים וכדומה ולידי חולאים עד כדי סכנה רח"ל. וכל זאת מחומר המודעיות בקרב ציבור הנשים החרדיות, כי עדיין לא נתינמדה מרפאה על טהרת הקודש ובדרך הצניעות המתאימה לבת ישראל אשר כל כבודה בת מלך פנימה... שרה סעמיאטיצקי תחי' קיבלה על עצמה לייסד מרפאה מיוחדת שיהי' לאישה מקום התאום לרוחה לבא לעצה ותושי' ולעזר בכל ענייניה אשר ודאי יושיע לנשים רבות."

הגאון ר' משה שאול קליין שליט"א

"...[בשבילך] [היא] מרפאה מיוחדת לנשים הפועלת על צד יותר טוב, הן בדרכי הרפואה...והן בדרכי הצניעות כראוי...והנה מאחר שישנם נשים המזלזלות בשמירת הבריאות ואינם מטפלות בעצמן בדרכי הרפואה כראוי, ע"כ הנני להביא לידיעתן את דעת מרן **פוסק הדור רבינו שמואל הלוי ואזנר שליט"א** שחובה גמורה להתנהג בדרכי הרפואה לשמור על בריאותן. וכן יש לבדוק עצמן מזמן לזמן על המחלות השכיחות בנשים ח"ו שמן הניסיון שאם מטפלים בזמן אזי הרפואה קרובה יותר."

הגאון ר' משה הלברשטאם זצ"ל

"כי דבר טוב ומועיל אשר יהנו מזה קציירי ומריעי כלשון חז"ל, ומצוה מאד נשגבה לפנינו..."

הגאון ר' רפאל צבי ובר שליט"א

"הנני מקריאה עבור המפעל החשוב הנקרא "בשבילך"... יש כאן פניה לנשים המזלזלות בבדיקות הנצרכות להם מחשש מחלות המצנים. שיש חובה לבודיקם בשלבים מוקדרמים על מנת שיוכלו לטפל בהם ולמעט הסכנה. ויש בזה חובה גמורה של ונשמרתם לנפשותיכם. ובזה אני מצטרף לקריאת הרבנים האונים שקראו לקבל המלצות של מפעל חשוב זה להיבדק בזמנים קבועים."

Figure 1.5. The inside of the brochure from Bishvilaych contains a full page of approbations from rabbis. Reproduced with permission of Sara Siemiatycki, founder and executive director of Bishvilaych.

While Bishvilaych's ability to provide comprehensive health care to women who otherwise may not prioritize nonreproductive health care is undoubtedly a step in the right direction, the welcoming of rabbinic participation in medical care raises questions about whose needs are prioritized. In her analysis of three controversial events in Israeli medical care, Hadas Ziv finds that the medical community in Israel routinely acts based on stereotypes about particular ethnic groups. Ziv explains, "Directors of hospitals boast of the wonderful relationship among their staff members of different ethnic origins—but are oblivious to the fact that the existing power relationships are based on the silence of the minority, that what they hold as 'consensus' as a given 'fact' is to others a question."[54] When we think back to the way the administration at Bikur Cholim hospital showed off their Haredi-friendly birthing rooms, we can see that all of these actions send multiple messages. On the one hand, doctors who make accommodations for Haredi patients are aware of and friendly toward their religious needs, cultivating an environment of cooperation and possibly increasing the chances that a religious patient will seek out medical care. On the other hand, a doctor who is already familiar with rabbinic instructions about a particular practice might find it hard to make space for a woman's preferred course of treatment, especially if she would like to follow a course not generally approved by rabbinic authorities. When doctors acquiesce to rabbis, they are basing their medical care on the demands of a small group of rabbinic authorities, overlooking women's reproductive agency and reinforcing the unequal power dynamics in the Haredi community. Haredi women, we will see, appreciate smaller accommodations but recognize that often they reflect a larger network of cooperation between doctors and rabbis that results in the restriction of women's reproductive options.

RELIGION, MEDICINE, AND ETHICS

Cooperation between doctors and rabbis, hospitals and religious authorities, can, to be sure, have positive effects on medical care. Bishvilaych is a prime example of this. However, among the women I spoke to, doctors and rabbis represent obstacles toward their reproductive agency. Effectively, as women gain more reproductive experience, they come to resent the network of rabbinic and medical cooperation that exists around them because this network does not prioritize a woman's embodied experience of pregnancy. It is important to understand the dynamics of this relationship in order to see why Haredi women feel challenged by these other sources of knowledge and authority.

On the one hand, medicine and religion exist in harmony in institutional bioethics in Israel. Many praise the medical and rabbinic cooperation as a synthesis between religious and secular values, part of what makes Israel a Jewish democracy, and a unique type of bioethics that is more communitarian than Western bioethics.[55] Whereas autonomy remains a principle of Western bioethics, Israeli bioethics claims to draw on community and kinship for priorities in the ethical regime.[56] State and hospital bioethics committees are composed of doctors, philosophers, and rabbis who meld religious norms regarding the sanctity of life, for instance, with more secular principles of dignity, privacy, and self-determination. Amos Shapira explains that the bioethical discourse in Israel has evolved within a "unique mix of religious orthodoxy and secularist lifestyle, of fundamentalist paternalism and permissive individualism, of traditional proscriptive tenets and liberal precepts of privacy, autonomy, and self-determination."[57] Bioethicists in Israel, responding to the sociopolitical nature of the country, established a method of compromise between religious and secular values as the driving force behind ethical decisions in medical care and research.[58]

However, the relationship between doctors and rabbis in Israel reflects the complex ways in which medicine and religion attempt to resolve their competing epistemologies in the daily interactions between representatives of each of those fields. Although doctors and rabbis can work together to resolve disputes in medical care or improve health care among certain populations, their close relationships can also pose a challenge to quality medical treatment. As we have seen in this chapter, doctors and rabbis create a context in which Haredi women are pawns in a larger epistemological competition. Instead of working together toward holistic, ethical medical care, doctors and rabbis cooperate to serve their own interests. Rabbis supervise doctors because they fear being pushed aside by the authority of the hegemonic and technologically rich medical system in Israel, and doctors work with rabbis to maintain a large Haredi client base of reproductive women. Working with these motives, doctors and rabbis are not always interested in providing Haredi women with personalized reproductive health care.

In this context of medical professionals and religious authorities attempting to direct women's reproductive health care, Haredi women develop reproductive agency. Reproductive agency does not refer to a woman acting autonomously and independently but rather to her taking action within a particular framework of possibilities. Doctors and rabbis in Israel have established a closed network that excludes Haredi women, and Haredi women recognize their exclusion from this network. Women prioritize their own embodied experiences after expressing their mistrust for rabbis and doctors who are not working in their best interest. This leaves a space for Haredi women to draw on their own embodied authority for medical decision-making. The next chapters will address how Haredi pregnancy books and women's embodied experiences of pregnancy help women internalize the mistrust for doctors and rabbis and then navigate an opportunity for reproductive agency.

NOTES

1. See Ivry, *Embodying Culture*, for this competition between doctors and patients in Israel in particular, and Ivry, "Kosher Medicine and Medicalized Halacha," for more on the triadic relationship.

2. There is a history to this relationship between Jewish religious leaders and Jewish medical authorities, both within Israel and outside of it, which is beyond the scope of this chapter. See Barilan, *Jewish Bioethics*; J. Efron, *Medicine and the German Jews*; Shvarts, *Health and Zionism*; Rosner, "Autopsy in Jewish Law and the Israeli Autopsy Controversy"; and Steinberg, *Encyclopedia of Jewish Medical Ethics*.

3. Jordan, "Authoritative Knowledge," 56.

4. Tsarfaty and Blais, "Between 'Cultural Enclave' and 'Virtual Enclave'"; Campbell, "Religious Engagement"; Neriya-Ben Shahar, "For We Ascend in Holiness and Do Not Descend."

5. Campbell, "What Hath God Wrought"; Rashi, "Kosher Cell Phone in Ultra-Orthodox Society."

6. Lehmann and Siebzehner, "Holy Pirates."

7. For a thorough analysis of how Haredi authorities perceive the internet and other media to be threatening, see Caplan, "Media in Haredi Society in Israel," and Cohen, *God, Jews and the Media*.

8. Finkelman, "Ambivalent Haredi Jew," 268.

9. Ivry, *Embodying Culture*.

10. Weingarten and Kitai, "Consultations with Rabbis," 138. See Keshet and Liberman, "Coping with Illness and Threat," on why even nonreligious Jews consult rabbis on healthcare issues.

11. Firer, "Lots of Ways to Help Heal."

12. Fader, "Ultra-Orthodox Jewish Interiority, the Internet, and the Crisis of Faith."

13. Ibid., 196.

14. Ibid.

15. Boas et al., *Bioethics and Biopolitics in Israel*, 12.

16. Shalev and Goldin, "Uses and Misuses of In Vitro Fertilization in Israel."

17. Haelyon, "Longing for a Child," 181.

18. Ivry, "Kosher Medicine," 667.

19. Kahn, *Reproducing Jews*.

20. Ibid.

21. Kahn, *Reproducing Jews*, 89.

22. Hashiloni-Dolev, "Effect of Jewish-Israeli Family Ideology," 122.

23. Strathern, "Displacing Knowledge," 346.

24. Kahn, *Reproducing Jews*, 115.

25. Calling these women mashgichot is interesting, as it is the same term used to refer to rabbinic authorities who oversee the kosher certification of restaurants. Here, too, the concern is preventing the improper mixing of substances, which would render food ritually impure. I will return to this later in the chapter.

26. Goodman and Witztum, "Cross-Cultural Encounters between Careproviders," found something similar among Haredi rabbis writing referral letters to a mental health clinic in Israel.

27. Kahn, *Reproducing Jews*, 116.

28. Hashiloni-Dolev, "Policy Regarding Reproductive Technologies," 123.

29. Kahn, *Reproducing Jews*, 116.

30. Ivry, "Kosher Medicine," 663; Fader, "Ultra-Orthodox Jewish Interiority, the Internet, and the Crisis of Faith."

31. In recent years, some clothing stores also display signs of approval from Haredi rabbis. These signs certify the modesty of the clothing sold within the store and serve to attract a particular clientele while requesting women not dressed modestly enough to remain out of the store.

32. It is important to note that clinics, unlike restaurants, do not have certification from the Rabbinate. The Rabbinate does not approve of certain clinics or doctors over others. This would be politically problematic and extremely unethical as the clinics are supported by the government-sponsored health care system, and the Rabbinate is also a state-sponsored political post. The certification of medical organizations is a practice limited to Haredi rabbis.

33. Sztokman, *War on Women in Israel*, 31–32; Bronner and Kershner, "Israelis Facing a Seismic Rift over Role of Women."

34. Rabbi Firer has also come under criticism recently for conforming to Haredi norms of gender modesty at his fundraising events. See Chajut, "Shlomo Artzi Denounces Ban."

35. El-Or, *Educated and Ignorant*, 143.

36. Ibid.

37. Fader, "Ultra-Orthodox Jewish Interiority, the Internet, and the Crisis of Faith," 192.

38. Ivry, "Kosher Medicine," 668.

39. In the Haredi community, negative views toward psychological disorders lead to the social stigma surrounding the presence of psychological disorders within one's family. This can damage the family's standing and make it difficult for siblings or children to find a "good" mate.

40. Ziv, "Cognitive Dissonant Health System," 76.

41. Fobersky, "Bikur Cholim Belongs to the Haredi Community."

42. Ibid.

43. Gil, "To Give Birth in Bikur Cholim."

44. National Insurance Institute of Israel, "Covering the Mother's Hospitalization Expenses."

45. Ziv, in "Cognitive Dissonant Health System," remarks that the combination of racism and monetary incentives affects maternity wards in particular, making the struggle much more difficult to fight.

46. M. Shabbat, 2:6.

47. See Sered, "Religious Rituals and Secular Rituals," for an overview of how women incorporate religious and secular rituals into childbirth. My explication here is not meant to be exhaustive but merely indicative of how the hospitals cooperate and facilitate women's observance of certain rituals.

48. See Baumel, *Sacred Speakers*, for a comprehensive discussion of *Mishpacha* magazine and other magazines that cater to Haredi women.

49. Erring on the side of stringency is a practice that has become common in the Haredi community. Especially regarding laws of menstruation, when conception during the niddah period could have a significant impact on the religious status of that future child, women are more likely to be stricter in their observance.

50. One religious doctor, Daniel Rosenak, is leading a crusade in opposition to this practice, advocating instead for changing the law, but most doctors comply unquestioningly. See Ivry, "Kosher Medicine," 674.

51. Isak, "Morbidity Characteristics," 81.

52. Ibid., 130.

53. katzeyefilms, "Bishvilaych—The Evelyne Barnett Women's Comprehensive Medical Center."

54. Ziv, "Cognitive Dissonant Health System," 77.

55. See, for example, Shapira, "In Israel, Law, Religious Orthodoxy and Reproductive Technologies," and Ravitsky and Gross, "Israel: Bioethics in a Jewish-Democratic State."

56. See Hashiloni-Dolev, "Policy Regarding Reproductive Technologies."

57. Shapira, "In Israel, Law, Religious Orthodoxy and Reproductive Technologies," 12.

58. For more on Israeli bioethics, see Siegal, *Bioethics Blue and White*.

TWO

—◊◊◊—

BOOKS AND BABIES

Pathways to Authority

AS DOCTORS AND RABBIS ATTEMPT to manage Haredi women's reproductive care, women themselves struggle to express their preferences. Pregnancy advice books help pave the way for women's authority over pregnancy and reproduction. By critically examining the significance of books and book learning in Haredi life, I argue that as women performatively use pregnancy advice books geared toward this community of women, they situate their agency within Haredi norms of knowledge production. Although they display these books proudly on their shelves, women I spoke to claim to never have looked to the books for guidance. When I asked women what they learned from the books, or what advice they had gained, they could not think of anything. Some did not remember what the books contained, and others provided me with broad summaries of the content without indicating what they had actually learned. As I read the pregnancy books, this surprised me because the themes in the books seemed to parallel themes from women's reproductive narratives. This chapter explores the paradox of women owning and displaying pregnancy books that they claim never to have read. I maintain that for Haredi women, having these books lends them some legitimacy and externally recognized authority in the Haredi world, but attributing to the books any authority over their own prenatal decisions would challenge their embodied agency. Although women might have learned something from these books, this becomes irrelevant because Haredi women do not prioritize books in their development of reproductive agency. Instead, they prioritize their embodied experience.

To analyze women's unique use of pregnancy advice books, it is necessary to understand the gendered spheres of Haredi life. Broadly, men belong to the world of books and women to the world of babies. Each is crucial to the maintenance and protection of Haredi cultural and religious norms, but they remain distinct. Men and women both are expected to conform to the laws in the books and recognize the authority of books and previous rabbinic leaders. Men, however, are those who write the laws and study the books, while women are those who do not have direct access to those same books. Instead, women have direct access to pregnancy and childrearing. Pregnancy advice books offer women a bridge between those two spheres, and women showcase the books to receive normative Haredi validation while subverting Haredi author- ity structures. It is through pregnancy and women's usage of pregnancy books that women can subvert the entire authority structure in Haredi Judaism.

BOOKS AND BABIES: GENDERED SPHERES OF HAREDI LIFE

Books and babies hold a kind of symbiotic status for Haredim, which can be explained using an example from one of my interviews with Devorah. Four weeks from her due date for her fourth child, Devorah's fetal ultrasound revealed that her fetus was not head-down but rather in a breech position. Her doctor told her that there was a chance the fetus would flip again before labor but that, at this point, there was a higher chance of C-section because he would not deliver a baby who was in the breech position. As we talked about Devo- rah's desire to avoid a C-section, she remembered a segulah she had once heard about flipping a fetus in utero. We briskly walked home, and Devorah started scanning the bookshelves in her living room. The front door of her apartment opened into the living room where a dilapidated couch sat against the wall on the right-hand side of the room. Her living room was sparsely decorated. Immediately in front of us as we entered her apartment was an entire wall of bookshelves, filled with *seforim* (sacred books).[1] Gleefully, Devorah pulled a few books off the shelves and turned them around so that they were standing up straight. With each flipped book, she whispered a prayer asking God to hear her request. According to the segulah, if the seforim in one's house are upside down, flipping them could flip the fetus into the right position. This was the ritual she remembered, and she hoped that by turning the books in her house, she could turn the fetus in her uterus as well.

Women told me about other segulot that echo a similar relationship between books and babies.[2] When a woman is in the ninth month of pregnancy, her hus- band is often given the honor of opening the ark containing the Torah scrolls during morning prayers. This action is a segulah meant to ensure a woman's womb begins to open for an easy delivery. Waiting until his wife is in the ninth month of pregnancy to ask him to open the ark, the congregation makes it clear that they do not want the delivery to come earlier than the ninth month. In this segulah, the ark parallels the womb and the Torah scrolls inside the ark are like the fetus inside the womb. Judaism's most holy books, the Torah, are seen as being similar, at least in this segulah, to a fetus. Here, a pregnant woman's husband is granted the ability to not only protect the fetus from an early delivery but to actually begin the process of labor for his wife. Although the origin of these segulot is not clear, we can see that they establish a relationship between holy books and babies. In these segulot, the directionality flows from books to babies. What men do with the books, or what women do with their husbands' books, will affect the fetus in some way.[3]

This relationship speaks to the two gendered spheres of Haredi life. Haredi Judaism is often referred to as a "book tradition," a phrase that highlights both men's participation in yeshiva study, or book learning, and the primacy of book knowledge, or halakha.[4] Just like the directionality of the segulot described, the books are meant to control and proscribe the authority of life experience (women's sphere). In the 1950s, the Israeli government began to offer financial support to young men who remained in yeshiva, a Jewish learning institution for traditional texts. This led more Haredi men to study in this environment as a source of income.[5] The yeshivot (pl. of yeshiva) encouraged the education of young men much more stringent in Jewish law than their parents, which in turn led to "the delegitimization of the traditions and practices of the families from which they came" and the dissemination of strict practices that had been approved by particular rabbinic leaders.[6] These yeshivot became not just places of learning but social formation—locations where stringency to the law could be institutionalized and spread through the intensive training of young men. The social pressure to enter these schools, combined with the exemption from military service in Israel provided one remained in a yeshiva or kollel once married, created a situation in which young men remained in learning communities their entire lives.[7]

Each yeshiva is a little different, following its own traditions and approaches to Judaism, but the centrality of books is universal. Although the yeshivot are generally lacking significant decoration, seforim are found all over the place. Many of the books found in a yeshiva are volumes of the Babylonian Talmud and codes of Jewish law, but one can also find prayer books, books on moral guidance, and Bibles. Before an individual puts a book back on the shelf, or if he drops it accidentally, he kisses the book. Samuel Heilman explains, "It is in this sense that one may consider these books not just items of study but objects of reverence, icons of the yeshiva."[8] The primary structure of learning is in the format of a *shiur*, or lesson, from the Rosh Yeshiva (head of the yeshiva), and *chevrusa* study (learning done in pairs). Heilman provides a picture of learning within the yeshiva:

> Typically, during the shiur the rosh yeshiva stands in the front of the room, leaning against a lectern or shtender, his volume of Talmud open before him. The students sit or stand next to similar shtenders or sit on pews around long tables, their books open to the same page. They follow along in the text as he recites, explores, and interprets the text. He also draws upon auxiliary texts ... the assumption is that the students will have reviewed the text and all the auxiliary sources so that they can more easily follow his line of thought.[9]

Although the Talmud is one of the most popular volumes in most yeshivot, it is only one link in a chain of rabbinic interpretation that begins with the Mishnah, continues with the Talmud, moves on through medieval rabbinic exegesis, and eventually gets to the contemporary rabbinic leadership. The students in yeshiva "are the last links in that long chain."[10]

The rabbinic discussions and laws found within the books are meant to be authoritative, presenting readers with normative guidelines for living a Jewish life. Having many books in your home, therefore, symbolizes your adherence to these codes. All of the Haredi homes that I entered looked similarly to Devorah's. Decorations were sparse, furniture was worn, toys were strewn throughout the house, and bookshelves overflowing with books on rabbinic law were placed in the main room of the house. A house with a lot of books conveys to visitors that the men within the home have devoted considerable time to learning the contents of those books. This is a marker of status for a Haredi family.[11] It demonstrates not only that a man has the intellectual ability to learn what is considered to be very difficult material but also that the family has devoted itself to this ideal lifestyle of the *avrech* family, where a husband stays in a learning community while his wife supports the family. Heilman explains, "Among haredim, education was everything: the purpose of Jewish existence and at the same time a barrier against its decay. It was the essence of what they believed was demanded of them as Jews."[12] Although many leaders and students in the Haredi world are beginning to realize that this lifestyle is not financially sustainable across the entire population, it is still considered the ideal way of living as a Haredi Jew.[13]

The books also symbolize something else. They remind all who enter the home (and that includes all those who live in the home) that one is expected to conform to rabbinic authority. After all, the yeshivot intend to create a culture of stringency, of young men who follow the letter of the law and cultivate uniformity in practice. Learning and adhering to the contents of particular rabbinic literature facilitates that kind of adherence. Importantly, Nurit Stadler's research on young yeshiva students highlights a certain level of rebellion against the rabbinic leadership. The yeshiva is not just reinforcing stringencies but also redefining these "time-honored models and shifting the understanding of the sacred."[14] While young Haredi men may be challenging certain fundamentalist ideologies, it is still the case that Haredi rabbinic leaders of today are seen as extensions of those who wrote the books on their shelves. Therefore, Haredi men do not look through the books and make a decision on their own when they have a question. Instead, bringing the knowledge of the laws within the books to their meeting with a rabbi, they ask how a certain law applies to their situation. Only these rabbis can correctly interpret the laws and provide guidance, and it is because their community has granted them this "larger-than-life authority."[15] Having an abundance of books in one's home is an expression of one's commitment to the general structure of authority in the Haredi world, an "homage to these icons" of Haredi life.[16]

Although Haredi women have never been exposed to the same kind of rigorous and advanced study of religious texts, they are expected to support their husband's studies and maintain the same level of conformity to Haredi rabbinic authority and respect for yeshiva education. In this way, they live "in the shadow of men."[17] And yet women are tasked with raising children, who exist at the center of Haredi life. While their husbands contribute to the maintenance of Haredi Judaism through their study of rabbinic texts, women enable the future of Haredi Judaism through reproduction and childrearing.[18] This is why women's spheres within Haredi Judaism are frequently referred to as "life tradition."[19] A woman's religious identity is tied to her reproductive abilities and her parenting of these future Haredi Jews. Babies are markers of status in a similar way that books exist as markers of status. In public, a Haredi woman pushing a stroller or leading a family of children has achieved the status of a good Haredi woman who is contributing to the future of Haredi Judaism. Furthermore, as Heilman explains, "parenting and education were at the front lines of the struggle against moral decay."[20] This is because despite living in enclave communities, Haredi children are also surrounded by the temptations of secular Israeli life. They must be guarded from these temptations and sustained on the Haredi path. This is the only way to guarantee that the future of Haredi life looks just like current Haredi life. Although much of this education happens in schools, women are those rearing children for the first number of years before they enter formal schools.

Scholarship on Haredi Judaism notes this gendered discrepancy. Many scholars have explored the lives of Haredi men by focusing on their extensive learning and adherence to laws.[21] Notable exceptions are Lynn Davidman's work on the embodied experiences of Haredi men who leave the tradition and Iddo Tavory's analysis of the way Orthodox men live their Jewish lives in public.[22] Research with Haredi women, meanwhile, has emphasized the lived, embodied actions of young girls,[23] older women,[24] and women new to Orthodox Judaism.[25] Tamar El-Or's research on Haredi women engaged in religious education offers an interesting exception, as does Ada Rapoport-Albert's extensive research on Hasidic women.[26] El-Or argues that just as scholarship has become of ultimate importance for Haredi men, Haredi women are also seeing an increase in the number and structure of their educational options. The goal of women's education, though, "is to duplicate the Jewish mother's home in Poland."[27] Women's education "strives to pragmatize the social reality and emphasize the material side. Women's education generates an ongoing translation of complex problems into simple actions. It levels questions of morality, faith and justice into instructions for action in daily life."[28] Women's education, then, returns to the lived and embodied experience.

The relegation of Haredi men to the important areas of education and book learning and women to the home, where childrearing and living Judaism exist as similarly crucial, brings us to the conclusion that although men and women occupy two distinct spheres of Haredi life, they each contribute significantly to the future of a Haredi Jewish society. However, Haredi society is predicated on the understanding that books provide knowledge and authority over living Judaism. "Life tradition" needs to be controlled and managed by the laws contained within the books.[29] Haredi women have internalized this message, and when they use pregnancy advice books to cultivate their authority over reproduction, they occupy both the male (book) sphere of authority as well as the female (pregnancy) sphere of authority. Books and babies are each markers of status in the Haredi world, and when women display their books about pregnancy, they earn a kind of doubled status. By displaying pregnancy books on her bookshelves, alongside her husband's seforim, a woman proclaims her homage to books and the significance of books in the Haredi world. Additionally, because they are books about pregnancy, in displaying the books, women are publicly declaring that they have children and are committed to the centrality of children in the Haredi world, in much the same way a woman pushing a stroller down the street publicly demonstrates her commitment. This demonstration, however, is done in the way men exhibit their commitment to the norms of Haredi life—through acquiring and showing off their books and respecting rabbinic authority. In this way, a Haredi woman's ownership and display of pregnancy books is both subverting her gendered role in the community and reinforcing it simultaneously. Her display of pregnancy advice books suggests that her reproductive authority exists on the same level as rabbinic authority.

WHAT TO EXPECT WHEN YOU ARE HAREDI AND EXPECTING

Young Haredi women, pregnant for the first time, must learn how to navigate the overlapping authorities of doctors and rabbis. To do this, they have to gain "prenatal literacy," or the ability to read, understand, and apply all the pregnancy signs and symptoms, tests, and ultrasounds.[30] This is when they buy pregnancy advice books geared toward their community. These books advance women's knowledge of pregnancy in a religiously appropriate way while also teaching women how to engage with the network of control described in the previous chapter. The authors of these pregnancy advice books intend to teach women what it means to be a good, Haredi pregnant woman.

When I visited Haredi women in their homes, I asked them whether they used any pregnancy advice books during pregnancy. Many women stood up to point to two specific books on their bookshelves: *B'Shaah Tovah: Madrich Refui Hilchati Lherayon v'Leida* (In a good time: A medical and halachic guide for pregnancy and labor) and *Hachana Ruchanit L'Leida* (Spiritual preparation for labor). Some removed them from their shelves to show me. As I held these two books in my hands, I noticed the differences between these books and all the other books displayed on their shelves. The majority of books on their shelves have black or brown covers with gold writing indicating the contents. These other books belonged primarily to their husbands, who had spent hours poring over their contents, sometimes learning them word for word. Amid dozens, if not hundreds, of books on rabbinic literature and sacred texts, women kept these two pregnancy books. *B'Shaah Tovah* and *Hachanah Ruchanit* both have colorful covers; one even has a picture of a baby. Aside from some prayer books and perhaps a copy of the Hebrew Bible, these pregnancy and labor advice books were women's contribution to scholarship in their homes.

B'Shaah Tovah was cowritten by a nurse-midwife, Michal Finkelstein, and her husband, Rabbi Baruch Finkelstein. The book was first written in English in 1993, as the Finkelsteins are American by origin, and then translated into Hebrew in 1996. The Finkelsteins released a revised and expanded version in English in 2001 and in Hebrew in 2002. The women I spoke to had the more recent Hebrew version, so I refer to that version here.[31] Feldheim Publishers, a large publishing house in Jerusalem and New York, published the book. *B'Shaah Tovah* is a phrase congratulating someone upon hearing of her pregnancy. It

Figure 2.1. Cover of B'Shaah Tovah pregnancy advice book.

Figure 2.2. Cover of *Hachana Ruchanit L'Leida* pregnancy advice book.

means "in a good time," or "in a good hour," meaning that the birth should come at the right time. The second book, *Hachana Ruchanit L'Leida*, is an anthology of writings primarily by women about labor and delivery. Another married couple, Moshe and Dafna Hasdai, edited and published this anthology, and although there is no publication date in the book, Dafna Hasdai remembers publishing it over twenty-five years ago, in the late 1990s.

Through a careful analysis of the content of these books, I will trace two themes that arise in Haredi women's prenatal literature. First, I will show how *B'Shaah Tovah* provides women with a framework for combining medical and religious guidance during pregnancy. The Finkelsteins assume that women are receiving a great deal of information and instruction from both doctors and rabbis, and their task, therefore, is to help women harmonize that information. Then I turn my attention to *Hachana Ruchanit L'Leida*, in which many authors stress the importance of women having authority over the doctors during pregnancy and birth. This theme is found less in the specific instructions regarding which tests to request, for instance, and more in the attitude women should take toward their role in prenatal care. Although this might seem like a departure from the first theme, the authors frame women's authority in religious terms. Although different from the way the Finkelsteins understand harmonizing medicine and religion, the authors of *Hachana Ruchanit L'Leida* see women exercising authority over doctors as another way of integrating religion and medicine. Both these themes are prominent in women's narratives of reproduction, which I will address in the following chapters.

How to Negotiate the Medical and Rabbinic Authorities

As we saw in the previous chapter, doctors and rabbis do not always agree on the best course of treatment for Haredi individuals. Each comes to the discussion with his or her own interests and reasons for suggesting a particular path, and the patient is left to decide, amid great pressure from both sides, which authority he or she will follow. The stakes are especially high for a pregnant woman, whose decisions affect not only her health but also the health of her developing fetus. *B'Shaah Tovah* introduces women to the ways in which doctors and rabbis, medicine and religion, can be considered simultaneously. This pregnancy advice book structures itself as a medical book about pregnancy *and* a religious book about pregnancy. Furthermore, by providing both medical and religious guidelines for pregnancy, the authors let women know that their religious needs can be met alongside their medical needs. Last, the book tackles the most significant question, which is whether one should put all her faith in either doctors or God. These attempts to show that medical and rabbinic information and guidance are consistent, integrated, or harmonious further blur the boundaries between rabbi and doctor in contemporary Israeli medicine. The Finkelsteins' efforts thus, though unintentionally, contribute to women's feeling that they cannot escape the network of rabbis and doctors.

In many ways, the structure of B'Shaah Tovah models how to combine medical and religious aspects of pregnancy. The first few pages of the book contain certifications from prominent Haredi rabbis as well as a certification from Dr. Chaim Yaffeh, the head of the Department of Obstetrics and Gynecology at Bikur Cholim Hospital. Rabbi Chaim P. Scheinberg writes that the book is "a necessary and useful book that deals with the wonderful process of the creation of a baby and the unique way in which God's partner in creation is to observe and act at each stage of development." Scheinberg praises B'Shaah Tovah particularly because the authors include God as an integral part of fetal development. Meanwhile, Dr. Yaffeh's letter compliments the book for its easy-to-read style. He thinks this will help reduce a woman's stress, particularly at the end of pregnancy. Yaffeh notes that the "connection between medical processes and Jewish law" is important for Jewish women. While rabbinic certifications are common in religious texts, providing the reader with a stamp of approval from a reliable source, other religious texts do not usually contain a letter from a medical authority as well. In seeking out and displaying medical approval, the authors of B'Shaah Tovah are demonstrating that this is a book the combines both medical and religious guidance and that Dr. Yaffeh's authority should be considered on par with that of Rabbi Scheinberg's. The Finkelsteins are suggesting that both medical and religious certification are necessary during pregnancy.

Another way the book displays the ability to follow both medical and religious guidance is seen in how the book brings these two realms of consideration to bear on the various stages of pregnancy. For instance, on two pages facing one another, the book outlines the stages of pregnancy. On the right-hand side, readers find guidelines for prayer during each of these stages. "In the first three days: a person should ask for mercy that the pregnancy will be accepted by the body. From the third to the fortieth day: one can pray for the sex [of the baby] that he wants."[32] These prayers operate according to a rabbinic understanding of fetal development. Because one can only pray for things that have not yet happened, it is clear that the rabbis believe that the sex of the baby is only determined after the fortieth day of gestation. On the following page, and for a few pages thereafter, is a description of the ten months of pregnancy according to medical descriptions of fetal development. Referring to the first four weeks of fetal development, the authors write, "Four weeks after the last monthly period, the head of the fetus is a third of its total size."[33] They continue with the medical description of fetal development, noting that by the eighth week the fetus starts taking on the shape of a person, developing arms, fingers, limbs, elbows, and knees. The description then gets to the question of sex, and here the Finkelsteins blend rabbinic and medical knowledge: "External genitalia exist but the sex of the baby is not clear yet. Actually, the fetus has all that it would need to develop into either female or male, but he will acquire definitive male and female characteristics only at the end of the seventh week of development. The Talmud tells us that fetal gender is set within the first 41 days of its life. Therefore, we have an opportunity to pray for the establishment of fetal gender until the 40th day of pregnancy."[34] Here the authors intend to demonstrate that medical knowledge does not just exist alongside religious knowledge but can sometimes also be used to confirm the utility of prayer and conformity to a religious life. Although an embryo's chromosomes are determined much earlier in the pregnancy, the Finkelsteins are attempting to show that the rabbis of the fifth century understood the science of fetal development.

The Finkelsteins make a point of noting when medical and rabbinic knowledge is consistent: "The rabbis teach that the creation of the fetus begins from the head. Modern medical research confirms this fact and points to the direction of development from head to tail with the head developing first."[35] The authors know that women might have heard about fetal development from their religious leaders or from their husbands, and while they do not want to present inaccurate medical information, they also want to appropriately credit rabbinic teachings. This makes the book more palatable from a religious point of view. If they only presented medical information, it would not be appealing to a Haredi audience. By including the rabbinic commentary as well and noting when it is consistent with medical information, they state their respect for rabbinic authority and demonstrate that doctors are often in agreement with rabbis.

Elsewhere in B'Shaah Tovah, we find evidence that Haredi women are not just trying to find accuracy but instead come to the medical arena with a set of Jewish legal concerns. B'Shaah Tovah responds to these needs by sharing the relevant Jewish legal information for each stage of pregnancy. In a chapter on labor and birth, the authors write about the differences between real and fake contractions, how to recognize the signs of active labor, and what will happen when arriving at the hospital, for instance. Michal and Baruch Finkelstein recognize that many women arrive at the hospital only to be turned away because their labor has not yet progressed to the point of hospital admission, but they include a small note relevant for religiously observant women about "false alarms and niddah."[36] Although women might be very familiar with knowing when they enter into niddah status on a monthly basis, many are confused about when they become a niddah during labor. Thus the authors write, "If you have been sent home because your [cervix] has not opened, then you are not considered a niddah. However, if your cervix has begun to open, even if you are sent home, you are considered a niddah, even if you have not seen any blood."[37] Citing a variety of rabbinic sources, *B'Shaah Tovah* makes sure that Haredi women have not only the medical information they need but the halakhic knowledge also.

Some of the content in the book is primarily halakhic in nature. Chapter 7 is entirely about whether pregnant women can observe a ritual fast. The Jewish calendar contains six major fast days, and pregnant women are bound to come across at least one during the course of their pregnancy. While the chapter provides broad guidelines for how one can fast safely, and advises women who are having difficult pregnancies not to fast, the authors also remind women numerous times to consult with both doctors and rabbis: "It is very important to accept the fact that a woman who receives permission from her rabbi to eat on Yom Kippur is then obligated to eat; she is forbidden from fasting, and she needs to listen to the advice of her doctor and uphold the rabbi's instruction."[38] In this example, a woman received instructions from her doctor to eat on the holiest fast day of the Jewish calendar, and as a result her rabbi gave her permission. This should not be taken lightly, but rather she should understand his permission to eat as her being forbidden from fasting. Here a rabbi issued a permissive ruling based on the instruction of a doctor. The authors recognize that this is a prime example of how medical and religious needs can come together to accommodate a woman's health.

Another chapter that looks at rabbinic teaching extensively is chapter 11, which addresses rabbinic guidelines for ensuring a safe labor. Although other sections of the book consider medical elements of labor and delivery, this chapter begins with an infamous rabbinic teaching about three sins for which a woman would die during labor. The Mishnah states, "For three sins women die in childbirth: because they are not observant of the laws of niddah, challah, and the kindling of the Sabbath lights."[39] These are three commandments that women are supposed to perform, and although later rabbis struggled to understand this passage while not wanting to assign any guilt to a woman who might have died during childbirth, it remains a common teaching. Therefore, despite the terrifying nature of this passage, it is not surprising that it receives significant attention in this book. *B'Shaah Tovah* also includes a chapter on spending the Sabbath in the hospital after birth and how religious couples can be sure not to violate the Sabbath during this time. Like the chapter on fast-ing, these parts of the book raise the Jewish legal questions a Haredi woman is most likely to encounter, and the authors aim to answer these questions by considering both medical and religious interests.

In other places, the authors include references to biblical figures such as Abraham, Sarah, Isaac, and Rebecca. These references are not quite the same as the legal details discussed above, but they provide an appropriate frame of reference for Haredi women. Michal and Baruch Finkelstein draw on a rabbinic story about the birth of Isaac to teach that "pregnancy is not just a means to an end but is rather a gift itself. It gives a woman the special recognition that she is a partner in the creation of a human being."[40] Referencing Rebecca's complaints while carrying twins, another rabbinic story reminds Rebecca that she prayed for a pregnancy, not just for the birth of a son. The rabbis admire her for praying for a pregnancy because it shows women that even though pregnancy can be difficult, it is an important privilege.[41] Just as Haredi men see themselves as links in a chain of rabbinic knowledge, contemporary pregnant Haredi women see themselves in a chain of pregnant women that extends back to the Bible. This is why women struggling with infertility or women whose relatives or friends struggle with infertility visit the place where many believe that Rachel the matriarch is buried. Rachel, Jacob's favored wife in the Bible, was infertile for many years before giving birth to Joseph, who became Jacob's favorite son. Infertile Haredi women see Rachel as their predecessor, and when they visit her grave they sob while they pray for fertility. Contemporary Haredi women feel the same sadness and desperation that they are told Rachel felt, and they believe that the continuation of Jewish life rests on their wombs, just like it rested on Rachel's.[42]

Because of these sections, it is clear that this book is geared toward ultra-Orthodox readers with particular needs and specific narratives framing their understanding of pregnancy. In this way, the book provides them with practical guidelines for maneuvering as religious individuals in a medical framework. These narrative and legal sections are similar to the religious accommodations found in medical settings, which were discussed in the pre-vious chapter. They let Haredi readers and patients know that their concerns are legitimate and can be dealt with from both medical and religious perspec-tives simultaneously.

Other sections of B'Shaah Tovah provide advice for women who are trying to figure out how to broadly negotiate the competing epistemologies of medi-cine and religion. In the opening section of chapter 4, which is about medical treatment during pregnancy, the authors raise the question of whether one should have faith (*bitachon*) in God or in the doctor: "Faithful Jews sometimes ask themselves, why do they need to go for medical examinations when God is directing every detail of their lives. Isn't it enough to pray to God for health and healing? Why should one trust the wisdom of a mortal?"[43] The answer that follows raises a variety of rabbinic sources that have already considered this issue. Ultimately, the authors explain that one needs to find the right balance: "We found that the two extreme attitudes towards medicine are not correct: the one who relies on a miracle to protect his health is considered a fool. Those who think that their health is entirely in the hands of modern medicine and not in heaven's hands are considered to be nonbelievers. We are required to find the golden path that merges our faith [*bitachon*] and our effort [*hishtadlut*]."[44] I will return to these terms in chapter 4 of this volume, because they are terms that the women I spoke to referenced frequently. Here, it is important to see that Michal and Baruch Finkelstein require individuals to turn to their doctors while also encouraging them to have faith in God for healing. In other words, women should be involving both doctors and rabbis in their reproductive care.

In *Hachanah Ruchanit L'Leida*, Nurit Glazer has a different view on the relationship between doctors and rabbis but encourages women to bring religious considerations to the medical arena. In her essay, which has the same title as the anthology, she writes, "Many times when a woman arrives in the labor and delivery room, and they give her a gown, and they measure her blood pressure, everything they need to do, she enters into an entirely different world. She forgets that she also has her own considerations and she has a role in the matter. Suddenly she is just a minor part of the play. She forgets that she has the right to say no sometimes or to bring her own opinion and request something."[45] Glazer goes on to suggest that if a woman asks nicely, she can get what she needs from the doctors. For example, a religious woman who enters the hospital will be more concerned about covering herself modestly. Glazer wants religious women to learn how to ask nicely for a blanket instead of being embarrassed in the hospital gown. Here Glazer equates a woman's "own considerations" with her religious needs and insists that the medical arena tends to overlook women's religious needs. She advises women to stand up for themselves and let the doctors know—in a respectful tone—how they can recognize her needs.

Like the Finkelsteins, Glazer does not suggest women avoid medical care entirely. Although she does not see the natural integration between medicine and religion that the Finkelsteins illustrate, she encourages women to bring their religious needs into the medical arena. Importantly, the advice books maintain that one cannot fully ignore either medicine or one's faith and religious obligations. Instead, the two should be blended in reproductive health care.

How to Develop Authority during Pregnancy

In addition to showing women how their medical and religious needs can be satisfied during pregnancy, pregnancy advice books also aim to help women develop their own authority during this time. In some ways, this approach challenges the network established by doctors and rabbis and bolstered by *B'Shaah Tovah*, which leaves little space for women in their own reproductive health care. However, as we will see, *Hachanah Ruchanit L'Leida* understands a woman's authority to result from religious texts and theological beliefs. Therefore, even when a woman is encouraged to exercise authority over her medical care, this authority comes from traditional religious sources. This book stands, then, as another example of how religious and medical instruction can be combined, though perhaps not harmoniously. Unlike *B'Shaah Tovah*, the authors of *Hachanah Ruchanit L'Leida* start from the assumption that doctors and the medical system are hostile to religious integration. This might be because the collection was published a few years before *B'Shaah Tovah*, so the accommodations I documented in chapter 1 were not yet prominent. It also might be because the Finkelsteins are an embodiment of the synthesis between medicine and religion, while the authors of *Hachanah Ruchanit L'Leida* mostly draw on religious backgrounds.

Their religious orientations are reflected in the way they talk about women's special connection to God as providing them with unique authority. Glazer writes, "Labor is woman's opportunity, in a rare and concentrated way, to connect to God, and this is a forbidden opportunity to waste."[46] Sylvia Dahari and Tami Perlman suggest that prayer is critical during labor and delivery. They show that the letters of the word for birth in Hebrew, *leidah*, can be separated to spell *l'yad Hashem*, or "next to God." The authors say that birth, therefore, is an opportunity to be next to God in prayer: "This is the reality of the ability of very high prayers. Everything we pray will be received."[47] Ilana Berninson wants women to think of themselves as vessels for God during labor because women bring blessings to this world on behalf of God: "We are partners in something holy. At this time, we have to partner in this activity with God and not let any barriers interfere with that."[48] All of these authors acknowledge the pain and discomfort of labor and delivery; however, by giving women a different framework for thinking about birth, they hope that women will learn to embrace this time and their contributions to the process.[49]

Many of the authors in this anthology also point to the Haredi understanding that pregnancy and labor for a woman parallel exile and redemption for the Jewish people. Clarifying a complex rabbinic teaching, Bracha Toverdovitch writes, "Babies before labor are like the nation of Israel in the time of the exile. The moment of labor symbolizes the moment of redemption."[50] Toverdovitch continues to explain that a woman's good deeds during pregnancy, like the Jewish people's good deeds during exile, will lead to the redemption: "The stage of exile is the stage of preparation and growth for the arrival of the Messiah."[51] In other words, women—like the Jewish people in exile—are not just supposed to wait for someone else to bring about a healthy baby. Instead, "pregnancy is the critical stage in the future development of the baby. Every change in environment, diet, can influence [the fetus] for better for worse."[52] This language of exile and redemption and the parallels authors draw with pregnancy and birth not only elevates the physicality of a woman's experience by framing it in religious terms but also reminds women that they play a significant role in fetal development and the healthy birth of a baby.[53]

One of the purposes of framing pregnancy and labor with this language is to help women think positively about labor and delivery. Many of the authors talk about the fear women have in facing the pain of labor or the fact that during labor, "from one side, the gates of heaven are open and prayers are received and are very important. From another side, it is said that the grave is open. This is the time of our judgment."[54] Authors respond to this fear by reminding women that they have an important role to play during labor and delivery, and they can influence the outcome. Nava Merom suggests that by doing good deeds, one can positively influence the outcome. She provides an example from her eighth pregnancy. Merom writes that during this pregnancy she was teaching a class for women on Tuesday nights at eight thirty. Despite the large size of this baby and the fact that she struggled with a long labor and difficult contractions due to the baby's big head, "finally, when the baby exited to the outside world, it was eight thirty on Tuesday evening and a normal delivery."[55] Merom draws a direct line between the class she was teaching and the way her labor ended because the time correlated exactly. She explains that it was due to the fact that she had been teaching this class that she merited a healthy delivery.

As we will see, these themes are prominent in women's narratives of how they developed agency during pregnancy. Additionally, the theological language in *Hachanah Ruchanit L'Leida* is similar to the language many women I spoke with used to describe their own relationship to God during pregnancy and labor. By giving women the language and the tools to think about their contributions to labor and delivery, these authors encourage women to take a more active role, despite what they perceive as an overbearing medical system. Just like these authors, the women I interviewed spoke about their authority deriving, in part, from the theological importance of pregnancy and delivery.

Unlike *Hachanah Ruchanit L'Leida*, which attributes women's confidence to theological beliefs, *B'Shaah Tovah* maintains that education is the key to a positive birth experience and the cultivation of self-confidence. Baruch and Michal Finkelstein make it clear that although their book has a great deal of information, one should still ask her rabbi certain questions and allow a doctor to provide medical care.[56] However, they maintain that the information this book provides can ensure a more positive reproductive experience. Despite the abundance of books one can find in Haredi homes, the authors state, "Until now, pregnancy and labor, a topic so crucial to our lives, is simply absent from Jewish literature."[57] This book, then, is meant to provide women with information about pregnancy and birth:

> It is proven that the difference between a negative and unpleasant experience and an experience of labor that is positive is the correct preparation.... The absence of information leads to fears, trepidations, and suspicions that transform the adventure of labor to a terrifying event; the absence of knowledge can even cause serious complications during labor. When a pregnant woman understands the changes in her body and is sensitive to them, she will be in control of her situation and will exercise more self-confidence. A woman who knows things can engage with the medical staff with ease and can influence the type of treatment she receives.[58]

The Finkelsteins argue that information is the key to allaying fears and cultivating an attitude of self-confidence among women, regardless of whether it is their "first or ninth pregnancy."[59] Instead of feeling belittled by their doctors, women who read *B'Shaah Tovah* will, according to the authors, be empowered with the information needed to relate to the medical staff.

As before, these two pregnancy advice books model a way for integrating medicine and religion. The authors of both books maintain that the integration will be positive for women, because they can enter the medical field with the information and the authority they need to receive personalized reproductive health care. The authors credit these books with providing women with the tools and knowledge they need in order to pierce the closed network of doctors and rabbis. Although the women I spoke to seem to agree that they can pierce the closed network of doctors and rabbis, they have a different idea about the origin of that information and authority. In women's reproductive narratives, they deny the role these pregnancy advice books have played in their reproductive agency.

CONCLUSION: BOOKS AND BABIES AND
THE AUTHORITY THEY PROVIDE

The next few chapters will make it clear that women's expressions of agency sound a lot like the content of these books. Haredi women emphasize their ability to deftly maneuver between medical and rabbinic authorities, sometimes ignoring one or the other based on their own preference and analysis. They talk about the importance of being informed and approaching the doctor with knowledge. Women also use theological understandings of pregnancy, labor, and delivery that are very similar to those in the pregnancy advice books. They talk about the importance of being a vessel for God and how birth is like the coming of the Messiah. Women claim that all of these factors contribute to their authority over reproductive decisions. Haredi women are able to make reproductive decisions without the advice of doctors and without asking their rabbis because they are informed by their knowledge of pregnancy and emboldened by their special relationship to God during this time.

So, why do women claim to not have learned anything from these books, despite displaying them prominently and repeating many of the same ideas and tropes in their own reproductive narratives? In the chapters that follow I argue that one of the most central elements of women's reproductive agency is their experience of embodying pregnancy. Although women in their first or second pregnancies may turn to books or external authorities, women in later pregnancies come to rely much more on their previous reproductive experiences. It is precisely because pregnancy happens in their bodies—and not their rabbis' bodies—that they understand themselves to be the authoritative sources on pregnancy. While women have come to internalize the themes popular in these pregnancy advice books, citing these books would negate the experience they gained from the embodiment of pregnancy. Instead of prioritizing book knowledge, women prioritize their embodied knowledge of pregnancy.

Furthermore, citing the books would validate men's method of being Haredi as superior. It would further prop up the yeshiva world and book learning, to which women are not exposed. And because books symbolize the entire authority structure in the Haredi world wherein rabbinic leaders determine the norms and actions of adherents, referring to content from these pregnancy advice books would lend justification to the idea that they *should* be visiting a rabbi every time they have a question. Instead, women prefer to rely on their own experiences of pregnancy. Having these books, however, and displaying them on their shelves alongside their husband's seforim make it possible for women to subvert Haredi norms. As objects, these books provide the veneer of conformity and respect for Haredi authority. By appearing to conform to Haredi male norms, women are able to authoritatively and safely reject these same rules and expectations. Having the books, therefore, paves the way for women's embodied authority.

Importantly, as women prioritize their embodied knowledge, they reverse the directionality of the relationship between books and babies. Recall that books, when used symbolically in segulot about fetal positions and the timing of the birth, are thought to influence the pregnancy. Additionally, male authority figures expect women to follow the instructions contained within the books and the advice of those who know the content of the books. In relying on their embodied experiences to determine whether they turn to the books for either content or symbolism, Haredi women are demonstrating that the relationship flows in the opposite direction as well. Women recognize that without their contributions—namely, pregnancy, birth, and childrearing—Haredi society cannot continue. Without more children to fill the study halls, the yeshiva as an institution would be obsolete. The way they make pregnancy decisions demonstrates that the books are not directing Haredi life but rather that the creation of life in the Haredi world makes the books relevant.

NOTES

1. *Seforim* literally just means "books," but when my Haredi informants use it, it refers to their sacred books.

2. For more on segulot and my use of the term, see the introduction to this volume, n100.

3. These rituals could be imagined as forms of couvade, wherein fathers take on certain behaviors of childbirth with the purpose of either establishing their paternity, protecting the fetus, or creating a physical bond with the baby. See Tylor, "On a Method of Investigating the Development of Institutions"; Tylor, *Researches into Early History of Mankind*; and Riviere, "Couvade: A Problem Reborn."

4. M. Friedman, "Life Tradition and Book Tradition."

5. See Berman, "Sect, Subsidy, and Sacrific," for more on the income generated by yeshiva study. I will return to the financial issue in chap. 5.

6. M. Friedman, "Life Tradition and Book Tradition," 140.

7. Don-Yehiya, "Orthodox Jewry in Israel and in North America." For more on the history of the yeshiva, see Stadler, *Yeshiva Fundamentalism*, 38–49.

8. Heilman, *Defenders of the Faith*, 245–46.

9. Ibid., 257.

10. Ibid.

11. Benor, *Becoming Frum*, 63. Benor points out that most Orthodox families display these books prominently as a demonstration of their attachment to these texts. Individuals and families who are becoming Orthodox do not get rid of the English-language books they might own. Instead, new books on Jewish law are added to their bookshelves. See also Yaffe et al., "Poor Is Pious."

12. Heilman, *Defenders of the Faith*, 171.

13. Stadler, *Yeshiva Fundamentalism*, 75.

14. Ibid., 4. Stadler discusses extensively the ways that Haredi men are challenging the norms of Haredi society in a way that causes these norms to shift.

15. Heilman, *Defenders of the Faith*, 176.

16. Ibid., 246.

17. Ibid., 237.

18. See also Stadler, *Yeshiva Fundamentalism*, on norms for men and women in the Haredi world.

19. M. Friedman, "Life Tradition and Book Tradition."

20. Heilman, *Defenders of the Faith*, 170.

21. See, for example, M. Friedman, "Haredim and the Israeli Society" and "Life Tradition and Book Tradition"; and Heilman, *Defenders of the Faith*. Stadler, in *Yeshiva Fundamentalism*, shows how this is beginning to shift as young men embrace non-yeshiva life.

22. Davidman, *Becoming Un-Orthodox*. Iddo Tavory, in *Summoned*, does not consistently look at Haredi men but broadens to Orthodox men in general.

23. Fader, *Mitzvah Girls*; S. Levine, *Mystics, Mavericks, and Merrymakers*.

24. Sered, *Women as Ritual Experts*.

25. Davidman, *Tradition in a Rootless World*; Benor, *Becoming Frum*.

26. See, for example, El-Or, *Educated and Ignorant*, and Rapoport-Albert, *Hasidic Studies*, and "Emergence of a Female Constituency."

27. El-Or, *Educated and Ignorant*, 89.

28. Ibid., 90.

29. M. Friedman, "Life Tradition and Book Tradition."

30. Han, *Pregnancy in Practice*, 24.

31. Translations from the Hebrew version are my own. The title of the revised English version is *Nine Wonderful Months: B'Sha'ah Tovah; The Jewish Woman's Clinical and Halachic Guide to Pregnancy and Childbirth*.

32. Finkelstein and Finkelstein, *B'Shaah Tovah*, 28.

33. Ibid., 29.

34. Ibid., 30.

35. Ibid., 28.

36. For more on niddah, see chap. 1, p. XX.

37. Finkelstein and Finkelstein, *B'Shaah Tovah*, 157.

38. Ibid., 74.

39. M. Shabbat, 2:6.

40. Finkelstein and Finkelstein, *B'Shaah Tovah*, 65.

41. Ibid., 66.

42. For more on Haredi women visiting the tomb of Rachel, see Sered, "Rachel's Tomb."

43. Ibid., 34.

44. Ibid., 36.

45. Glazer, "Spiritual Preparation for Labor," 18.

46. Glazer, "Spiritual Preparation for Labor," 17.

47. Dahari and Perlman, "Labor—Next to God in Prayer," 35.

48. Berninson, "Time of Labor—Time of Cancellation," 51.

49. I return to these metaphors in chap. 4.

50. Toverdovitch, "Towards Spiritual Motherhood," 36.

51. Ibid., 39.

52. Ibid., 38.

53. See Gribetz, "Pregnant with Meaning," for more on these metaphors. I address them more fully in chap. 4.

54. Glazer, "Spiritual Preparation for Labor," 16.

55. Merom, "Spiritual Treatment," 62.

56. Finkelstein and Finkelstein, *B'Shaah Tovah*, 7.

57. Ibid., 8.

58. Ibid.

59. Ibid.

THREE

—⚊—

THE EMBODIMENT OF PREGNANCY

CHANA, A MOTHER OF ELEVEN children whom I met while observing in one of the hospitals in Jerusalem, came to the ultrasound unit already in labor, because the doctor wanted her to get another scan before they proceeded. Chana described herself as a "yaldah tovah yerushalayim," roughly a "very good girl," meaning she gets all the tests her doctor wants. Unexpectedly, for two of her earlier labors she had cesarean sections, and she decided that for this one, she would do all she could to prevent another. Though she had already given birth vaginally since her C-sections, Chana was concerned that the doctor this time would force her to have a C-section because earlier scans indicated she was carrying a large baby. Chana called her rabbi, who told her to call Dr. Abramov, the head of obstetrics at the hospital. Abramov is sympathetic to Haredi concerns and works frequently with this community and with the rabbis in charge. I asked Chana why she did not want another C-section, and her first response was "I know my body." For Chana this was less about whether or not a C-section was medically indicated and more about the fact that she knew, based on previous experiences, that she could give birth vaginally. She added another concern, though, when she stated, "If I get a C-section now I'll always need one." Chana, then, was thinking about not only her past pregnancies but also her future ones as she made the decision to proceed with a vaginal birth.

Chana's reliance on her past experience continued during the ultrasound. As she was scanning Chana's abdomen, the technician asked her, "You've already had a C-section?" When Chana confirmed this, the technician excitedly responded, "So what are you doing here? Go get a C-section!" Chana objected with confidence as she said, "I'm having a regular labor, and the birth will be today. I already gave birth naturally twice since the C-sections." The technician at this point eased off the topic of the C-section and tried to focus again on determining an accurate weight for the fetus, because in Israeli medical practice, fetuses that measure greater than 4.0 kilograms (about 8.8 pounds) are generally recommended for a C-section birth. As the technician measured the fetus to get an accurate weight, she asked Chana, "What weight do you usually birth?" Chana said, "About 4.0." The technician said she was measuring about 4.0 or 4.2 kilograms. "But I could be wrong. I'll keep scanning." Chana shared with the technician that frequently the measurements on the ultrasound are incorrect, either estimating a fetus much bigger or much smaller than what emerges. The technician had her own stories like Chana's so she kept measuring until she was able to write down measurements that would allow Chana to give birth vaginally. In the end the technician admitted, "The ultrasound is not precise."

Chana refused to heed the advice of her doctors, called her rabbi only to get the name of a doctor who would listen to her, and even convinced the ultrasound technician to read the scans in such a way that confirmed her patient's experience. Chana's reproductive agency was based on her previous experiences. For Chana and many other women I spoke to, experience—the embodiment of pregnancy and the cultural participation in reproduction—educates Haredi women about pregnancy itself and about how to develop one's authority as a Haredi woman.

As the previous chapters have demonstrated, Haredi women experience pregnancy and reproduction within a medical and rabbinic context that attempts to limit women's authority over reproduction. Additionally, the gendered divide in Haredi life reinforces the authority of books over women's embodied experiences. Haredi women, however, draw extensively on their embodied experiences when making decisions about pregnancy and childbirth. This chapter and the next show how this happens in a way that is consistent with Haredi cultural and theological norms. In this chapter I argue that women's reproductive agency develops as a result of their embodied experiences of pregnancy and cultural and religious context. This chapter traces how Haredi cultural and religious norms embolden women to draw on their embodied experiences and how Haredi women's repeated pregnancies foster their embodied authority. In this patriarchal culture, therefore, women are actually capitalizing on their bodies, the sites of their gendered limitations in Haredi society, to cultivate their agency.

I first provide a description of the cultural and religious context that makes room for pregnant Haredi women to turn to their embodied experiences for reproductive authority. In the private realm, the makeup of Haredi families and the gendered structure of family life make it possible for Haredi women to act independent of the male authorities. Although heavily regulated within that authority structure, Haredi women's bodies can become sites of agency during pregnancy. The second part of this chapter considers the ways a Haredi woman relies on her previous reproductive experiences for authority. A Haredi woman's subjectivity in her community and sense of authority change throughout—and as a result of—her reproductive life. I continue this discussion in the next chapter as I address the ways women understand Haredi theology to bolster their reproductive authority.

PART I: MAKING ROOM FOR A WOMAN'S AGENCY

It might seem odd to suggest that by participating in reproduction a Haredi woman is able to exert agency and authority. The maternal body is, after all, understood to be the "reproduction of the social body,"[1] and in our case, the pregnant Haredi body reproduces the male-dominated religious and cultural norms of Haredi life. How can women find agency by participating in this structure of domination? Following the work of Saba Mahmood, I define agency in terms of the "capacity for action" enabled and created by the "historically specific relations of subordination" in which Haredi women's identities are formed.[2] Thus, to make the case that Haredi women do have a capacity for action during their pregnancies—that is, agency, which manifests as authority—I will first argue that the context in which they live, pray, work, and raise families actually facilitates and creates a space for women to act with authority.

The Private Realm: A Problem of Zugiyut

Shira, a mother of five, is an eighth-generation Jerusalemite, and she has seen the Haredi community change over the course of many generations. As a social worker for the Haredi community, Shira focuses on problems of *zugiyut*, or "couplehood." The term has a positive connotation, but Shira finds that this positive element of marital relationships is lacking within Haredi households, due partly to the ways in which Haredi men and women meet and begin their marriages and partly as a result of the financial stressors on Haredi families. The lack of zugiyut makes it possible for Haredi women to possess some independence from the male-dominated Haredi cultural context. Specifically, the nature of a Haredi woman's relationship to her husband allows her to make reproductive decisions without his knowledge and therefore without the involvement of their rabbi. This is because Haredi women do not turn to their rabbis directly. Instead, they ask their husbands to approach a rabbi with a question.

Shira explained that one of the most significant problems facing Haredi couples is that there is a lack of education within the Haredi world about how to communicate with one's spouse and how to build a loving home. Some of this, Shira explained, is due to the fact that couples marry very young after a short or nonexistent courtship and begin having children before they even know each other. Haredi women are generally married around the age of twenty or twenty-one and men perhaps a year or two later. Their marriage is set up by a matchmaker and approved by the respective families, though sometimes a family member serves as a matchmaker.[3] Matchmakers play an important role in the maintenance of social priorities. The matchmakers and other community leaders often teach young girls and boys how to judge their intended: by particular characteristics that should be compatible, including religious perspectives and observance. Hasidic parents are generally more involved in choosing their son's/daughter's intended than parents of Lithuanian descent.[4] Matchmakers also ensure that strict boundaries are maintained between Sephardi and Ashkenazi young men and women to prevent the marriage of the two different religious practices.[5] The young couple also must agree to the match. Though they do not "date" for very long, a young couple on a match date will meet in a hotel lobby or other public place and get to know each other. They may discuss their families, their plans for the future, how many children they would like to have, where they would like their children to be educated, religious inclinations they share, and where they would like to live. If the match is suitable to the couple, then their parents will begin planning for the wedding, a community affair that usually takes place within a couple of months of the match.

Before marriage, young women and sometimes young men attend gender-segregated premarital education classes, where they learn about their roles in marriage and the observance of menstrual laws, an entire body of Jewish law that has been hidden from them until the eve of marriage.[6] These marital preparation courses teach women in particular about the values of selflessness (such as the importance of giving rather than receiving) and the need to communicate with one's spouse and find common ground, especially on religious issues. Women learn about the laws regarding family purity and how to mark their menstrual cycles in accordance with halakha, but they learn very little about physical intimacy. Brides are eager to learn about this, but their teachers, older Haredi women who have not been trained to provide this type of instruction, are embarrassed and reluctant to discuss these topics with young women.[7] Esther Goshen-Gottstein writes that when Haredi mothers and daughters talk about sex, it "is usually given with much embarrassment, which prevents the daughter from asking further questions."[8] Though girls discuss these issues with their peers, the information usually involves fantastical stories and horror tales about men.[9] Meanwhile, boys learn about a woman's world as one full of emotions, much different from the rational, text-centered world of Haredi men.[10] These classes, then, do not sufficiently prepare young men and women for the new sexual encounter that faces them on their wedding night. After having grown up in a completely sex-segregated community and not ever exposing one's body to a member of the opposite sex, the wedding night can be a terrifying experience.[11]

Thus, during the first few years of marriage Haredi couples struggle with their new lives as a couple while they are also raising young children. Haredi women are still the primary caretakers in their families, despite some recent changes in social norms. Haredi men have begun taking on more responsibilities and are frequently seen walking the streets of Haredi neighborhoods with strollers and children in hand and sitting at playgrounds with their children.[12] Rabbinic leaders have encouraged Haredi men to take a more active role in family duties to help their wives and prevent the family duties from taking too large a toll on women. In Nurit Stadler's account of literature for Haredi men, she finds that men are taught to be aware of "the emotional instability of ultra-Orthodox woman [sic] and the 'stumbling blocks' that female frustration is liable to mount on the road to maintaining a functional family."[13] With this in mind, leading rabbis in the Haredi world teach their students the importance of being more sensitive to their family's needs. While the women I spoke to mentioned that their husbands often helped with childcare, they also discussed the segregation between their private lives and those of their male spouses. This, it turns out, becomes relevant when they make reproductive decisions.

Shira clarified, "We see many situations where there is a lack of knowledge, where couples need help with zugiyut, and pregnancy and birth put lots of stress on these already rough relationships." I saw this phenomenon repeatedly among the women I spoke to. None articulated it quite as well as Dalia, who described herself as a "nontypical Bei[t] Yaakov girl." Beit Yaakov is the school system for Haredi girls and young women. The education of a Haredi woman who will provide for her growing family begins in early childhood education and continues throughout adulthood.[14] The Beit Yaakov school system provides young women with both a Jewish and a secular education. The school's mission is to train ultra-Orthodox Jewish women to become teachers within the ultra-Orthodox school system.[15] In addition to providing basic education to Haredi girls up to the age of eighteen, the schools aim to instill in young women the importance of supporting their future spouses. As young Haredi men are encouraged to devote themselves completely to Torah study, they need wives who can support them, both financially and domestically. By the end of the 1950s, this became the trend in Israel: young women graduated from the Beit Yaakov school system and married yeshiva students who continued with their yeshiva education while their wives pursued an educational career in the Haredi world.[16] After some time, due to a surplus of women graduating from the Beit Yaakov schools, there were not enough teaching positions available. Thus, still with the mission of supporting their husbands, these young women pursued higher education and went into other fields, such as business, clerical jobs, other educational initiatives, or the arts.[17]

While "typical" Beit Yaakov girls eagerly marry Torah scholars, Dalia met over twenty potential suitors—all scholars—before she decided on her current husband when she was twenty-one years old. They quickly got married, but Dalia knew she was not ready to become a mother. Instead, because she loves dancing, she joined a Haredi dance group in her neighborhood. Soon she opened her own studio for young Haredi girls to learn dance. Ten years ago, this was a radical business venture, because girls in the Haredi world were not encouraged to dance or perform publicly.[18] Due to her success, however, her husband began working on the business end of the studio while Dalia still functions as the artistic director. Dalia knew that getting pregnant would not only interrupt her dance and performance schedule but also lead her to define herself anew, and she was not quite ready for that.

Unexpectedly, though, Dalia became pregnant quickly. When we met, she was a woman in her thirties with four young children. Dalia attributes her decreasing anxiety and increasing confidence with each pregnancy to the improvement of her marriage. She recognizes that as a young bride with a husband she barely knew, she did not enjoy being married or getting pregnant. With the help of marriage counseling, though, her marriage stabilized, enabling Dalia to embrace her identity as a dancer. She explained,

> I knew that my basic instinct was as a dancer, and today I just know that is the way it is. I don't even try to change it. I'm just also a mother. . . . At the beginning it was embarrassing for me. What is wrong with me? Why is everyone different? Why does everyone want to be a mother and I want to be a dancer? It wasn't something I mentioned to anyone because it was such an embarrassment. In the Haredi world . . . motherhood is put on a pedestal, but in fact we're all human beings. We all have our issues. . . . Even when it [motherhood] is great, it's not easy.

Dalia also explained that attitudes toward big families began to shift in the last ten years, leading to more satisfying marital relationships, and Shira confirmed this. Now, it is more likely that rabbis will permit the use of birth control when a family already has a few children and the couple would like to wait a little while before having more. Dalia remarked, "Today birth control in the Haredi world is wide open. In my days, in the last twelve years, it was different. I know because I see my sisters and the way they talk to their friends. They talk about birth control freely. In my circles, we never discussed these issues. Today it's not even an issue. In my days, we never spoke about it between friends." Dalia told me that her rabbi has become increasingly supportive of couples using hormonal birth control, expressing his opposition to big families in the Haredi world. His opinion is that these big families lack love, support, and financial stability, thus leading to unhappy marriages, children, and women. Despite the fact that Dalia's rabbi would easily give her permission for birth control, she said that now "if I feel like I need birth control, I'll take it right away," meaning she would not ask her rabbi for permission. She feels that his consent is unnecessary. Ten years ago, Dalia would not have asked her rabbi because she would have been too nervous that he would judge her or her husband negatively for wanting to limit the number of children they raised. She also would not have discussed it with her friends, and she probably would not have even used birth control. She explained, "I would not have even mentioned it to my husband. I would have avoided the topic." According to her reproductive ethic now, however, Dalia maintains that it is solely *her* decision to use birth control. In fact, birth control is widely used among Israeli Orthodox families, even though there are still some who refuse it.[19] Dalia's attitude toward birth control changed in the last ten years due in part to the shift in religious norms but also due to her growing comfort and confidence as a mother who feels that she can make these decisions on her own.

Furthermore, marital norms enable Dalia to keep many decisions secret from her husband. This lack of communication among young Haredi couples plays out in a practical way when it comes to making decisions about pregnancy. For instance, the silence between a woman and her husband on issues related to pregnancy and the lack of direct communication between a woman and her rabbi leave an opening for a Haredi woman to act with agency on matters related to pregnancy. As we saw with Dalia, when a woman is not comfortable discussing her desired use of birth control (for either personal, professional, or financial reasons) with her husband, then her request will never reach her rabbi. Furthermore, if her husband considers it immodest to attend a doctor appointment with her or if he is busy at kollel all day, then a pregnant woman can receive ultrasound scans that might otherwise be forbidden by the community. Viewed in this way, we see that the nature of private relationships and a woman's role in her family actually help create women's agency by leaving space for women to act without the regulation of male authorities.

The Public Realm: A Fertile Lacuna

In the public realm, pregnancy is seen as so normative that it is not usually a topic of conversation. Thus, unlike in North America, where a woman may be subject to a stranger's hand placed on her pregnant stomach or the persistent "Do you know what you're having?" inquiry, pregnant Haredi women in Israel are so conventional that they garner little attention. Pregnancy is such a common and unremarkable occurrence that when I introduced myself to Haredi women hearing about my research for the first time, they were often puzzled about why this would be interesting to anybody. One woman remarked, "Yeah, so what? We're pregnant a lot. It's not a big deal." Others said, "Well, you won't have a hard time finding pregnant women to talk to!" Indeed, walking down the streets of Haredi neighborhoods one can easily spot dozens of pregnant women—pushing strollers, running to a meeting, or picking up some groceries. Despite its seemingly common occurrence in Haredi life, a woman's pregnancy is not discussed, even among close friends and family.

This is not to say that pregnancy or pregnant women are ignored, however. One reason for this silence is the observance of prominent segulot. In an effort to avoid attracting the evil eye, Haredi men and women do not discuss a woman's pregnancy. Additionally, it is common to avoid purchasing clothing, furniture, or other supplies for a new baby before the birth.[20] Haredi women do not hold baby showers or name their babies until the ceremonial naming after birth. Yet due to these segulot, a woman's pregnant body is constantly under the fearful gaze of the Haredi community. This is because it is considered a rather dangerous time for both a woman and her fetus. For instance, in a class setting, I observed two pregnant women searching the floor on their hands and knees for a nail clipping that had accidentally fallen. Surrounded by other pregnant women, these two did not want others to step on this nail because they adhered to a segulah that stepping on a nail clipping would cause a miscarriage.[21] In this way, although the pregnancy is seemingly shielded from public conversation, the avoidance of this conversation is an active choice and places pregnancy under the silent and fearful gaze of the community.

Tsipy Ivry discusses this cultural tendency, which she calls the "trivialization of pregnancy," among secular Israeli women. Despite the fact that motherhood is a central element of Jewish Israeli female identity, individual pregnant women do not garner any special attention.[22] Ivry explains that pregnancy is recognized "as a fertile enterprise only retrospectively, after a healthy baby has been born."[23] This is because the possibility of catastrophe during pregnancy drives much of Israeli prenatal care. Ivry argues, "Pregnancy is basically a chaotic process in which nature is liable to make mistakes."[24] In her focus on the genetic emphasis of Israeli reproductive health care, Ivry finds that doctors, ultrasound technicians, and geneticists enter as saviors, as the health of future Israelis is threatened by the natural course of pregnancy. Although Haredi individuals do not tend to rely on prenatal testing to the same extent as their secular counterparts, the possibility of disaster looms large over both religious and secular Jewish populations in Israel.[25]

The absence of societal and familial discussion leaves a fertile lacuna for a Haredi woman to make reproductive decisions. Additionally, the tension between the trivialization of pregnancy and the fear of reproductive catastrophe leads women to understand that their decisions are important but should not be discussed with others. As a result, a Haredi woman feels the authority to make decisions regarding prenatal testing, ultrasounds, or birth control because pregnancy carries such great risk, which she is responsible for, and she can do so without fear that her community will judge her as long as nobody talks about her pregnancy. If nobody asks her which prenatal tests she is getting because her community considers such discussions of pregnancy to be segulah, she does not have to tell anyone that she might have made a decision that is counter to what her rabbi may advise. For an individual Haredi woman, this space to experience her pregnancy free from the involvement of the community results in her ability to make reproductive decisions independently.

And yet Haredi women do not take this responsibility lightly. They understand their reproductive actions carry great weight individually, communally, and religiously, and they draw on their embodied experiences to justify these choices.

PART II: EMBODIED EXPERIENCE CREATES AUTHORITY

Now that we see how Haredi life makes space for women to exert agency, we can look more closely at how Haredi women draw on their previous reproductive experiences for their reproductive agency and how a woman's embodied experience of pregnancy informs her authoritative knowledge. As is the case for many participants of a variety of religious traditions, embodied rituals are a significant part of ultra-Orthodox women's religious lives. These rituals—in dress, behavior, eating, language, and sexuality—influence women's experiences by helping them distinguish themselves from outsiders, transform themselves, and cultivate a relationship with the divine.[26] Although pregnancy does not start as a bodily ritual with the ability to transform one's identity, the repeated pregnancy experiences of Haredi women become part of what shapes not only her identity but also her religious authority. Furthermore, I argue that the lack of religious signification for pregnancy (few prayers, laws, or blessings exist for pregnant women) leaves a space for *women* to make this bodily practice religiously relevant and formative. Accustomed to expressing their religious identities through bodily practices, Haredi women's reproductive experiences come to provide them with unique access to agency.

One of the most fundamental bodily practices within the Haredi community is the regulation of dress codes, which begins at a very young age. By kindergarten, young girls are taught that their bodies, unless completely covered, can lead men to have sexual thoughts about them.[27] Girls and women wear long skirts, thick stockings, quiet shoes, long sleeves, and shirts that cover them up to the neck.[28] Young girls are expected to have their hair pulled back neatly and not flowing freely over their shoulders.[29] Married women cover their hair with a variety of options: hats, wigs, scarves.[30] Although some variations exist between different Haredi groups, Haredi women can be identified by their conformity to these norms.[31] These dress codes are meant to maintain cultural norms of modesty within the community, protecting social and sexual boundaries between the genders, and to distinguish Haredi adherents from non-Haredi individuals.[32]

Once she is married, a Haredi woman must follow the laws and procedures of *taharat hamishpacha* (family purity). These laws regulate her and her husband's actions when she is a niddah, usually during menstruation and for the seven days following. Each month, for at least twelve days (and more if her period lasts longer than five days), Haredi women refrain from touching their spouses. They sleep in separate beds, do not share food from the same plate, and observe a variety of other rituals meant to maintain distance. During her seven "clean" days, she must check herself with a cloth twice a day to make sure she is not bleeding. If she does find a drop of blood on the cloth during the seven days following her period, a woman must bring this cloth to a certified rabbinic authority who will determine whether the size and color of the cloth indicates that she must start counting her seven clean days all over again. At the conclusion of seven clean days, she immerses naked in a ritual bath, a mikvah, while a trained observer confirms that all parts of her body have been covered in water. After this ritual, she can return home to her husband and engage in sexual activity.[33]

These bodily rituals foster a femininity that is meant to be hidden and protected from the male gaze. Yafeh argues that "they are designed to make the body and its material needs 'fade away,' disappear."[34] In fact, even the rituals themselves are shrouded in secrecy. Entering a rabbinic office for him to check a stain on a cloth involves a woman anonymously walking into an unmarked room. However, maintaining secrecy about one's internal bodily processes is extremely difficult when a Haredi woman becomes pregnant and her bodily shape changes significantly and publicly. When her body's very routines, shapes, feelings, and needs differ significantly from what she is used to, and when her body's material needs—more space on a couch, cravings for particular foods, extra time sleeping—are unable to be ignored, the laws of modesty no longer align with her embodied experience. As Yafeh points out, "The emphasis on concealment, alongside the cultural preoccupation with bodily practices, only intensifies the body's presence in the girls' lives."[35] At a certain point, a pregnant body cannot be concealed and its material needs cannot be ignored. Simultaneously, Haredi women are used to the intensified meaning of their bodily practices, leading them to weave their reproductive embodiment into this cultural framework.

Importantly, although others have analyzed Haredi bodily rituals as important factors in self-formation, pregnancy is not often thought of as a bodily *ritual*, even for Haredi women who experience pregnancy more often than most other women. Unlike dress codes, prayer, and food practices, which are daily routines, and the monthly observance of family purity laws, one completes a ten-month pregnancy at most yearly. Furthermore, during pregnancy, one's bodily practices are constantly changing.[36] Therefore, although it is hard to say that pregnancy can become routinized or ritualized like these other bodily practices, Haredi women speak about their third pregnancies as if it has become a ritual in which they have authority. This is important because it places pregnancy squarely within other Haredi bodily practices, where devotion to Haredi life, distinction from the outside world, and relationship with God is established through the repeated action. This alignment with Haredi norms is what ultimately provides women with the agency to make decisions without their rabbinic leaders.

With each pregnancy, a woman gains more bodily experience that then informs her future reproductive decisions. Writing about shyness resulting from certain bodily actions among Muslim women, Saba Mahmood explains, "Action does not issue forth from natural feelings but *creates* them."[37] Similarly, Haredi women do not intuitively express authority during pregnancy but the repeated action of pregnancy cultivates women's authority.[38] Through a comparison of women's reproductive agency in their first and second pregnancies with their agency in the third pregnancy and beyond, I will show that as their reproductive lives progress, Haredi women come to make decisions based on their previous embodied experiences, not on the advice of rabbis, doctors, or family. This unique embodied agency becomes their reproductive ethic.

A Growing Sense of Authority

Hadassah, an Orthodox nurse-midwife who has provided medical care for Haredi women for decades, teaches prenatal classes to Haredi women in Meah Shearim. The six-week course that I attended was populated predominately by Lithuanian-descended Haredi women who were pregnant for the first time. Thirty women in their early twenties sat around a large conference table in Bikur Cholim Hospital to learn from Hadassah. They turned to her as a certified nurse, a midwife, and an Orthodox woman who could provide them with medical guidance that is sensitive to their religious needs. She begins a new course every two to three months, and these courses are always enrolled at capacity. Each session of the course lasts about three hours, but Hadassah stays after answering a variety of personal questions for her students. The class costs NIS 500 (approximately $125),[39] but some of the health plans subsidize up to 50 percent of the course fee. Though this expense could still be onerous for a Haredi family struggling to make ends meet, I did not witness any woman complaining about the cost or requesting a discount from Hadassah.

The course included medical information about pregnancy that is likely common in many prenatal classes in Israel as well as basic sex education. Hadassah covered topics such as menstruation cycles, gynecological examinations, picking a hospital in which to birth, prenatal care and testing, the birthing process, and the postpartum period. After treating thousands of Haredi women during her extensive career as a nurse-midwife in Jerusalem, Hadassah knows what Haredi women do not know, and she uses her course as an opportunity to educate them for the future.[40] Most Haredi women do not receive basic science lessons as part of their regular education, so many are ignorant of the physiological elements of their menstrual cycle. Additionally, although most of the women were already in their seventh month of pregnancy when they began the course, Hadassah used a slide presentation on the first day of class to show them how they got pregnant. This anatomy lesson was about a normal ovulation cycle and how fertilization occurs during this period. Though she used medical terms to label the parts of the female anatomy, Hadassah did not actually say where the sperm comes from, preferring instead to talk about the male anatomy abstractly. As she is aware of Haredi modesty norms, Hadassah knows that using the word *penis*, even in a medical setting, would be inappropriate and therefore make women uncomfortable. Instead, she referred to "men" but not their body parts.

The Ministry of Health encourages women to get an early ultrasound in their first trimester so that doctors can date the pregnancy and check the location of the placenta and the location of the fetus to make sure that it is not an ectopic pregnancy. Hadassah repeated these guidelines and then, in a more casual and friendly voice, added one of her own: "Listen, already at the beginning you're experiencing a number of changes like nausea, dehydration, exhaustion, and you want to know if there is something there. You don't feel it and you don't have a stomach yet, so you might not know you're pregnant, especially in your first pregnancy." From her experience, Hadassah knows that Haredi women do not immediately recognize the signs of pregnancy when they are pregnant for the first time. As newlyweds who have not received comprehensive sexual education, these women may not even know that they are pregnant until the doctor tells them. Though women in her classes have long since passed the early signs of pregnancy, Hadassah gives them this advice for their next pregnancy, an event that may equally surprise them.

My observations in the ultrasound unit of a prenatal clinic in Geula confirmed this unawareness among Haredi women. One Haredi woman, twenty-one years old, came into the ultrasound examination with her friend, an unmarried woman who was equally surprised when the ultrasound technician told the newly married friend that she was pregnant. The young bride responded, "But we just got married last month! How could I be pregnant?" The technician, a woman in her early thirties with four children, knowingly smiled and said, "I guess you got pregnant on your wedding night." She responded, "I didn't know that was possible!" Of course, many non-Haredi women also are not aware that they can get pregnant when they engage in sexual intercourse for the first time. Some Haredi women were equally shocked to be pregnant for a second time so soon after giving birth to their first because they believed, mistakenly, that breastfeeding would prevent ovulation and conception. Except for Hadassah's prenatal classes, there are few resources available for a Haredi woman to learn about the biology of conception.

As a result of a lack of information regarding one's body and the process of pregnancy, labor, and delivery, Haredi women often have negative memories of their first births. Rivka, a doula from Ramat Beit Shemesh who moved to Israel with her family when she was thirteen years old, found Israeli Haredi women in particular talk about their first births as completely traumatic experiences, filled with surprises and unexpected pain. Rivka suggested to me that this is based on the general lack of knowledge that women have going into their first births. Rivka explained that the lack of education about pregnancy and labor only adds to a Haredi woman's inability to make decisions regarding labor and delivery. Because young Haredi women have been raised to turn to the rabbi with all of their questions, they become paralyzed when they are finally confronted with the need for a quick decision in the hospital during labor. Rivka has found this frequently among her Israeli Haredi clientele, as she has spent hours waiting for a rabbi's approval of a medical procedure during birth, much like we saw in chapter 1.

Another consequence of the absence of education regarding pregnancy and birth is that many women turn to their doctors for a great deal of information during their first pregnancies. During her first pregnancy, Miriam was upset with her doctor for not being more responsive. Though the doctor agreed to see her as a patient, Miriam remembers only one appointment, when she was thirty-six weeks into the pregnancy. Disappointed at the lack of care she received, Miriam admitted, "I knew the baby was growing. *I* knew, but it was still my first. They just should not have taken me on as a patient." Early in her reproductive life, Miriam did not rely on her embodied knowledge telling her the fetus was healthy. Instead, she expected (and wanted) the doctor to play a more active role. During her first pregnancy, she still prioritized medical knowledge. During labor, however, Miriam's attitude toward her own authority changed. She refused an epidural, believing that her prayers would be more "intense" if she could feel the pain of birth.[41] As a result, Miriam remembers that the birth was a powerful experience that changed her perception of herself. "After my first baby was born," Miriam explained, "I remember thinking, 'Now I really feel like a woman.' I never really understood, and now I feel like a woman. This is what a woman is, this is what happens, this is what I am." After she completed her first pregnancy Miriam finally "understood" herself differently. The experience of pregnancy and birth educated her to see herself as a woman in the Haredi community who would be repeatedly performing these acts and in this way could rely on her embodied knowledge instead of on that of her doctors.

Although Miriam felt a significant change in her identity and subjectivity in the Haredi community after her first pregnancy, most of the other women I interviewed began to see a difference only after their second pregnancies. Ultimately, their confidence increased as they experienced more pregnancies. This confidence was based on the knowledge gained from the embodied experience of pregnancy. With each subsequent pregnancy, women felt more comfortable challenging the received authorities—doctors and rabbis—and relying instead on their own reproductive agency. For them, this agency came from the knowledge and authority they gained from embodying pregnancy, and it allowed them to challenge the knowledge that had come from male authorities.

For example, Talya, a thirty-year-old woman with three young children and pregnant with her fourth when we met for the first time, came to fully rely on her previous experiences over the course of four pregnancies. She believes that women should possess authority over reproductive decisions, but she did not act on this authority until she had some reproductive experience. Talya said explicitly that during her first pregnancy, she went to the doctor all the time. She did everything they wanted her to do, without even thinking about it. "They did all the weighing, the blood pressure, the ultrasounds. But I was so busy. I was in seminary and I had to take off class to go. By the second pregnancy, I don't think I went at all! I know I went a lot less. With her [pointing to her third child], I went once." Late into her fourth pregnancy, Talya asked her rabbi if she should be going to the doctor, and he said, "Yes, you should be doing what needs to be done." This injunction from her rabbi was not sufficient for Talya. "Even the midwives say you should just go for one ultrasound at least to make sure everything is in the right place." For her first pregnancy, then, Talya relied entirely on the doctor's instruction. After she spent two pregnancies rejecting the doctor's involvement, she finally asked her rabbi, but even he did not convince her. Talya, like other women, made reproductive decisions based on the medical authorities for her first pregnancy but did not rely on medical or rabbinic authorities for the subsequent pregnancies. This change occurred gradually, as Talya went to the doctor fewer times with each pregnancy and even found her rabbi's advice to be irrelevant once she had experienced three pregnancies.

In Dalia's reproductive narrative, she characterizes her pregnancies based on when she began to reject male and medical authorities. Remember that she had always defined herself as a dancer and getting pregnant scared her because she was not eager to become a mother. Dalia's first pregnancy was difficult because, as she said, it "limited me physically." She wanted to continue dancing, but her husband was very scared that dancing would "hurt the baby." Conforming to the demands of others, she decided that she should "please him, please the baby, please everybody, just like all Haredi women." Here, Dalia expressed her tendency during the first pregnancy to do what others wanted of her; she knew dancing would make her feel better, but she abided by others' demands and requests in order to make them happy. This, as we have seen, is common throughout Haredi women's narratives of their first pregnancies.

Internally, Dalia began challenging this model during her second pregnancy. Because of some light bleeding at the beginning of her second pregnancy, the doctor instructed Dalia to go on bed rest for a few weeks. Dalia challenged this restriction. "I did have thoughts of 'what do I need this for?' It is not like I'm committed to babies. If not this one, another will come." She admitted that she would not have had an abortion because that is not "responsible," but her thoughts and feelings indicate that Dalia was beginning to express her own desires in this pregnancy, as opposed to the first. After she completed the short period of bed rest, Dalia's second pregnancy proceeded normally. It was easier than the first one, primarily because, as she said, she had "done this already." Dalia knew how she would balance her life afterward and knew she would love the baby, so she was not as anxious as she was during the first pregnancy.

Throughout the third pregnancy, Dalia remembers feeling more confident. She danced and felt comfortable with the fact that she would be welcoming a new baby into the world. In fact, immediately after she brought her third baby home from the hospital she recalls wanting a fourth. Although she struggled with depression during her third pregnancy, as soon as the baby was born she was excited for the next one. Dalia explained, "I knew it would be OK if I had more. I will not lose myself and my identity." In light of this, Dalia described her most recent pregnancy as asymptomatic. She had no nausea, she felt very light, and she danced throughout the entire pregnancy. This pregnancy blended seamlessly into the life Dalia had already grown accustomed to, and in this way, it made her the happiest. For Dalia, each pregnancy gave her more confidence to lead the life she wanted to lead, as opposed to what she perceived as the paradigmatic Haredi female life. Instead of emerging from each pregnancy exhausted and frustrated, as she had done after her first two pregnancies, Dalia learned how to make motherhood just one piece of her life. When she learned how to do that, Dalia became much more confident about her reproductive decisions.

The repeated embodied experiences of pregnancy enabled these feelings of confidence and authority. When she was pregnant for the fourth time, Dalia even disagreed with her doctor regarding a certain prenatal test he wanted to perform. She had used this same doctor for three pregnancies and liked him immensely, so she usually did whatever he asked of her. During the most recent pregnancy, however, Dalia felt she had enough experience to contradict him. "This time he wanted me to do more [testing]. He said, 'You're getting a little older. Maybe you should do *skirat maarachot*'," referring to an advanced ultrasound performed in the second trimester, wherein doctors check fetal development. Dalia said he did not push the matter, but it was also clear that she was going to be making this decision—not the doctor. "If I feel good, and I know that I'm OK, then I'm OK." Though for Dalia "feeling OK" about the pregnancy did not preclude a fetal anomaly, she relied on her instincts—a honed sense of what a pregnancy is supposed to feel like—because she had experienced this before. As a woman pregnant for the fourth time, Dalia expressed her reliance on her own embodied experience instead of the authority of doctors and rabbis.

This rejection of medical advice during third or fourth pregnancies was common among the women I interviewed. Sometimes, these expressions of agency resulted in women making decisions that were dangerous to their health or the health of their fetuses. Tamar, a twenty-seven-year-old mother of two and pregnant with her third, did anything the doctor asked of her during her first pregnancy, and she was worried all the time. By the second pregnancy, however, she felt that she needed to humor the doctor but not really take her doctor's authority seriously. When her doctor asked her to go through extensive screening for gestational diabetes, Tamar decided she would have one preliminary test but was "sure it will come back fine. [The doctor] will see there's nothing to worry about." When I asked how she felt so confident that the test would not reveal gestational diabetes, Tamar justified her decision by explaining her doctor's overcautious attitude. She added that she has never had gestational diabetes before and thus she is not worried. Of course, one can have gestational diabetes with one pregnancy and not with another. Tamar, however, felt that her previous experiences were sufficient in predicting any current and future prenatal experiences. Instead of listening to her rabbis or her doctors, Tamar relied on her embodied experience to guide her during pregnancy. An unfortunate consequence of this phenomenon is that sometimes a Haredi woman's embodied authority leads her to make decisions that are not medically sound. Authoritative knowledge is not necessarily *correct*, but it is, within particular social groups, recognized as moral and rational.[42] For Tamar and many other women I spoke to, their embodied experience informed their medical decisions despite their inaccurate assessment of medical risk.

It is sometimes uncomfortable to hear about women making decisions that put themselves and others at risk, and it might be tempting to write off these women as acting irresponsibly. However, it is important to first identify why women are prioritizing (sometimes misguided) embodied knowledge over that of medical authorities. As a mother of five and pregnant with her sixth, Hila, like other women I spoke to, doubted whether doctors are truly effective in preventing or treating certain issues that arise during pregnancy. Regarding gestational diabetes, she said, "Whether the test comes out positive or negative, women should be eating appropriately." Regarding high blood pressure, Hila said, "I know when my blood pressure goes down. If you listen to your body, you'll be OK." According to Hila, doctors claim they know what they are doing and that the tools they use are safe, but she insisted that this was not always the case. Hila had multiple interactions with doctors who denied her experience of pregnancy and prioritized their own authority and that of the rabbinic authorities in her community. This tendency to doubt scientific knowledge, therefore, must be seen within this context, familiar to many Haredi women. Furthermore, Hila and others combine this suspicion with the Haredi reliance on women's embodied identity, leading Haredi women to make medical decisions about their pregnancies without the advice of a doctor. It is important that these examples of women making poor medical decisions not lead us to question the virtue of women expressing their reproductive agency. Respecting women's agency means respecting that sometimes they will make poor decisions, like everyone. Hila and Tamar, and many other women I spoke to, reject their rabbis and their doctors because those two sources of authority do not respect their embodied knowledge. Therefore, they feel the need to act independently.

CONCLUSION: PREGNANCY EMBODIMENT AND HAREDI WOMEN'S RELIGIOUS AUTHORITY

In this chapter, I have taken up the threads of scholarship surrounding the embodiment of Haredi women's lives and the embodiment of pregnancy in order to advance an argument about agency and pregnancy embodiment as both consistent and in tension with Haredi norms. Haredi women's embodied experience of Jewish ritual is critical to the shaping of their religious identities.[43] Their bodies have been regulated, watched, judged, and discussed by male rabbinic authorities for indications of their status and availability. Additionally, many of the rituals that they observe as ultra-Orthodox Jews, not just as women, take place within their bodies. To live as a Haredi woman is to experience Judaism through the constant regulation of one's body. For adult Haredi women, pregnancy and birth are among the most central experiences in their lives. Given the fact that the embodiment of pregnancy is an important part of a woman's understanding of pregnancy and reproduction, it makes sense to consider how the embodiment of pregnancy affects Haredi women's religious lives.

As Haredi women draw on their embodied experiences of pregnancy, they both challenge and reinforce Haredi norms. By participating in biological reproduction, Haredi women reinforce the gendered norm that their bodies were intended for this purpose, a norm that buttresses inequalities and subordination. However, the norms that require a Haredi woman to remain in a state of pregnancy are those same norms that she draws on to resist male authorities.

The conditions that have led to her gendered role in the community—the requirement for her to reproduce and raise a family, her seclusion from the male sphere of decision-making, the emphasis placed on her body and when her husband can access it—have also been the sources for her self-formation and her ability to rely on those embodied experiences for authority.

This argument hinges on an understanding of bodies that are lived and enculturated. Israeli Haredi women come to see pregnancy as an authority-granting experience due to the embodiment of pregnancy in Haredi society. Iris Young explains, "The lived body is a unified idea of a physical body acting and experiencing in a specific sociocultural context; it is a body-in-situation."[44] In other words, the ways we move our bodies, dress our bodies, and communicate with our bodies are all shaped by the national, religious, ethnic, class, and gender context in which we live. Because Haredi women's bodies are essential to the way they are seen in the community—their menstrual cycle determines their sexual access, their identities as women limit their access to many religious spaces, the (in)visibility of their hair marks their marital status and religious identity—it is fitting for Haredi women to come to see their pregnant bodies within this same religious, ethnic, and gender framework. In this way, drawing on their embodied experiences of pregnancy is a natural extension of other Haredi embodied identities. A pregnant body marks a woman as a successful contributor to Haredi life.

However, as women draw on their embodied experiences of pregnancy for authority, they challenge Haredi gender norms. Instead of relying on religious authorities or medical authorities for guidance and instruction regarding reproduction, Haredi women come to find doctors and rabbis to be out of touch with their own embodied experiences of pregnancy. In the conflict between women's preferences and rulings from rabbis and doctors, Haredi women express agency and rely on their own embodied authority. Paradoxically, in their uniquely female participation in pregnancy, the moment they mark themselves as ideal Haredi women, it facilitates Haredi women's entry into the male sphere of decision-making. This is similar to the way anorectic women report gaining access into the male world because their bodies appear more male, without curves or breasts.[45] Although pregnant bodies do not look more masculine, Young maintains that pregnant women often experience the weight and materiality of pregnancy as "a sense of power, solidity, and validity. Thus, whereas our society often devalues and trivializes women, regards women as weak and dainty, the pregnant woman can gain a certain sense of self-respect."[46] A pregnant Haredi woman is able to avoid the constant male gaze on her body because she is pregnant. She is not subject to the laws of menstrual purity to the same degree, and pregnancy segulot mean that a pregnant woman can avoid the overt objectification of her body. Although all individuals—men, women, and genderqueer—live as embodied beings, for pregnant Haredi women, a body that is not constantly regulated in the way their bodies usually are is more like a man's body and therefore confers authority. In this way, pregnancy allows Haredi women to challenge the gender norms that otherwise structure her life.

This is because the embodiment of pregnancy actually changes a woman's subjectivity in the Haredi community. Giti, like many women quoted in this chapter, sees her identity as tied to her pregnant body. Giti has five children, and she was not pregnant when we first met. She told me that she feels ready to get pregnant again when she scolds herself for being so "selfish" with her body; when she begins to think of her body as "only her own," she knows it is time to have another baby. Between pregnancies, there are times when she says, "I cannot believe I am living my whole day and nobody is inside of me, . . . and it gets to that point where I want to be taking care of someone inside of me. Even though I'm taking care of everyone around me, there is something so special knowing that it's growing inside of me." For Giti, pregnancy means fulfilling her greatest responsibility to take care of someone else with her body. This is the task she understands as most crucial for her body and therefore herself. Giti's self-formation is tied to her body's participation in reproduction.

Yet we cannot come to see this self-transformation as unidirectional or even an uncomplicated transformation for Haredi women. Embodiment theories, such as those from Pierre Bourdieu and Maurice Merleau-Ponty, neglect to account for the pregnant subject, who is not a unified Cartesian self.[47] Young suggests that the pregnant subject is "de-centered, split, or doubled in several ways. She experiences her body as herself and not herself. Its inner movements belong to another being, yet they are not other, because her body boundaries shift and because her bodily self-location is focused on her trunk in addition to her head."[48] Giti cannot imagine her body without a fetus growing inside of it. When she is not pregnant, she is not comfortable in her body. Her body as herself is always a body with another body inside. Furthermore, the pregnant body itself is in flux, Young explains, and the pregnant subject is not always aware of "where [the] body ends and the world begins."[49] Therefore, the pregnant subject's embodiment is split in multiple ways: First, she is sharing her own body with another's body, but that other is not completely other, since it is part of her. Second, her body is not consistent but rather changing constantly, leading a pregnant subject to rediscover her body at every turn. This resonates with Dalia's reproductive narrative, as she constantly struggled to redefine her identity through her embodied experiences of pregnancy.

Regardless of how many pregnancies one has experienced, pregnancy is not a certainty, nor is the birth of a healthy child. Even for a complete pregnancy, it is temporary, and after it ends, women may not become pregnant again for some time. All of this means that a woman's pregnant subjectivity is constantly shifting as women phase through various reproductive experiences. It is an identity that is not constant, and in this way, it introduces unique tensions for women who come to rely on their embodiment of pregnancy for their authority. For instance, their authority is limited to areas of reproduction because their authority is based on their experience of reproduction. This is why Haredi women prioritize their embodied knowledge of pregnancy when it comes to matters of reproduction but not when it comes to other areas of their lives. They return to their rabbis for all non-reproduction-related questions because their subjectivity shifts to provide them with authority only with regard to issues that they embody, like pregnancy. Understanding how Haredi women's agency is conscribed to these particular areas is crucial for understanding how they see their agency functioning within the bounds of Haredi religious and cultural norms. In the chapter that follows, we will see how women draw on specific theological concepts as they make reproductive decisions. In so doing, they more firmly situate their authority over pregnancy and their bodies within their religious framework.

NOTES

1. Diprose, *Bodies of Women*, 25.
2. Mahmood, "Feminist Theory," 203.
3. Galahar, "Haredi Matchmaking Rates Skyrocketing."
4. Lehman and Siebzehner, "Power Boundaries and Institutions," 288.
5. Ibid.
6. For more on gender segregation in the Haredi community, see Stadler, *Well-Worn Tallis for a New Ceremony*, 70–72.
7. Porush, "Study of Pre-Marital Education Predominantly within the Haredi Community," 74.
8. Goshen-Gottstein, *Growing Up in Geula*, 6.
9. Ibid.
10. Lehman and Siebzehner, "Power Boundaries and Institutions."
11. At a film screening for a documentary about individuals who left the Haredi community, one such individual spoke about his wedding night as the "mutual rape" of both him and his wife. The community pressure for them to consummate their marriage was compounded by the fact that neither he nor his new wife felt comfortable with one another or with their own naked and now sexualized bodies.

12. Stadler, *Well-Worn Tallis for a New Ceremony*, 70.

13. Ibid., 79.

14. Yafeh, "Time in the Body"; El-Or, *Educated and Ignorant*.

15. For more on the history of Beit Yaakov schools, see M. Friedman, "Back to Grandmother"; Weissman, "Bais Yaakov"; Seidman, *Sarah Schenirer and the Bais Yaakov Movement*.

16. M. Friedman, "Back to Grandmother."

17. Geiger and Alt, "Haredi/Chabad Women's Acculturation Experiences," found that Haredi society did not restrict women's education, provided women could maintain their duties of motherhood while pursuing advanced degrees.

18. Still, the performances are only for female audiences.

19. Taragin-Zeller, "Conceiving God's Children."

20. Gaster, *Customs and Folkways of Jewish Life*. This is more common among Ashkenazi families than Sephardi, but it is a tradition that has spread among even secular Jews. See Ivry, *Embodying Culture*, for more on this cultural custom.

21. Sered, *What Makes Women Sick?*, includes a long list of amulets and various protections from the evil eye that religious Jews use during pregnancy and birth.

22. Berkovitch, "Motherhood as a National Mission."

23. Ivry, *Embodying Culture*, 187.

24. Ibid., 74.

25. This is somewhat similar to Barbara Katz Rothman's ideas about "tentative pregnancy."

26. Davidman, *Becoming Un-Orthodox*; Fader, *Mitzvah Girls*.

27. Yafeh, "Time in the Body."

28. Davidman, *Becoming Un-Orthodox*; Yafeh, "Time in the Body."

29. Yafeh, "Time in the Body."

30. Davidman, *Becoming Un-Orthodox*.

31. Men are also expected to follow dress codes, but they have fewer laws related to modesty (Heilman, *Defenders of the Faith*; Davidman, *Becoming Un-Orthodox*).

32. Yafeh, "Time in the Body." For more on the history of modesty campaigns, see Inbari, "Modesty Campaigns of Rabbi Amram Blau."

33. For more on niddah and fertility, see chap. 1.

34. Yafeh, "Time in the Body," 541.

35. Ibid.

36. Young, "Pregnant Embodiment."

37. Mahmood, *Politics of Piety*, 157. Unlike in the case of Muslim women, Haredi women do not see pregnancy as a process of disciplining.

38. Others have discussed intuition as it relates to reproduction. See, for instance, Davis-Floyd and Davis, "Intuition as Authoritative Knowledge."

Teman, *Birthing a Mother*, looks at how surrogates draw on their intuitive and embodied knowledge to counteract the doctor's "authoritative knowledge."

39. NIS here indicates the new Israeli shekel.

40. Admittedly, I do not know how Haredi women reacted to this information, since I did not interview those in Hadassah's classes. Although Hadassah gave me permission to sit in on the classes and told the women that I was a student observing the class, she did not want me approaching the participants.

41. I return to this philosophy in the next chapter.

42. Jordan, "Authoritative Knowledge and Its Construction," 58.

43. Davidman, *Becoming Un-Orthodox*; Fader, *Mitzvah Girls*.

44. Young, *On Female Body Experience*, 16.

45. Bordo, "Body and the Reproduction of Femininity."

46. Young, *On Female Body Experience*, 53.

47. See Csordas, "Embodiment as a Paradigm for Anthropology," for a complete discussion of Bourdieu and Merleau-Ponty on embodiment.

48. Young, "Pregnant Embodiment," 46.

49. Ibid., 49.

FOUR

—ᴧᴧ—

REPRODUCTIVE THEOLOGY

Embodying Divine Authority

THIS CHAPTER BUILDS ON THE argument of the previous chapter—namely, that Haredi women's cultural context facilitates their reproductive agency. Here I show how women's understanding and creative usage of particular Haredi theological concepts justify their reproductive authority. In particular, we see how pregnancy connects women to God, a connection that provides women with authority. For Haredi women, pregnancy facilitates a privileged position in relation to God, and they recognize their bodies to be the conduits for this relationship. Importantly, because reproduction—the act of creation—occurs through women's bodies, women maintain authority over reproductive decisions. I refer to Hardi women's reproductive theology as embodying divine authority because their particular use of theological concepts reinforces their belief that during pregnancy, they have authority that overrides that of the rabbis, and in fact, it is pregnancy that enables this shift. This line of authority runs directly from God to Haredi women, bypassing a rabbi's legal interpretation. Seen together with the cultural and economic context discussed in chapter 3, this theology helps us understand how women come to reject both doctors and rabbis during pregnancy. By framing pregnancy as the embodiment of divine authority, a Haredi woman can alter her own subjectivity in the community.

An example will help to elucidate what it means that Haredi women embody divine authority. At the conclusion of our two-hour interview in her apartment in Meah Shearim, Naomi walked me to the bus. Naomi and I had spent two hours talking about her pregnancies. While her husband studied in kollel, she has worked in a variety of Haredi schools. Naomi is thirty-seven years old and has nine children. Because she loves thinking about names

and their origins, Naomi asked me about the connect
namesake in the Hebrew Bible: "Do you know why N
children?" She was referring to King David's first w
King Saul. "Because she yelled at King David when h
streets with the Ark," I responded. In the biblical book
rebuked King David when she saw him celebrating the arr
the Covenant. Immediately afterward, the text states that she died w
having any children, leading many to believe that God punished Michal
with barrenness for rebuking King David. Naomi was not satisfied with my
answer, so she continued with the lesson: "Yes, but what did she yell at him
about? Michal yelled at David because he put God ahead of *malchut* [king-
ship]." Naomi explained that Michal's father, Saul, always considered himself
a king first and a servant of God second. As she saw her husband—King
David—dancing with the Torah in the streets, Michal thought he was putting
God ahead of his role as king, something that conflicted with her upbringing.

Until this point, I thought Naomi intended to teach me about the importance of humility, but here the lesson changed drastically. Naomi added
a *midrash* (rabbinic addendum) to Michal's narrative that helped explain
how Michal made up for the fact that she was barren—a curse too great
for Haredi Jews to fathom. "Michal also wore *teffilin* [phylacteries], and she
was the only woman who wore teffilin and was not yelled at by the rabbis."
Even though traditionally only men are commanded to put on teffilin during
the daily morning prayers, Naomi explained that Michal wore the teffilin
voluntarily to remind herself of God's presence in her life. "Unlike other
women who know God intuitively, Michal needed to teach herself, and she
did this through teffilin." Naomi clarified that whereas women who are able
to get pregnant "know God intuitively," Michal's inability to have children
prevented her from experiencing God through her own pregnant body. As
we approached the bus stop, Naomi concluded, "Pregnancy is that bodily
reminder of God. You cannot ignore God when you are pregnant or say
that anything is higher than God." According to Naomi, Michal used teffilin
to create the embodied experience of God, but for Haredi women, pregnancy is the embodied experience that enables their subjectivity to shift and
to experience God directly.

Pregnancy is an embodied experience in that it is a time when cultural and
religious norms are applied to the female body. Viewing pregnancy as the
embodiment of divine authority is not about seeing pregnancy as the physical
manifestation of God. Instead, it is about seeing pregnancy as a time of authority due to women's unique connection to God. Recall Iris Young's argument

chapter 3 that pregnant women experience a decentering or splitting of the
. Young elucidates a number of divisions in pregnant embodiment. Women
re at once self and other, as the fetus is part of them, yet as each day passes, it
becomes an increasingly separate being. As the pregnancy progresses, women
become more unaware of the physical limits of their body as they adjust to
their new size and shape as they move in the world. While pregnant women
may experience a heightened sense of their own sexuality, others may desexu-
alize them.[1] I add another splintering that Haredi women experience while
pregnant: A pregnant Haredi woman experiences her body as not just herself
and her fetus but also as that which carries divine authority. As she rediscov-
ers herself and her pregnant body with each pregnancy, a Haredi woman is
reminded of the divine act she is performing and therefore the authority she
is granted. A Haredi woman does not have this authority at other times, so it
is precisely this splitting that shifts her subjectivity in the community. Instead
of seeing her physicality as that which leads to male control over her body,
understanding pregnancy as the embodiment of divine authority leads her to
transcend male control. In so doing, she can exercise agency over her reproductive life. The embodiment of pregnancy leads one to consider these reproductive experiences as splitting the body and the self in a way that facilitates a
woman's authority.

In this chapter, I identify the sources of the reproductive theology that
informs Haredi women's agency. Then I will discuss the ways women draw
on this theology to challenge norms of gender and authority in the Haredi
community and show how Haredi women draw on the divine authority that
comes from the splitting of the self during pregnancy to counteract the medical community's attempt to alienate them from pregnancy. Young explains
that the medical field contributes to women's alienation from their own pregnancies and birthing experiences by controlling and defining women's experiences of pregnancy without sharing their goals or assumptions.[2] Like other
Western medical systems, the Israeli medical system carries an implicit male
bias, defines pregnancy as a dysfunctional condition, and relies on technology that devalues women's own experiences—all elements that contribute
to women's alienation from pregnancy. The women I spoke to invoke the idea
that pregnancy connects them directly to God, a unique subjectivity that
allows them to bypass the human authority figures in their lives. By referencing their embodiment of divine authority during pregnancy, and using that
to inform their reproductive decisions, Haredi women limit the authority of
their doctors and rabbis and remain tied to God through their reproductive
experiences.

HAREDI REPRODUCTIVE THEOLOGY: BYPASS THE
RABBIS AND GO DIRECTLY TO THE SOURCE

The theological belief that to be pregnant is to participate in a divine act and that pregnancy thereby sanctions women to make important reproductive decisions is found in educational materials for Haredi women. A number of women told me about audiocassette tapes they listen to during pregnancy, recordings of lessons provided by the wives of prominent Haredi rabbis.[3] Despite the fact that women refer to them as prenatal classes, the tapes do not teach them about the physiological aspects of pregnancy or the stages of birth. Instead, these classes teach them how to take a particular religious viewpoint regarding pregnancy and labor. The content of the lectures reinforces gendered norms about women's roles and the reasons why women experience pregnancy pain.[4] Meanwhile, women who listened to these lectures understand the lessons to be cultivating a sense of authority over reproduction.

In one such lecture titled, "Chava's Curse," the *rebbetzin* (rabbi's wife) criticizes women who view their pregnancies as an obstacle, who dread being pregnant because of the discomfort. She makes it clear that men and women have distinct roles in bringing the Messiah, and pregnancy is a woman's contribution. Women, the rebbetzin explains, are tested in their faith when they confront difficult pregnancies. If women complain about nausea, vomiting, and backaches during pregnancy, or if they decide not to have children, then they will be failing the test and thus preventing the arrival of the Messiah, essentially bringing an end to the world in its entirety. The rebbetzin's position reflects biblical and rabbinic ideologies about the connection—at least metaphorically—between a woman in labor and those waiting for Messianic redemption. Sarit Kattan Gribetz discusses the implications of this metaphor. "Several biblical texts use imagery of a laboring woman to emphasize the pain and suffering associated with moments of crisis: exile, destruction, judgment (e.g. Jer 4:31, 6:24, 13:21, 22:23, 30:6–7, 49:24, 50:43; Isa 21:3, 26:17). Laboring and birthing imagery is also invoked, however, to describe the specifically *temporal* dimensions of redemption."[5] Biblical and rabbinic authors employ the metaphor for a variety of reasons: just as pregnancy will eventually end, so too will the Messiah inevitably arrive; additionally, just as childbirth is a time of pain, new life, and often death, tragedy, and uncertainty, so too is the end of days. These similarities remain on the level of metaphor, however. Gribetz argues, "According to rabbinic theology and law, for example, women typically do not play an active role in hastening redemption."[6] For the rebbetzin in this tape, though, the way women handle the difficulties of pregnancy and the pains of childbirth will directly affect the end of days.

Furthermore, the rebbetzin maintains that the physiology of pregnancy and the embodiment of pregnancy and birth solidify this relationship to God. In her class, she refers to pregnancy as *chevel leida*, meaning literally, "the rope of birth," but a synonym found in biblical texts refers to the "pangs of childbirth." Rabbinic usage of the word *chevel* refers to *chevlei mashiach*, or "the birth pangs of the Messiah."[7] Here, again, we see a parallel between pregnancy/labor and the coming of the Messiah. In Modern Hebrew there is an additional parallel that the rebbetzin invokes: the word for umbilical cord is *chevel hatabor*. Building on the similarities between all of these phrases, the rebbetzin explains that like the umbilical cord that connects a fetus to a woman, pregnancy connects a woman to God. Using this metaphor, the rebbetzin makes the case that the physical experience—being tied to the fetus during pregnancy and experiencing the pain of childbirth—pull a woman closer to God by giving her the opportunity to display her faith in God and thus hasten the Messiah. As we will see later, when the umbilical cord is severed after birth, women also see their direct connection to God as severed.

This bodily connection to God through pregnancy is also buttressed through an understanding of the body as a *kli*—a vessel or conduit for God to bring about new life. Although we saw this concept used in the pregnancy advice books, Haredi women who draw on this concept do not attribute it to any particular source. For Chava, a mother of seven and a doula, being a kli means a woman must take care of her body because God is using it to increase the Jewish population. Thus, Chava's reason for eating organic food and staying slim is precisely that God is using her body as an instrument for populating the Jewish people. A Haredi woman who views her body as a kli for God then sees her task as divinely inspired. Any decision she makes—whether to seek out prenatal testing or what foods to eat—is a choice that has serious implications for the future of the pregnancy and the Jewish people. Thus when women are pregnant they see themselves as embodying God's creative powers.

Hila, who was pregnant with her sixth child when we spoke about her rejecting medical advice (in chap. 3), believes that embodying divine authority gives her the privilege to bypass rabbinic guidance as well. She considers this privilege to be written expressly onto her body. She explains, "God gave me this body, and I have to provide for it, and I have to take care of it. I am raising a child in me that's not only a child but a Jewish child." Hila and other Haredi women view their bodies as direct gifts from God, a gift endowed with great responsibility because of the religious identity of this future child. This responsibility is also what sanctions Hila's authority. Because God has trusted her with this responsibility, in other words, Hila has moral authority and does not need to trust anybody else to tell her what to do during the pregnancy. In fact, trusting someone else would contradict her obligation to God and her body. Significantly in the phrasing that she uses, *she* is raising the Jewish child, not God or her doctors, rabbis, or husband.

For some women, just being pregnant is not enough to facilitate this relationship with God. Women must actively see their bodies as pathways toward reaching God. Moriah, a doula, thinks that women focus too much on remaining modest in the birthing room or saying the correct psalms during birth; she wants them to look at pregnancy and birth as a gift from God and thus imbued with an opportunity for building a relationship. "You are so religious? You say blessings all the time? Start seeing God. God gave this to you. Know that. Trust that. Let him talk to you. . . . It's a very physical experience, but it is a paradigm for life. We have a spiritual goal for it. We can rise above the physical and touch the other side." Moriah emphasizes that it is through the physical act of pregnancy and childbirth (and not through the performance of more "minor" commandments) that women can reach God. Thus, women should feel free to moan during birth if that reduces the pain, hold their husband's hands even after they have technically entered a state of niddah, or remove articles of clothing that are too restrictive. All of these acts would be considered immodest by Haredi norms, but modesty, for Moriah, is a religious ideal that does not help women see that birth is already imbued with religious significance. Instead of remaining modest, Moriah requests that Haredi women remember that the ability to birth is a direct gift from God, and as such, it is a physical experience that transcends material realities and requirements.[8]

The embodied connection to God during pregnancy both grounds women in the physicality of pregnancy and allows them to establish a more intimate connection to God. In *Mitzvah Girls*, Ayala Fader explains that for young Hasidic women in America, the constant tension between the body and the soul or the material and the spiritual is resolved by those who "elevate the physical world of the body in order to serve God and eventually be rewarded in the world to come."[9] The elevation occurs through ritual for the Hasidic women Fader interviewed. The performance of divinely commanded yet physical rituals gives them a method for moving their bodies from the physical to the spiritual level. Similarly, Haredi women in Jerusalem grant metaphysical significance to the overtly material acts of pregnancy and childbirth by arguing that pregnancy is participation in a divine act. In this way they remove pregnancy from its gendered and physical limitations as an act performed through a woman's body and transform it into a Godly act that imbues women with divine authority.

This understanding of pregnancy is consistent with rabbinic claims about fetal development being almost entirely an act performed by God, yet women's claims of authority challenge this assertion as well. According to Gwynn Kessler's work on rabbinic reproductive theology, the rabbis ascribed minimal contribution to the male partner and complete passivity (if not outright danger) from the female partner while insisting that God was the primary creator of each fetus. Within this understanding, the kli metaphor seems to imply that women are just vessels for God's creative powers.[10] And yet the women I spoke to ascribe great influence to the choices they make during pregnancy. They understand their role as a kli to be fundamental and significant, demonstrating their rejection of rabbinic claims that women contribute nothing to the reproductive process. Haredi women creatively interpret rabbinic theological concepts in order to reinforce their own agency.

Rejecting rabbinic authorities allows women to draw more heavily on the divine connection they maintain during pregnancy. Recall that Haredi life relies on a particular hierarchical authority structure wherein one asks his or her rabbi for permission or guidance regarding issues related to all parts of one's life—religious or not. In this way, everything becomes a matter of rabbinic interpretation and application of Jewish law. According to this system, people are obligated to adhere to the answers of their rabbis, answers believed to derive from the sources of Jewish law and therefore seen as coming from God. Many women with whom I spoke grew resentful of rabbis who tried to tell them what decision to make during pregnancy precisely because women felt entitled to make these decisions on their own. They felt strongly that their physical connection to God afforded them a great deal of responsibility over the outcome of the pregnancy and the privilege to act contrary to medical and rabbinic authorities. This shift challenges the entire structure of Haredi Jewish life.

Talya faced a tough decision regarding the hospital where she would give birth to her fourth child. She preferred a particular hospital that is more inclined toward natural birthing and has a policy of allowing the baby to remain with the mother as tests are performed on the newborn. This hospital, however, is not "Shabbat oriented," meaning they do not observe the laws of the Sabbath, something that is problematic for Haredi Jews. The other hospital is Shabbat oriented but will take the baby away right after the birth and place him or her in the nursery. Talya hesitated before approaching her rabbi with the question. She registered at both hospitals and delayed asking him because she assumed he would want her to give birth at the Shabbat-oriented hospital, but Talya did not want to give birth there. At her husband's urging, Talya asked her rabbi. He responded to her dilemma by saying, "Which is more important to you?

To have the birth go exactly the way you want it or to have someone not work on Shabbat for you?" When Talya relayed the story to me, she quoted her rabbi as asking her this in a mocking tone, clearly insensitive to Talya's desires. This answer hurt Talya, since he undermined her preferences for natural labor in favor of observing the Sabbath. Talya continued, "It's not an easy thing for a woman. This is my *avodat Hashem* [service for God]. I carry this child for nine months, and I *do not* want someone taking it away from me after it's born." Her response can be seen as responding both to her rabbi's words and to what would occur in the Shabbat-observant hospital. Talya's rabbi had taken away from her the ability to make her decision based on her embodied preferences, which she felt entitled to exercise. Instead, he wanted her to decide on a hospital because of its observance of Jewish law.

Another reason Talya wanted to avoid the Shabbat-observant hospital was that by removing the baby from her after the birth, this hospital removes the source of a Haredi woman's authority immediately after it leaves her body. Many women shared with me their sadness at birth because someone else takes the baby away from them. After birth, the umbilical cord no longer connects a woman to the baby, and moreover, once the umbilical cord is severed, it is as if a woman's direct line to God is severed as well. Talya acknowledged the importance of Jewish law and observing Shabbat. She questioned her preference for the natural birthing hospital by saying, "Who am I to put my emotional needs before Shabbat?" In the end, however, she went into labor early in the week and did not have to decide between the two hospitals. Talya gave birth to her fourth child in a hospital that was not particularly Shabbat oriented but that allowed her to stay with the baby immediately after the birth. As she shared this story with me, Talya described prioritizing her "emotional needs," despite the fact that the timing of her labor released her from any concerns about Shabbat. Talya's desire to privilege her own pregnant positionality even after the birth indicates that the authority she derives from the embodiment of pregnancy exceeds her sense of obligation to the primacy of Jewish law. Allowing someone else to decide for her or to tell her that she needs to prioritize Jewish law during pregnancy, birth, or the immediate postpartum period would violate what Talya sees as her divinely ordained role.

Maya also understands pregnancy to be the performance of God's work and therefore as something that supersedes the law. She was six months pregnant with her fourth child when she talked with me about pregnancy as a prime opportunity to connect with God. Maya's reflections on a woman's connection to God during pregnancy and labor bolstered her views on the irrelevance of rabbinic legal rulings for pregnant women. Not only is the Talmud outdated on issues related to pregnancy, Maya claimed, but the rabbis know nothing about pregnancy and birth. Maya did not mean that the rabbis do not possess basic information about reproduction but rather that their bodies have not been imbued with significance by God as a woman's pregnant body has. This intimate relationship—expressed through a woman's body—gives women authority over pregnancy and birth, an authority that the rabbis do not possess simply because they are all men. Pregnancy, then, allows women to connect with God in a way that men cannot.

The fact that women connect with God through their bodies should, according to Maya, teach women that they should rely on their bodies more. Maya explained that relying on one's body is closer to what God wants from us than what one may find in a book. Sarcastically she insisted, "You trust doctors, you trust medicine, you trust everybody, but you do not trust yourself. Trust anybody because they went to school and they learned. Don't trust yourself even though you've lived in your body for twenty years." Relying on one's body for knowledge during pregnancy is, for Maya, relying on God. During her third pregnancy, Maya was diagnosed with cytomegalovirus (CMV) at fourteen weeks gestation.[11] As Maya remembers, the doctors wanted to perform an amniocentesis at twenty-six weeks to check whether the baby was also carrying the disease. Because a baby born with CMV can sometimes develop health problems throughout infancy and childhood, some physicians suggest aborting fetuses diagnosed with the virus, and in fact, a number of women shared with me that Haredi women often abort when their fetuses are diagnosed with CMV. Maya and her husband, Eitan, agreed to the procedure and booked the appointment. As the date approached in her twenty-sixth week, however, they began to feel hesitant. Around this time, Maya had emergency root canal surgery, and she took this as a sign that God was trying to communicate something to her. "God brought me this tooth thing that totally knocked me out. It made Eitan say, 'What are we doing? I don't want you to go and have to deal with more things.' God brought it in the moment, and I really saw that right now, that's it." Eitan did not want Maya to have to consider whether they would have an abortion if the test came back positive. Maya understood the physical ailment of root canal surgery to be a direct message from God. She believed that God communicated to her through her body, and she understood that it meant she should not go through with the amniocentesis.

Maya gave birth at home a few months later to a baby who appeared to be completely healthy. Because of what she describes as bureaucracy around registering babies born at home, Maya never even tested her daughter for CMV to find out if perhaps she had a mild case of it. There were times when the baby was an infant and a toddler when Maya and Eitan were concerned that she might have hearing loss. At the time of our interview a few years later, Maya said their daughter was healthy. Maya interprets her daughter's confident and calm attitude to the fact that she and her husband "chose her, and she knows that. There was a certain point where we made a choice that if she was given to us she was supposed to be with us." I asked Maya what led her to make that choice, and she said she learned a really important lesson: "If I listen in the moment I'll be told exactly what I need to do." Maya interprets her canceling the amniocentesis to be an active choice that she made. She attributes this choice to her daughter's identity. That is how significant it is that *she* made this choice. And yet it was a choice made because of a message from God, told to her through her body (the toothache). Maya's embodied relationship with God allowed her to make the choice to not have an amniocentesis or an abortion.

Hila also came to rely on her pregnant body and when I asked her when she might turn to her rabbi with a question, Hila could not think of anything she would ask her rabbi. She said that if a test revealed a fetal disability, first she would either do research or ask her mother. After pausing to think about what she would ask her rabbi, Hila stated, "I never had to [ask my rabbi] a question, but if you're bleeding, then you have to." Here we see that Hila would ask her rabbi about her status as a niddah if she were to begin spotting during pregnancy. After thinking for a few moments she added that if there was a question of whether she would need to be induced to begin labor, she might ask her rabbi. This, however, is not so simple "It's a difficult thing because some rabbis only listen to what the doctor says and not all doctors necessarily do what's medical." She corrected herself by saying, "Well, they don't do the right thing." Although Hila admitted that there might be some cases where the fetus is diagnosed with a serious disability that would warrant asking a rabbi about an abortion, she also leaves room for her rabbi's opinion to be disregarded. Hila sees her doctor as a potential adversary and her rabbi as slightly unnecessary during pregnancy, save for the few legal questions one might have. Instead of these two authorities, Hila relies on herself and her embodied experience of pregnancy to make reproductive decisions.

By viewing pregnancy as the embodiment of the divine act of reproduction and thus sanctioning their reliance on their bodies, Haredi women are changing the hierarchical structure inherent to this branch of Judaism. They relegate their rabbis' opinions to minute legal questions, rejecting the prominence of da'at Torah. When constructing their reproductive agency, these women found that being pregnant granted them all the knowledge and authority they needed to make reproductive decisions. This stance is based on their applications of the theology of pregnancy and reproduction that Haredi women hear frequently.

By explicitly rejecting rabbinic influence and the authority that Jewish law holds, Haredi women are rejecting the book tradition and, by extension, the rabbinic authority structure that is now prominent in the Haredi community. Instead, women rely on their lived and embodied tradition—the experience of pregnancy and the theology that it engenders. They draw a direct line to God through the embodiment of pregnancy, thereby justifying all their preferences and desires. Haredi women see pregnancy as a distinct domain where rabbinic authority does not hold any weight. The divine authority that they embody informs their choices and their reproductive agency. In the next section, we will see how women draw on two specific theological concepts to articulate their connection to God and use these concepts to inform their reproductive ethic.

CREATIVELY EXPANDING ON THEOLOGICAL CONCEPTS: HISHTADLUT AND BITACHON

On a warm fall afternoon, Devorah and I sat in a park near her apartment in Jerusalem, watching her two-year-old boy play in the sand. Devorah was seven months pregnant with her fourth child when I asked her about two terms I had heard frequently in my interviews with other Haredi women—*hishtadlut* and *bitachon*. Women seemed to use them to refer to a wide range of actions and choices during pregnancy, and I struggled to understand their application. In Modern Hebrew, *hishtadlut* means "endeavors" or "attempts." The verb form of this noun, *l'hishtadel*, means "to make an effort" or "to lobby." *Bitachon* means "security" or "confidence" and can be used to refer to safety, a guarantee, or confidence—as in *bitachon atzmi* (self-confidence). According to Devorah, these concepts describe a dynamic relationship between a Jew and God, a relationship that a Jew must constantly be cultivating. She explained, "God rules the world, but he created the world in such a way that we have choice. Jews are not ruled by the constellations." Devorah switched to a pregnancy example: "If someone is going to drink alcohol the entire pregnancy, the way God created the world, there is natural course of events. That means that the baby will be born with alcohol problems. If you want to walk in the middle of the street with a hundred cars going, you're not going to get extra protection. *Ein somchim al ha'nes* [We don't rely on a miracle]. But if you're doing a certain amount of natural safe-guarding, then God will help you." According to this explanation, then, God has a plan and he "rules the world," but humans are expected to do their hishtadlut—put forth a good faith effort.

Furthermore, if humans do their part, God will take care of them. This is bitachon—knowing that one is in a relationship with God that guarantees

God's protection as long as one has already taken particular actions and lob-
bied for herself. In other words, bitachon is not just faith in God's existence
but rather faith that God will intercede in one's life. Bitachon expresses the
guarantee of that relationship with God, and even though hishtadlut implies
that human actions are required in this relationship, one with bitachon can be
sure that God will intercede if she does not perform enough hishtadlut.

This section looks at how Haredi women see their relationship to God and
how their accountability for pregnancy outcomes change during pregnancy.
It also considers how women understand the unavoidable reality of biological disasters that threaten to limit a Haredi woman's control over her pregnancy. Through an analysis of hishtadlut and bitachon—concepts rooted in
the Haredi theology of humanity's relationship with the divine—I argue that
women understand their impact on the process of fetal development to be
significant and apply these concepts to their reproductive lives in order to
control the involvement of doctors and minimize the significance of medical
contributions to pregnancy.[12] In so doing, they associate themselves and their
relationship to God directly with the outcome of the pregnancy. We will also
see that women manipulate their usage of these terms in order to theologically
rationalize their own limitations over pregnancy outcomes (of which they are
acutely aware) and as such maintain a sense of dignity when even their best
intentions and actions do not yield their desired results.

Hishtadlut: Bodily Autonomy

Haredi women understand their hishtadlut during pregnancy to be the actions
they can take to shape the physical development of the fetus. A woman imag-
ines her role—and her greatest responsibility—to be forming the fetus. Some
of this work begins even before a woman meets her spouse, but it continues
through conception and pregnancy. In contrast to recent scholarship that highlights a genetic determinism in Israeli fetal medicine,[13] I found that Haredi
women believe their actions—their hishtadlut—influence fetal development.
By claiming these actions as part of her hishtadlut, women attempt to cultivate
a mutual relationship with God. Moreover, as they see themselves influencing
the development of the fetus to such a great degree, women elevate otherwise
routine activities and ascribe great importance to their actions.

Hishtadlut Is Proper Nutrition
Maternal nutrition is a major health concern in the Haredi community, and
many women emphasize the importance of healthy eating during their pregnancies. For some, eating healthy is their hishtadlut. A petite woman in her

early forties, Batya has eight children, including two sets of twins. Though she describes the pregnancies as not particularly pleasant—with nausea, bed rest, and nightmares—Batya was so happy to be pregnant and thrilled to have an excuse to eat a lot, because, she explained, "You're eating for someone else." She took great pride in her food intake throughout her pregnancies. Batya explains that eating is avodat Hashem. When she was pregnant with twins for the first time, Batya made eating her hishtadlut. Separating every syllable of the word to give emphasis to her effort, Batya said, "It was *a-vo-da* [work], with meaning and intention." Following the instructions in a prenatal advice book for carrying twins, Batya—five feet two and 110 pounds—ate four thousand calories a day, including two thousand milligrams of calcium and ninety grams of protein. She did not want to say, "God you do everything and make everything OK," meaning she did not want to rely on bitachon.

Batya contrasts her pregnancy to her friends' pregnancies at the same time because they did not pay as much attention to their eating habits. These women, Batya claims, gave birth to twins two months early and the babies were in the hospital for weeks before being released. Batya's twins, however, were born only a month early, and "they were both five pounds, so they were OK. They were really OK. Thank God." Despite the fact that Batya adds the commonly used phrase *baruch Hashem*, meaning roughly "thank God," to the end of her statement, she still says, "Eating was a really serious thing." According to Batya, her healthy eating habits led directly to the birth of her healthy twins.

Like Batya, Ronit understands her hishtadlut during pregnancy to be her eating habits, which immediately change when she becomes pregnant. Ronit was twenty-nine years old and pregnant with her fourth child when we met. Her husband studied in the kollel near their house, and she worked for a computer software company from home. During her first pregnancy, she told me she instinctively stopped drinking coffee and eating white flour and junk food and began craving only vegetables and natural, healthy food. Now pregnant with her fourth, she explained, "Knowing I'm carrying children, it's a huge responsibility." Ronit clarified that this responsibility of "making a child" extends to everything a woman sees, hears, and thinks because this all "goes into this child." When walking through non-Haredi neighborhoods Ronit takes off her eyeglasses so that she does not see the immodest billboards and posters around her. Ronit said, "It's written somewhere that the thoughts of a pregnant woman affect this baby." Ronit expressed here a segulah that I heard a few times: if a woman sees a certain figure or animal during pregnancy, the baby will end up looking like that other being.[14] Thus, many pregnant women who share this concern will avoid visiting the zoo during their pregnancies. Ronit extends the segulah to sounds, smells, tastes, and even thoughts.

When she prays, Ronit pleads, "God, please don't let me hear things, do not let me see things because there is a *neshama* [soul] in me."[15] Notice that Ronit is not asking directly for God to guarantee the correct development of the fetus. Instead, the fulfillment of the prayer is filtered through her actions. Ronit must see, hear, and eat the correct things in order for the fetus to be healthy. By asking God to prevent her from seeing or hearing the wrong things, she ensures her own role in the process of fetal development. She could have asked God to give her a healthy baby, but she knows that she should not formulate that prayer. First, if she asks for a healthy baby and is not given one, Ronit will question why God did not give her what she wanted. But moreover, Ronit's prayer must include her own contribution to the fulfillment of her request. This is what hishtadlut means; she is a required part of the equation. Furthermore, Ronit considers seeing, hearing and eating to contribute to the baby's soul, not just to the baby's physical development. Instead of seeing food as merely a contributor to biological development, Ronit equates eating with the metaphysical development of the fetus. As such, her food choices become religiously significant, thereby elevating the importance of her contribution, her hishtadlut.

It is important to note that Haredi men and women already sacralize the mundane act of eating through the consumption of kosher food, the process of food preparation, and the blessing of food before and after eating.[16] Esther, a Hasidic mother and prolific teacher of Hassidut in Jerusalem, taught in one of her classes that eating becomes a holy act through both "external" and "internal" actions. External actions are all the things one does to purchase and prepare kosher food and then to recite blessings before and after eating. Esther explained that the internal actions have to do with "what we think about while we eat and what we do with the energy it [the food] provides." All of these actions, Esther stated, are necessary to elevate the importance of this routine and physically indispensable act.[17] Esther looks at pregnancy in a similar way. She said it becomes a holy pregnancy when it results from a "kosher relationship and where the focus is on bringing children into the world to serve God." These can be seen as external actions. Esther adds that a woman can elevate the holiness of a pregnancy when she "realizes that she is involved in something holy." This is an internal action. We have seen in this chapter that Haredi women find great significance in their nutritional efforts during pregnancy, understanding these as external and internal actions that sacralize pregnancy. Using the language of hishtadlut to refer to healthy eating during pregnancy allows Haredi women to mark the religious significance of their commonplace and extremely physical experiences (eating and pregnancy) and understand their actions during pregnancy as religiously and theologically significant. Indeed, it is these actions that ensure the correct formation of the next generation of Haredi Jews.

Medical Hishtadlut

Many Haredi women interpret any prenatal care they procure as their hishtadlut. Rachel, a young mother of two and pregnant with her third, maintains that going to the doctor, napping, and taking vitamins are important elements of her hishtadlut during pregnancy. Rachel explained, "You cannot say, 'Everything will be OK.' You have to make an effort for your child. That is my job as mother." In other words, she knows that she has to do those things to show that she is not taking her pregnancy for granted. Bayla, a mother of five, told me, "The hishtadlut I was doing was going to the doctor and taking my prenatal vitamins and making sure I was eating healthy and taking care of myself and sleeping. In general, taking care of myself was my hishtadlut." Instead of seeing these actions as reinforcing the doctors' role, these women understand procuring prenatal care as a reinforcement of a woman's role in fetal development.

When I asked Yael, twenty-six years old with three children, what her hishtadlut was during the pregnancy, Yael said that hishtadlut is performing all the tests that will be helpful to her during the pregnancy. Any test that provides information that she cannot use, Yael does not consider part of her hishtadlut. What she means is that she does not want to ever be in a position to get results from a genetic test that would make her consider an abortion. It is not surprising that Yael links prenatal testing to abortion; it is widely documented in Israel.[18] Because hishtadlut regarding medical intervention has so much to do with a woman being able to take credit for the creation of a healthy baby, prenatal tests that might require a woman to make a decision about abortion put her in a precarious position, one that would possibly require her hishtadlut to work *against* her desired end.

Yael and other Haredi women can avoid genetic testing and many other prenatal tests during pregnancy because they have already participated in genetic testing before marriage. Much of a woman's reproductive hishtadlut begins even before a young man and woman meet for the first time. As high school students, Haredi men and women take a genetic test for disorders that occur most commonly in their particular ancestry.[19] Dor Yesharim, meaning "straight generation,"[20] is the organization that tests Jews for their carrier status and then helps establish "good" matches. After Dor Yesharim tests their blood, individuals receive an identification number, but they do not get the results of the test. Matchmakers use these identification codes to find out if the suggested pair will pass on a genetic disorder to their children. If both individuals carry the gene for the disorder, the organization tells the matchmaker they are not a good match. As a result, the matchmaker never knows—and thus nobody in the community knows—which disorder they both carry. In this way, individuals avoid the stigma of the community knowing they are carriers of a particular genetic disorder.[21] Due to the prominence of Dor Yesharim, the Haredi reproductive hishtadlut includes genetic testing even before marriage.

Genetic testing features prominently in Israeli medical care, where, as Tsipy Ivry has argued, "Responsibility to bear a healthy fetus, in the geneticist truth regime, rests with the mother, but she must rely on diagnostic technologies to be able to fulfill this responsibility to her family and to society."[22] Though Haredi women recognize the importance of genetic testing and support the medical establishment's diagnostic usage of these technologies, Haredi women in Israel see this testing as part of their hishtadlut. As they frame their participation in Dor Yesharim's premarital genetic testing as histhtadlut, they see it as an action that will lead to a healthy baby and a positive relationship with God. This different perspective on the procurement of genetic testing reveals that women do not view genetic testing as part of the medical community's purview but rather as something that falls under their responsibility. Haredi women reappropriate the prominence of genetic testing, so procuring these tests is not seen as contributing to the "fatalism" of Israeli medicine but rather something women can use to control the process of fetal development and limit possible outcomes.

When I asked women to specify what tests they did or how frequently they saw their doctors, they answered with something like "whatever tests we usually do" or "I did whatever the minimum tests are." A woman's generalized response to this question indicates that she recognizes that her hishtadlut—the effort she is required to take—is shaped by communal practices. Haredi women recognize that doctors and modern medicine are unavoidable elements of their pregnancies. Sometimes, this is because a woman cannot get pregnant without the help of her doctor or particular drugs, but more frequently, this is because the practice of medicine is currently an integral part of the prenatal experience for Haredi women. It is important to see here that despite the fact that Haredi women see prenatal tests and doctor visits as hishtadlut, it is more in the form of social obligation or an abstract requirement to involve one's doctors. For instance, Yael's rejection and diminishing of medicine shows that Haredi women limit the significance of medical involvement. In turn, they elevate the impact of their own efforts. When women understand these medical and physical actions as part of their hishtadlut—as actions that are required of them in order to rely on God when needed—they emphasize both the practical effect of their efforts and the religious significance of these actions. Lea Taragin-Zeller refers to this type of negotiation between God's reign over reproduction and the influence of modern scientific attitudes as "flexible decision-making."[23] As Haredi women respond to the multitude of choices for prenatal health and tests that they face, it is clear that the concept of hishtadlut is situationally defined and in many cases individual—in other words, flexible.

One of the reasons women had difficulty defining hishtadlut was because despite the fact that women speak of a "normal" or "accepted" hishtadlut, there is actually very little consistency between women's hishtadlut. Some of this is due to the fact that medicine has advanced and prenatal tests have become more commonplace in medical practice. Devorah explained that for some, getting an ultrasound is now expected, but fifty years ago, getting an ultrasound was not part of any woman's hishtadlut. Seeing a doctor, too, is part of common hishtadlut now, even though regular visits with a doctor were not normal in the past. Devorah rationalizes the situation as follows: "So you have to do what general hishtadlut is. If general hishtadlut is to get ultrasounds, then many rabbis say that you should do it. But if it's not general hishtadlut, and it's more, then you don't have to do it." Though the ideology of hishtadlut acknowledges that there is a natural course of events that is, to a certain extent, unavoidable because it is preordained by God, the influence humans have in this natural course of events changes throughout history.

As they identify which actions are hishtadlut and which are not, Haredi women attribute religious and theological significance to their prenatal care. Therefore, as they view their nutritional choices and their procurement of medical tests and interventions as hishtadlut, women claim that these actions contribute to a relationship with God wherein they can clearly be seen to be "doing their part" in the required exchange. Furthermore, as they see these actions as hishtadlut, women classify their actions as having a direct effect on fetal development. In this way they continue to see pregnancy as a woman's partnership with God.

Bitachon: Divine Intervention

Now we turn to the other half of this relationship with God, a feature that appears primarily (and most clearly) during labor and delivery. Bitachon refers to one's faith in a God who is actively involved in one's life and indicates a security with that relationship and an understanding that a woman must do certain things to create that relationship and ensure that God's involvement is positive. One woman told me, "If you don't include God in your life, he will put himself in your life," indicating that women are at times fearful of God's strength. Bitachon points to the fact that women are aware of God's power and the fact that they are taking a risk with each pregnancy. Each time, they risk a variety of reproductive catastrophes—miscarriage, fetal disability, maternal death—and they rely on a personal relationship with God to prevent any of those disasters from harming them. If they do not show their trust in God—their bitachon—then they are placing themselves and their families at risk. Thus, to create a positive relationship with God, women must know how to express their bitachon—their confidence in relying on God. In this section, we will see how women draw on bitachon during labor and delivery in order to express an intimate relationship with God while simultaneously limiting the involvement of medical authorities. This expression is shaped both by the doulas who factor prominently in the birth process as well as by the fact that pregnancy—and therefore a woman's agency—ends with the birth of the baby.

The connection between faith and relationship in Haredi women's understandings of bitachon is reminiscent of Emmanuel Levinas's interpretation of *emunah*. In *A Covenant of Creatures*, Michael Fagenblat describes emunah in Emmanuel Levinas's ethics. Fagenblat distinguishes the Jewish concept of emunah (faith) from a more generic understanding of belief in Levinas's ethics by saying, "Levinas's ethics of faith is not a belief *that* the other is such and such but a faithfulness *to* the other."[24] Levinas rejects "belief" because it is individualistic and cognitively based. An ethics based on faith, however, is an ethic that is "fundamentally social and nonindividualistic."[25] Fagenblat explains, "To say, then, that someone is faithful is to say that she is a person who exhibits or can be counted on to exhibit loyalty."[26] This is precisely what we see with Haredi women's expressions of bitachon and the loyalty they expect from God as a result.[27]

Maya, who rejected medical control through her avoidance of hospital births, said, "When it comes to the actual birth, of course the bitachon takes over. We are not in control. . . . Hishtadlut is a *mitzvah* [commandment], and it's a good thing to do hishtadlut. But the results are not in our hands." Women, then, view the pregnancy as part of the process and thus intricately linked to hishtadlut and the effort each must expend, but the birth is the result—a result that is not dependent on a woman's effort but rather on God's. A number of factors contribute to Haredi women shifting from hishtadlut to bitachon when it comes time to give birth to their babies. First, Haredi women generally give birth in hospitals, and they draw on the concept of bitachon to confront the medicalized and patriarchal birthing practices prominent in Israeli hospitals.[28] Although during pregnancy women can—to a certain extent—selectively avoid medical interventions, this choice is harder during birth. While Haredi women may have been able to avoid a medicalized pregnancy by expressing their authority over reproductive decisions, once they are in the hospital, they are not able to easily express the authority that otherwise pervades their reproductive experience because the hospital becomes an all-consuming experience. During birth, then, the only recourse Haredi women have to reject the authority of medical knowledge is to draw on their relationship with God. They refer to this as "releasing control" to God while they simultaneously control the influence of medical authorities. Haredi women use the concept of bitachon as an alternative to medical intervention as they remind themselves and the doctors that God is in charge. Though Haredi women might feel powerless when they confront the medical field, drawing on an intimate relationship with God connects them once again to a superior source of authority.

To help them negotiate medical authorities, many Haredi women hire doulas to assist them at the hospitals. These doulas reinforce bitachon during labor as a concept that is both consistent with their ideology of women needing to release control and Haredi theology that requires them to rely on God. The doulas whom many Haredi women employ grew up in America during the 1970s feminist movement.[29] They follow the teachings of Ina May Gaskin, a famous homebirth midwife whose book *Spiritual Midwifery* (1975) introduces pregnant women, doulas, and midwives to the natural birthing process and encourages women to pursue this path for their own births. The doulas in Jerusalem who work with Haredi women espouse Gaskin's ideology and express an antimedicalization tendency, although most of them do not attend to women who choose to give birth at home. In fact, only one woman I spoke to gave birth at home, and many cited the material benefits they receive from the state as one significant incentive to giving birth in the hospital.[30] Additionally, many of the Haredi women I spoke to, like the doulas or like Gaskin, were not opposed to medical interventions on principle. Instead, Haredi women hire doulas to help them negotiate what they perceive to be an overbearing medical community. Furthermore, many Haredi women hire doulas so that they can have someone by their side during the labor and delivery in the hospital. Because of menstrual purity laws and modesty laws that restrict the physical involvement of one's husband beginning at an early stage of the labor, Haredi women invite doulas to help them manage the pain of labor and delivery and to encourage them through the birth. Many of the doulas identify as Orthodox Jews, and they incorporate a familiar theology into their coaching that helps Haredi women combat the medicalized birthing practices.

Haredi women's use of doulas and God language during birth has some elements in common with homebirth practices in America. Pamela Klassen observes that although the revival of home birth in the 1960s and 1970s had a decidedly feminist and anti-Christian tone, some strands of midwifery at the time began drawing on what they called "spiritual homebirth." Notable among them was Gaskin's countercultural community in Tennessee.[31] The women in Klassen's study were drawn to spiritual home birth because they felt that "official" religion did not have language for the transformative experience of childbirth. Instead, they draw on religious language to make meaning of the "embodied memories and human connections forged in the process of childbirth."[32] In a more recent study of religious "nones" in America, Ann Duncan finds that women involved in the Sacred Living Movement reject the medicalization of birth and seek to mark pregnancy as a rite of passage while creating community around motherhood. Without formal religious affiliations, these "nones" sacralize the physical experiences of pregnancy and birth through journaling, birth art, sex, belly adornments, and group retreats, for example.[33]

Although Haredi women exhibit marked differences from the religious "nones," they too attempt to sacralize their physical experiences in order to counteract the influence of medical interventions on pregnancy and birth. For Haredi women in Jerusalem, however, this is because the official religious language falls short of their goals for childbirth. Halakha provides a significant amount of regulation surrounding childbirth; however, similar to women in Klassen's study, Haredi women felt that this language did not encapsulate the significance of the experience for them. Furthermore, the language of bitachon that Haredi women import into childbirth provides them with authority that supersedes the medical community. This is because bitachon implies a relationship wherein Haredi women can rely on God, who they see as more powerful than the medical community. This, then, is more like what Klassen found among devout Christian home-birthing women, who submit to their husbands' authority and reject any others—doctors and midwives—in order to preserve the chain of command from God to husband to wife. By drawing on bitachon, Haredi women reject the incursion of doctors *and* husbands in order to maintain the connection between a birthing woman and God.

Many women maintain that the first step in this rejection of medicalization is to educate oneself. Despite a woman's lack of control over things that fall within God's realm—the birth of a healthy baby and the survival of the mother—doulas teach women that they do have control over certain medical interventions. Aliza, a doula and a young mother, feels that it is her responsibility to educate women about birth. She is saddened that doctors "rush" women into C-sections, increasing the amount of medical interventions; moreover, Aliza is unhappy that women are not educated enough to say otherwise. Though she blames doctors for cultivating this practice, Aliza also blames women for not doing "their homework." She continues, "They come in and they don't know anything about birth, or they read one book, which is not enough. They just do not know." She relayed a story to me of a recent birth she attended:

> After this birth the husband said to me, "You know, you totally have to have *emunah* [faith] when you birth." And I said to him, "It's true, and you also have to have *yeda* [knowledge]." You have to have knowledge. Especially if you walk into a hospital, you need to show them that you know. Once they see you know, they back off a little bit, or once they see you have someone with you who knows, they back off. That's why doulas at births in hospitals end up with fewer C-sections, fewer epidurals, fewer interventions, because someone there knows. It helps to know.

Rina, a doula who also provides childbirth classes for Haredi women, talks about the importance of rejecting medical intervention because women can only feel in control when they are working with God. She provides two linguistic examples of this relationship. The letters of the word *leidah* [birth] in Hebrew can be split into two words, *l'yad Hashem*, meaning "next to God." This means that birth is inherently about being near to God. This linguistic tool was found also in the pregnancy advice books noted in chapter 2, but Rina does not attribute it to anyone in particular. Secondly, *emunah* contains the word *em*, which means "mother." Becoming a mother, Rina claims, is about exerting faith through bitachon. In the doulas' estimation, a woman can either embrace medicine or religion, but embracing medicine means not demonstrating one's bitachon.

One of the primary ways women are taught to reject the involvement of doctors is by avoiding pain medication during birth. This is largely because doulas understand labor pain to be a central element in reminding women that although they should be in control of doctors, they are not in control of the birth. Though many women connect the pain of childbirth to the biblical story of Eve's sin in the Garden of Eden, doula Shula offers a different view. She explains that Eve's curse was not due to eating from the forbidden tree but rather due to her desire for control. As a punishment, women are eternally reminded—through the pain of childbirth—that they are not in control. Many of the doulas I spoke to encourage women not to control or limit the pain of childbirth, because by feeling the pain, they insist, women embody their connection to God. This is similar to Klassen's findings about women in North America who chose to undergo the pain of vaginal childbirth without any anesthetic interventions. These women justify this choice in religious language that "describes the newfound knowledge of self, and sometimes tells of renewed or novel intimacy with deities and loved ones."[34] Similarly, Haredi women are encouraged not to anesthetize the pain of childbirth because only by feeling the pain can one show her loyalty and submission to God.

Though women are encouraged to release control to God, doulas also remind them of the importance of maintaining control over the medical establishment. Aliza emphasizes the difficult paradox for Haredi women: "What I've always believed in is really empowering women. Not that she's in control. She's not in control." She wants women to know that they are "active participants [in the birth]. She's having the baby.... Don't sit there waiting for someone to have the baby for you. You have to get up. You have to move. You have to be informed." Aliza wants women to know that while they are in control of the doctors, God is in control of the outcome.

Ronit fully embraced this tension. As we walked back from her ultrasound in the thirty-second week of her pregnancy, Ronit explained that planned C-sections are opposed in the Haredi community precisely because they place too much faith in doctors. The result of this misguided faith, she claims, is that women do not have the opportunity to show their emunah and bitachon. When a woman understands the pain of childbirth as part of her relationship with God, she shows that the only way of dealing with the pain is to acknowledge God's role in it. By rejecting certain medical interventions, such as pain relief, women have an opportunity to show their bitachon—their faith in God's ultimate control. Thus the exchange is reciprocal. To show that they are not in control of birth but rather that God is, women must mitigate the involvement of the medical field; simultaneously, to mitigate the involvement of the medical field, women must surrender to God's authority.

Women's creative application of bitachon demonstrates once again how participating in this divine act of reproduction makes it possible for a Haredi woman's body to become the source of her agency. Here, a woman draws on bitachon as a way of surrendering the authority that she maintained throughout the pregnancy. It is only by surrendering to God that she can gain authority over medical decisions. During birth, she must accept the pain of childbirth and express her bitachon to once again gain control over the doctors. During birth, she must exert control over the medical establishment, but to do this, she must surrender to God's control.

Reproductive Catastrophe: Manipulating Hishtadlut and Bitachon

As we have seen, by drawing on the ideology of hishtadlut and bitachon to define their tasks during pregnancy and labor, women theologically bolster their cultural and religious roles in Haredi society as they display how pregnancy and birth bring them into an intimate relationship with God. In this way, Haredi women ensure that others appreciate their importance and significance in reproduction. This responsibility over the outcomes of pregnancy becomes threatening when women are faced with reproductive catastrophe. According to the current theological framework as outlined here, a miscarriage, stillbirth, fetal defect, or maternal death might indicate that a woman did not act correctly or (worse) that she did not cultivate the proper relationship with God to ensure divine protection. When faced with reproductive catastrophe, though, women manipulate their usage of hishtadlut and bitachon in such a way that preserves their dignity. As Haredi women manipulate the understanding of hishtadlut and bitachon, they avoid blame and ascribe to God (or another acknowledged authority) the responsibility for undesired outcomes.

Rachel, who had already taught me a great deal about hishtadlut, relayed to me a story of reproductive catastrophe. A young, healthy Haredi woman she knew went through her entire pregnancy without any problems, but at the very end, she started having seizures and died after the baby was delivered. Rachel told me that when this happened, it made her obsessively nervous for months, especially during her own pregnancy. After discussing it with her husband, she concluded, "It's clearly from God. Something so crazy like that has to be clearly from God. She gave birth to her baby and then died." The episode taught her "that we have no control." After being nervous that there was something perhaps this woman should have done or that Rachel should be doing—hishtadlut—to prevent the same thing, Rachel concluded that this was completely in God's hands. According to Rachel, God was responsible, not the woman.

Other women find that they have no control over their fertility itself. Orah learned this after various fertility treatments failed. Orah remarked that not being able to have the amount of children she always wanted "humbled" her: "You see that you are not in control." Orah particularly felt she was being controlled by God because having a baby was simple for her at the beginning of her marriage. After three healthy children Orah suffered from secondary infertility, and she felt that God had suddenly said, "You know what? No more. God 'humbles the haughty' and he has humbled me many, many, many times." In the case of tragedy (as opposed to normal conception, pregnancy, and birth),

Orah understands that control is something that either a woman has or God has, never both. This is in direct contradiction to what we saw, for instance, with birth. In a normal birth, a woman is expected to work *with* God and to utilize her authority to make a space for God's involvement and mitigate the doctors' role. It is a woman, then, who facilitates God's presence in a normal birth. In the case of infertility, Orah claims God is fully responsible.

Just as women understand bitachon to free themselves from control or responsibility, they also refer to hishtadlut when they want to show that they have done all that the community requires of them. I posed a question to Yael about a hypothetical woman who found out late in a pregnancy that the baby was not going to survive for long after the birth. I wanted to know, according to Yael, if abortion would be justified in that case. Yael first said that probably most rabbis would not allow an abortion, though she admitted there are probably differences of opinion on the matter. Then she thought about how she would respond:

> To wait nine months and then after all that time, he's dead? That's really
> difficult. So let's say you go to the rabbi and he tells you not to get the
> abortion. Obviously that's a halakhic answer, but maybe it's also possible to
> calm you from a psychological perspective. There might be differences in
> rabbinic opinions, but you did your hishtadlut. You asked. On the other hand,
> if the rabbi tells you to have an abortion, then that could also calm you. It's
> too much to decide something like this on our own. It's not that everything is
> out of our hands, but not everything is in our hands.

Yael claims here that just asking her rabbi for his advice or for halakhic governance on the matter is hishtadlut. In this way, Yael removes herself from the responsibility of making this difficult decision. Though many Haredi women I spoke to attribute the entirety of their prenatal choices to hishtadlut, by asking her rabbi and considering that to be hishtadlut, Yael effectively makes the rabbi accountable. By manipulating what constitutes hishtadlut, Yael avoids having to decide about the abortion of a fetus.

Reproductive catastrophe presents women with a reality that threatens not only their theologies but their images of themselves. Throughout pregnancy and birth, women claim a degree of authority and control over the outcome, which they base on the relationship that their embodied experience establishes with God. Exhibiting this certainty in their relationship with God is the gendered expectation for Haredi women. However, when women consider the possibility of reproductive catastrophe, they are forced to confront their uncertainty and the faith that is required of them. Women are eager to

claim responsibility for a healthy and successful pregnancy, but the alternative threatens their understanding of a relationship of protection from God.
Teman and Ivry refer to Haredi women's negotiation of these risks, both physical and spiritual. They write, "Faith serves as a tool for coping with uncertainty
but simultaneously contributes to additional pressures on pregnant women
who are trying to fulfill the ideal gendered model of faith in their community."[35] Their hishtadlut should cultivate that certainty, but it often does not
because these women know that reproductive catastrophe is always possible.
Thus, they are expected to maintain both hishtadlut, an acknowledgment of
human contribution, and bitachon, faith in God's influence, simultaneously.
When faced with the random tragedies sometimes seen during pregnancy
and birth, women turn to bitachon to express faith in God's ultimate plan or
the rabbinic authorities. In this way they can avoid blaming themselves for a
lack of hishtadlut and instead demonstrate the gendered ideals of certainty in
God's plan.

CONCLUSIONS

When seen within the Haredi cultural context discussed in chapter 3, it becomes
clear that Haredi women's reproductive theology both challenges and reinforces the gender norms that make space for women's reproductive agency.
By creatively complying with dominant theological and cultural norms about
reproduction, Haredi women exert their authority over their bodies and their
pregnancies. Furthermore, despite Haredi women's insistence that they make
reproductive decisions without their rabbis, by drawing on these theological
concepts, they are connecting themselves to the Jewish past and the Jewish
future (the hope for Messianic redemption). In this way, their rejection of rabbinic authority does not imply the rejection of Judaism in its entirety. Instead, it
is a reclaiming of concepts in order to prioritize women's embodied experiences.

Haredi women's application and manipulation of theological concepts to
bolster their authority is similar to what Elizabeth Bucar found among US
Catholic and Iranian Shiite women who creatively conform to their religious
texts and authorities to produce moral knowledge. Bucar found that "women
negotiate with powerful clerical moral guidance" through a concept she calls
"dianomy." Dianomy encapsulates Bucar's argument that women are relying
"neither exclusively on the self nor exclusively on religious traditions as a source
of moral authority."[36] Similarly, Haredi women in Jerusalem are drawing on
both their embodied experiences (the self) as well as Haredi theology (their
religious traditions) as a source of authority. Their reading and application of

theology is explicitly informed by their embodied experiences of pregnancy. Wanting to avoid being controlled by rabbinic and medical authorities, Haredi women interpret theological concepts in a way that depicts women as the embodiment of divine authority and as those who are crucially important to the process of reproduction.

Importantly, Haredi women's theology of embodying divine authority changes prominent structural characteristics of the Haredi world and the construction of moral knowledge. First, despite the fact that rabbis are involved in the daily activities of their Haredi constituents, when Haredi women cultivate a relationship with God through reproduction, they can avoid not only medical intrusion (as much as they want) but also, more importantly, rabbinic involvement. Whereas in other areas, rabbis act as intermediaries, interpreting God's will for Haredi individuals, during pregnancy and birth, women draw a direct line to God through their use of hishtadlut and bitachon, thus cutting out the middlemen. Furthermore, as women use these terms to make meaning out of the very physical experience of pregnancy and childbirth, they emphasize the importance of bodily practices in religion and in Judaism specifically. By using theological terms to make meaning out of their bodily practices, these Haredi women demonstrate that women's bodily practices are also to be incorporated into the corpus of religious tradition. Pregnancy is a "rite of passage" for Haredi women,[37] and while medicalization and rabbinic interference threaten the transformative possibilities of pregnancy, women draw on a wealth of religious resources to cultivate their agency during pregnancy. In the next chapter, we will see how Haredi women apply a similar model to pregnancy terminations.

The prominence of doulas also enables the exclusion of rabbinic authorities from pregnancy and birth. As Kimberly Kelly demonstrated in her study of conservative women's authority in crisis pregnancy centers, "Gender essentialism can be a unique resource that legitimates autonomous sex-segregated spaces . . . and places explicit limits on men's power."[38] When Haredi women give birth, it is already a somewhat sex-segregated space. As Haredi women bring female doulas, instead of husbands or rabbis, into the birthing room, they legitimate this space as one that is intended to be all-female, not just a space without men. Furthermore, the feminist-inspired theology that the American emigrant doulas bring with them works to further exclude any male influence on the space. Although Haredi women would not claim that their actions are feminist, their use of doulas and the reproductive theology that they create intends to bolster women's authority over pregnancy and birth.

NOTES

1. Young, *On Female Bodily Experience.*

2. Ibid., 55.

3. While each tape represents the viewpoint of that particular teacher, in disseminating tapes they are attempting to broaden their message and unify the variety of perspectives that exist. For more on these audiotaped classes in the Haredi world, see Caplan, "God's Voice"; Fader, "Nonliberal Jewish Women's Audiocassette Lectures in Brooklyn"; Leon, "Political Use of the Teshuva Cassette Culture in Israel."

4. Fader, in "Nonliberal Jewish Women's Audiocassette Lectures in Brooklyn," found similar trends in tapes for ultra-Orthodox Jewish women in Brooklyn.

5. Gribetz, "Pregnant with Meaning," 180, emphasis in the original.

6. Ibid., 177.

7. Ibid., 178.

8. In "Like a Snake in Paradise," Nicolas Stadler and Lea Taragin-Zeller also found that young Haredi women in Israel reinterpret norms of modesty to carve for themselves a "direct path to 'the All Mighty'" (138).

9. Fader, *Mitzvah Girls*, 37.

10. Kessler, *Conceiving Israel.*

11. Cytomegalovirus is an infection that can be passed from the woman to her fetus in utero. It passes through the placenta and can lead to developmental disabilities or hearing loss among infants born with CMV.

12. This is starkly different from Kahn's findings in "Making Technology Familiar" about the way infertile Haredi women in New York use Hebrew prayers, Yiddish aphorisms, and English slang to "frame, understand, and negotiate their infertility." While Susan Martha Kahn maintains that Orthodox Jews use this language to help them make sense of the treatments and cope with the outcomes, Haredi women in Israel use these religious concepts to support their selective avoidance of medicine. See Kahn, "Making Technology Familiar," 468.

13. See Ivry, *Embodying Culture.*

14. Gaster, *Customs and Folkways of Jewish Life*; Ivry, *Embodying Culture.*

15. Although *neshama* could refer to both "soul" and "person" in Hebrew, I found that when Haredi women use the term, they are referring to the person's soul.

16. See Fader, *Mitzvah Girls.* As Fader argued in her ethnography of Hasidic women, Jewish religious practice is making the mundane sacred.

17. Bynum, *Holy Feast and Holy Fast,* is helpful for thinking about this argument. Bynum states, "Not only was food a more significant motif in late medieval spirituality than most historians have recognized, food was also a more important motif in women's piety than in men's" (4). Sered, "Food and Holiness," also points to the importance of food preparation in elderly Middle Eastern Jewish women's religious experience.

18. See M. Weiss, *Chosen Body.* This is not just an Israeli phenomenon, however, as other scholars of reproduction have noted the ways that prenatal testing often creates a feeling of a "tentative pregnancy" until the result is one that the woman wants. See Rothman, *Tentative Pregnancy.*

19. This list of disorders is constantly growing. Currently, a person of straight Ashkenazi lineage is recommended testing for twelve genetic disorders.

20. Also defined in some places as "upright generation."

21. This stigma can be very powerful, in some cases preventing all of one's siblings from being paired because of the fear that the family's genes are somehow problematic. See Raz and Vizner, "Carrier Matching and Collective Socialization in Community Genetics." Yael Hashiloni-Dolev, in "Effect of Jewish-Israeli Family Ideology," discusses how the Israeli-Jewish favorability toward genetic compatibility testing speaks to the centrality of the family as a whole in Israel and not on the autonomy of a child-to-be.

22. Ivry, *Embodying Culture,* 11.

23. Taragin-Zeller, "Conceiving God's Children."

24. Fagenblat, *Covenant of Creatures,* 146, emphasis in the original.

25. Ibid., 145.

26. Ibid., 146.

27. This comparison is especially appropriate since, as Halbertal, in "On Belief and Believers," points out, in Modern Hebrew, *emunah* is connected to *bitachon* (cited in Fagenblat, *Covenant of Creatures,* 147).

28. Portugese, *Fertility Policy in Israel,* and Kahn, *Reproducing Jews,* discuss the medicalization of conception as seen in Israel's widespread support of reproductive technologies. Ivry, *Embodying Culture,* finds that medicalization is a critical piece of prenatal care.

29. See Rock-Singer, *Prophetesses of the Body,* for a more thorough analysis of how American doulas import ideas about Western medicine and natural birthing to the Israeli religious birthing scene.

30. Brusa and Barilan, "Childbirth in Israel," connect the history of Israeli policy toward homebirth to the rise of newborn screening programs. See also Fuchs, "This Time I Was a Person," for more on Orthodox Jewish women who gave birth at home in Israel.

31. Klassen, *Blessed Events,* 31.

32. Ibid., 64.
33. Duncan, "Sacred Pregnancy in the Age of the 'Nones.'"
34. Klassen, "Scandal of Pain in Childbirth," 75.
35. Ivry, Teman, and Bernhardt, "Pregnancy as a Proclamation of Faith," 78.
36. Bucar, *Creative Conformity*, 1.
37. Davis-Floyd, *Birth as an American Rite of Passage*.
38. Kelly, "In the Name of the Mother," 204.

FIVE

—ᴍ—

ABORTIONS, FINANCES, AND WOMEN'S REPRODUCTIVE AUTHORITY

IN MY INTERVIEWS WITH HAREDI women, none admitted to having an abortion. Most, however, told me about a friend who had had an abortion. When I asked them hypothetical questions about a fetus diagnosed with a disability, women offered accounts of their friends to whom this had happened or stories of a "woman in the neighborhood" who had to decide whether to terminate a pregnancy. They often lowered their voices while telling me about abortions or found something to fiddle with, like a rubber band. Women were nervous while telling me about their friends, in part because many women were pregnant during our interviews and were fearful that they would find similar abnormalities the next time they went to the doctor. I reminded them that we could change the subject at any time, and I trod lightly during our conversations about this sensitive topic. Deciding to terminate a pregnancy seems to challenge Israeli and Haredi pronatalist norms. Unlike other reproductive decisions that are made in the interest of ensuring the birth of a baby, abortion appears to be the opposite. A Haredi woman who has an abortion is often understood to be acting contrary to the pronatalist norms and the paradigms of her gender identity. Because of this, even Haredi women themselves had a hard time discussing abortion.

In many ways, however, pregnancy termination is also the result of Haredi educational and economic norms and should be seen as flowing directly from women's reproductive ethic. My conversations with Haredi women and research with the EFRAT organization, an antiabortion nonprofit group in Israel that has a special relationship with Haredi women, reveal that there are three scenarios where Haredi women would consider terminating a pregnancy: (1) after a prenatal test reveals a fetus will be born with a disability or a severe illness, (2) when a woman's life is in danger, and (3) when she cannot afford another child. The severity of the fetal diagnosis often determines whether one will terminate the pregnancy, but most women said that if the continuation of the pregnancy posed a risk to her life, she would get an abortion. While women understood these scenarios to be more acceptable reasons for abortion, financial considerations also drive family size. Sometimes this means terminating a pregnancy one cannot afford. Women make these decisions within a socioeconomic context that requires them to serve as the breadwinners and primary caretakers for their families while glorifying a life of poverty. Deciding whether one can raise another child is a complex negotiation of whether one has the mental, physical, and financial capabilities to do so.

As I will argue, this deliberation is consistent with how Haredi women think of reproduction as an act laden with responsibility. In thinking about their divinely inspired responsibility to bear children, Haredi women understand each pregnancy as something that either fulfills or challenges that responsibility. This is consistent with how Rebecca Todd Peters has described "childbearing as a deliberative moral act" because it is an act that women undertake after careful consideration of the risks and consequences, which include their existing moral obligations.[1] When Haredi women consider terminating a pregnancy that they cannot afford or that might result in the birth of a baby with a severe disability, they are worried about how their existing children might fare, and they are contemplating whether they can continue to work outside the home or bring in enough money to support this family. These considerations are built into the Haredi cultural setting, making women's moral deliberations about childbearing consistent with Haredi norms regarding family size and women's earning potential. In this way, the decision to terminate in certain circumstances is also consistent with Haredi gender norms.

This chapter explores the tensions in Haredi women's approaches to pregnancy termination. I will weave together interviews with Haredi women with ethnographic research at EFRAT to demonstrate how Haredi women think about pregnancy termination. When women exercise reproductive authority to terminate a pregnancy due to financial concerns, or when they limit their family size for the same reason, they view this decision as contrary to Haredi cultural norms. In this way, this chapter diverges from the rest of the book, wherein I demonstrate that women see their reproductive agency and all decisions that flow from it as consistent with Haredi cultural and theological norms. Abortion due to financial difficulty is the first instance of a Haredi woman doing something she considers rebellious. However, as I broaden the picture to show how Haredi women's fertility has long been in tension with their financial reality, it will become clear that financial considerations are integral to considerations of pregnancy termination.

ABORTIONS IN THE HAREDI COMMUNITY

Leah was twenty-nine years old and pregnant with her fourth child when I conducted my first interview with her. Although she was far enough along in the pregnancy to have already gone through a series of prenatal tests that revealed she was carrying a healthy fetus, Leah was still anxious while we talked about the possibility of a fetal diagnosis. She lowered her voice considerably, and her demeanor changed. Instead of cheerfully talking about her pregnancies as she had for the last hour, Leah became serious and concerned as we talked about the possible need for an abortion. She mentioned a friend of hers who found out she was carrying a fetus with anencephaly. Anencephaly is a neural tube defect that results in a fetus's brain or skull not developing. There is no cure for anencephaly, and almost all babies born with this diagnosis will die shortly after birth.[2] Leah's friend did not have an abortion. Instead, she continued with the pregnancy and gave birth to a child who survived for just minutes after he was born. Leah talked about her friend with a great deal of sadness, and she made it seem like this was an unusual decision. She told me, "I personally would not be able to handle an anencephalic baby. I would not be able to handle going through the pregnancy. I would have spoken to a rabbi and received permission for an abortion."

When I asked what a woman might do if she were in a position like her friend, most women, like Leah, responded that they would ask a rabbi for an abortion. This was often the first time in my interviews where women referenced turning to a rabbi with a question about pregnancy or birth. Asking a rabbi when considering getting an abortion marks a drastic shift in women's reproductive agency. Instead of jettisoning rabbinic authorities, women turn to them when they have a question about pregnancy termination. On the one hand, as Leah's response indicates, a woman first makes the decision about terminating her pregnancy and then turns to a rabbi who will confirm that decision. In this way, turning to a rabbi at this point is not about getting advice but rather about receiving validation for a decision. However, women's eagerness to receive rabbinic support for abortion, even if only nominal, indicates that decisions about pregnancy termination are unique in the realm of reproductive decisions. This is because her authority over reproductive decisions is based explicitly on the fact that as a pregnant woman, she is fulfilling gendered and religious expectations. A Haredi woman who terminates thinks she cannot do so from the position of reproductive authority. Instead, she turns to a rabbi.

Asking a rabbi about pregnancy termination reflects Yael's belief, noted in chapter 4, that turning to a rabbi with a question of this magnitude is a woman's hishtadlut. Asking a rabbi is a way to avoid making the decision oneself, to release that burden of responsibility to someone else. It is also how Haredi women negotiate the tension between seeing all reproduction as a blessing from God and confronting scientific knowledge that threatens God's divine plan.[3] Importantly, though, women did not leave this decision to just any rabbi. Leah said she did not know which rabbi she would go to, but she would find one who would permit an abortion. Many women knew exactly which rabbi they would ask about getting an abortion—namely, a rabbi who would permit the abortion in their particular case.

When we discussed whether they would terminate a pregnancy after a fetal diagnosis, women expressed a few important considerations to this decision. These considerations reflect the way Haredi women think about each pregnancy as one of many. An abortion after a fetal diagnosis allows a Haredi woman to preserve her mental and physical health for the children she already has and those she wants to have in the future. Leah had a clear understanding of what made a diagnosis serious enough to merit an abortion, and a lot of it had to do with her emotional investment in the pregnancy. Leah said she "does not understand" women who get abortions when they have received a positive diagnosis of Down syndrome in the fetus, because those babies are going to survive. Leah thinks that she would be able to raise a child with Down syndrome and does not consider it serious enough to terminate. However, she seeks out a variety of prenatal tests because, as she told me, "I do not want to go through nine months of pregnancy to have a baby who does not survive." Leah's pregnancies are not particularly challenging. She told me about morning sickness and sensitivity to certain smells, but she considered these discomforts nothing out of the ordinary. Although her labors are long and often painful because she avoids any pain medications, Leah's recoveries have been easy. When she says she does not want to go through nine months of pregnancy, it is not because the pregnancies are so difficult but because she knows that every pregnancy and birth carries risks to her own life and her ability to care for her other children. Additionally, Leah wants the labor she puts in and the risks she takes to yield a baby who is going to live. That is why abortion seems like a better option if a woman finds out she is carrying a fetus who will die soon after birth. In these cases, abortion allows her to terminate the pregnancy before she has spent forty weeks gestating a fetus, cultivating an emotional relationship with that child, and risking her own life for this fetus. Moreover, women shared with me that finding a rabbi who would permit an abortion after a fetal diagnosis was not difficult because they, too, see these terminations as a way of preserving a mother's health for the children she already has and those she will have in the future.

While women were willing, though slightly uncomfortable, to think about when they might consider an abortion after a fetal diagnosis, they all knew that they should not be thinking about an abortion for financial reasons. Although most women expressed an understanding of the financial stressors that another child can add to a family, they told me that it is "forbidden" to have an abortion or even go on birth control if the reasoning is that they do not have enough money to support another child. Women told me that no rabbi would approve an abortion or birth control for this reason, though most women, like Dalia in chapter 3, would start taking birth control without rabbinic permission. None, however, shared that they knew anyone who had an abortion because of concerns about financial stability. This might be because of the stigma surrounding abortions for financial reasons, but it also might be because these abortions likely happen early in the pregnancy, before someone even appears pregnant, unlike abortions after a fetal diagnosis, which often happen in the second trimester. However, through my research with EFRAT, I discovered that financial considerations often motivate reproductive decisions and challenge the pronatalist ethic that otherwise drives Haredi reproduction. EFRAT is an antiabortion organization based in Jerusalem that works to prevent abortions among Jews by serving as a social welfare group and providing financial support to Israeli Jews who are considering abortions. Haredi women turn to EFRAT when they are pregnant and unable to afford caring for another child, and EFRAT offers them significant financial help, even beyond what they provide non-Haredi clients.[4]

Although women would not admit that poverty motivated pregnancy termination, it is important to understand that abortions after a fetal diagnosis are also related to communal rates of poverty. Distinct from the example at the beginning, of a child who would not survive outside the womb, in less severe fetal diagnoses, babies born with disabilities often require extra care and support services. These services require financial means and an adult who can care for a disabled child. A Haredi woman who decides to raise a disabled child might face more financial challenges and the inability to work full time. Haredi families depend on a woman working to support the family materially; if a woman is instead a caretaker for a disabled child, she will not be able to work outside the home. This is due in large part to the lack of satisfactory services for disabled individuals in Israel and insufficient support given to their parents.[5] As the spouse more likely to be involved in full-time employment outside the home, a woman who is facing the possibility of caring for a disabled child will be thinking about the financial consequences of this decision. The added costs associated with raising a disabled child therefore relate pregnancy termination in the case of fetal diagnosis to limited financial resources; disabilities, then, are not inherently burdensome for Haredi women, but the social reality of having a disabled child makes this particularly difficult.[6]

This complicated issue demonstrates that Haredi women are negotiating competing ethical considerations of material survival for their whole family and the expectation that they reproduce at high rates. These priorities naturally intersect as more Haredi women enter the workforce and monetary stipends from the government decrease. In this way, terminating a pregnancy when a fetus is diagnosed with a disability or when a pregnancy puts a Haredi family in a more precarious financial situation is becoming more consistent with Haredi norms. This is why, even though abortion itself is not widely accepted within Haredi communities, women can easily find rabbis who will permit abortions after a fetal diagnosis. Even though abortion *seems* like it challenges Haredi gender and pronatalist norms, abortions after fetal diagnosis are actually a way of preserving those norms. Women can have more children if they are not overwhelmed (physically, mentally, or financially) with caring for a child with a disability. It is much harder, however, for a woman to find a rabbi who will permit an abortion if she shares that her reasoning is that she cannot afford to raise another child. This is because, as many women shared with me, one is not supposed to determine family size based on financial considerations.

ABORTION LAWS IN ISRAEL AND ANTIABORTION ORGANIZATIONS

Abortion has been legal in Israel since the late 1970s. The law—referred to as the Penal Law of 1977, or the Pregnancy Termination Law of 1977—makes it legal to procure an abortion in the following circumstances: (1) a woman is under the age of thirty-three or over forty;[7] (2) the pregnancy is the result of rape, incest, or extramarital relations; (3) there is a possibility the baby will be born with a physical or mental disability; (4) or the continuation of the pregnancy could endanger a woman's life or mental health. Legal abortions follow the approval of a three-person committee, of which there are forty in Israel. These committees are composed of a gynecologist; a doctor with another medical specialty such as internal medicine, psychiatry, family medicine, or community health; and a social worker. At least one of these committee members must be a woman. In many cases, a woman interested in an abortion must meet with a social worker who will help her fill out a request form. The two-page document requests a great deal of private information before arriving at information about a woman's age; marital status; the age of her children, if any; whether she was using birth control and which kinds; if she has had previous abortions; and any other relevant medical history. The last, and forty-eighth question, asks for the reason she is requesting permission for an abortion, asking her to select one of the approved options. That form is sent to the hospital's abortion committee, which decides whether it satisfies one of the supplied stipulations. Because of the intrusiveness of this form and the process that regulates whether a woman can terminate her pregnancy, Delila Amir and Orly Benjamin describe abortion as a "complex mechanism of social control."[8] Focusing on the way a woman became pregnant and her use or nonuse of contraceptives, the process reflects how "society punishes what it defines as lack of sexual control or irresponsible sexual behavior by true lack of control, where the responsibility and the ability to choose are taken from the woman and transferred to the committee."[9] These committees approve 98–99 percent of the requests for abortion, demonstrating that even though most applications are approved, Israeli law does not want a woman procuring an abortion without the social control mechanism of the abortion committee. A woman whose request was denied has the right to appear before the committee and request they reevaluate her case.

The clauses above make it possible to procure an abortion for many reasons, and if an abortion fits within these circumstances, then abortions are subsidized by national health insurance. The state pays for abortions for women under the age of thirty-three and over the age of forty, absent any other consideration. However, even for women between thirty-three and forty, the state pays for the cost of the abortion (approximately $2,500) if the pregnancy is the result of rape or sexual abuse or in the case of medical emergency. Some women want to avoid the obstacles to obtaining a legal abortion and instead pay between $600 and $850 for an illegal abortion. Women and physicians are rarely prosecuted, despite claims that half of all abortions performed in the country are illegal.[10] The law also recognizes that sometimes abortions are necessary to immediately save a woman's life, and in these cases, they are not subject to committee approval and are fully subsidized. The same applies to abortions that occur in the course of other procedures.

Furthermore, abortions are legal until the end of the pregnancy. In December 1994, the Ministry of Health created "high-level regional abortion committees" that consider late abortions (after twenty-three weeks of pregnancy).

Since then, if a woman wants an abortion during her third trimester, she must appeal to one of the six high-level committees located in various hospitals around the country. The high-level committee includes five members: three who have a vote (the head of the hospital, the head of the department of obstetrics and gynecology, and a senior social worker) and two who serve merely as advisors (the heads of the neonatal department and the genetic institute). Because these high-level committees are located in only a few, select regions of Israel, women who need an abortion after the twenty-fourth week of gestation face a slightly more difficult task. That being said, during the years 2006–9, these committees approved 92–97 percent of all those women who appealed to them, with 87–90 percent referencing the fetal disability clause.[11] Of the approximately twenty thousand applications for pregnancy termination each year, 1 percent are for abortions in the last trimester of pregnancy.[12]

According to data published in 2008 by the Israeli Ministry of Health, most abortions occur in the first trimester. The majority (58 percent) occur in the first seven weeks of pregnancy, with another 32 percent in weeks eight to twelve. Only 10 percent of abortions occur after week thirteen. Out of all abortions approved by committees, 55 percent are approved under the second clause, that the pregnancy was the result of an extramarital relationship; 18 percent under the fourth clause, that the pregnancy would result in a risk to the mother's life or health; another 18 percent because of a fetal diagnosis; and 9 percent for a woman's age.[13] 62 percent of the abortions approved in the thirteenth week or beyond were approved because they satisfied the third clause. In other words, most of the abortions that occurred in the second or third trimester were the result of a fetal diagnosis. More than half (57 percent) of abortions approved according to the fourth clause, that the pregnancy might risk a woman's physical or mental health, occurred in the first seven weeks of the pregnancy.[14]

The liberal abortion law in Israel belies the pronatalist history in Israel's reproductive policies.[15] EFRAT, an antiabortion organization in Israel, enters the scene to ensure that this abortion law does not challenge Jewish demographic growth. I spent a year conducting interviews and observations and volunteering at EFRAT. Ruti Tidhar, the assistant director, was thrilled to have another native English speaker in the office who could do some translation work for them. Ruti immigrated to Israel almost thirty years prior. She agreed to allow me to collect research data as I volunteered. First Ruti gave me simple tasks—putting together a mailing, finding addresses for donors—but within a couple of months, she wanted me to call donors and thank them for their support and also call EFRAT's clients, women who were considering an abortion. I was shocked that Ruti asked me to help in this way, considering my lack of social work training and the fact that she did not really know my position on abortion. For Ruti, though, it did not matter whether I was in favor of or opposed to abortion, because she saw her organization as a "pro-woman" group, instead of a "pro-life" group. This became clear to me when she would not sign the consent form giving me access to EFRAT until I changed the descriptor of the organization to "pro-woman." In her mind, and reflected throughout EFRAT's mission, anybody who is supportive of women will help them have children.

The ideological seeds for EFRAT began in the 1950s, when a Holocaust survivor moved to Israel and discovered—to his surprise—that Jewish women were having abortions. Ruti explained this survivor's reaction to me, "After we had lost so many of our people, and he came to Israel and saw how many abortions were being done, he was horrified." In 1962, this Holocaust survivor founded the Association for the Encouragement of the Increase in the Birth Rate among the Jewish People.[16] Years later, in 1977, Dr. Eli Schussheim, a doctor previously unconnected to the issue, founded EFRAT and decided to devote all of his time to preventing abortions among Jewish women in Israel.

EFRAT has two primary objectives: to prevent "unnecessary" abortions and to increase the Jewish birth rate. "Unnecessary" abortions are those performed because of a family's financial struggles. In an interview with Dr. Schussheim, he explained the distinction between necessary and unnecessary abortions: "We are not opposed to abortions! We are for women who want to have their babies but cannot." EFRAT is not opposed to all abortions. Its medical experts determine when an abortion is necessary to preserve the health and life of the mother, and it provides support systems to women who discover during pregnancy that their fetuses will be born with disabilities. They counsel such women about whether abortion or birth is a better option for them. These are what EFRAT refers to as "necessary" abortions. EFRAT is, however, opposed to women having abortions because of economic difficulty. These are what EFRAT refers to as "unnecessary" abortions. EFRAT prevents these "unnecessary" abortions by offering financial incentives and gifts meant to offset the cost of raising young children. The distinction between necessary and unnecessary abortions demonstrates that EFRAT is aware of the fact that many women in Israel consider abortion due to financial difficulty. EFRAT maintains that although broadly abortion should be available, financial distress should not be a reason one terminates a pregnancy.

There are three antiabortion organizations in Israel today, but EFRAT is by far the biggest and the most prominent. EFRAT maintains four thousand women as clients each year. As a result EFRAT is much more well-known in

Israel, particularly among Haredi women. One of the other organizations is Bead Chaim, a name that means literally "pro-life," and is run by Messianic Jews, many of whom emigrated from English-speaking countries. Bead Chaim's primary mission is to prevent Jewish women from having abortions, a task its organizers see as hastening the arrival of Jesus Christ. Bead Chaim "saves" approximately seventy babies a year. EFRAT, however, claims it has prevented approximately forty-five thousand abortions since the early 1980s, including about four thousand per year for the last few years. The last antiabortion organization, Nefesh Achat B'Yisrael, translated by the organization as "Just One Life," has experienced significant funding challenges in recent years, and a lot of its work these days is more oriented toward helping women in the Russian immigrant community. According to the organization's director, although it began as a subset of EFRAT's work, its ideological differences led Just One Life to separate and form its own organization. It does not have the funding stream that either Bead Chaim or EFRAT maintains and, at the time of my research, was not focused on abortion prevention.

EFRAT is not explicitly religious, but due to its ties to the Haredi community and the prevalence of Haredi women who work there, EFRAT is often fielding questions about whether it is a Haredi organization. Chani, one of the Haredi women who has been working at EFRAT for ten years, told me she receives daily calls from women who are not Haredi and think that therefore they will not receive any help from EFRAT. Ruti also often fields these questions, and she answers, "No we are not a religious organization. We are a Jewish organization." What she means by this is that "we would never use religion as a reason. We would never come to women with a Jewish legal reason why she shouldn't have an abortion." Although they are concerned about abortion rates among Jews, this antiabortion organization is not concerned with the legalization of abortion or the procurement of an abortion because of religious or theological opposition to ending fetal life.

Despite the fact that the organization does not claim to be based on any religious principles, the Haredi community has come to ascribe to the organization some religious authority regarding abortions. Many Haredi women told me about "Rav" Schussheim, a rabbi who can help a woman determine whether she should have an abortion. Although Dr. Schussheim, the founder of EFRAT, is eager to point out that he will seek out rabbinic advice and is not a *rav* for the organization, the conflation of these titles among Haredi women is an indication of the overlap between medical and religious authorities, discussed in chapter 1. Schussheim is a doctor and serves as the medical director for the organization and a medical advisor for religious women and rabbis.

For instance, before Yom Kippur each year, EFRAT sets up a phone line for two nights where Schussheim is available to answer women's questions about fasting while pregnant. EFRAT has come to hold such an esteemed status in the Haredi community precisely because its approach to abortion prevention aligns with that of the Haredi rabbinic authorities. By offering medical advice in the case of fetal anomalies and counseling women on how to procure an abortion in these scenarios, yet recognizing that financial need is a common and generally unacceptable reason for terminating a pregnancy, EFRAT reflects Haredi attitudes toward abortion. Because of this, EFRAT has a unique relationship with the Haredi community in Israel.

FETAL DIAGNOSIS AND PRONATALIST CONCERNS

Recall Leah, who shared that she would immediately go to a rabbi for permission to terminate a pregnancy if it was discovered that the fetus would have a disability or die soon after birth. Leah and other Haredi women explained that it is easy to find a rabbi who will permit an abortion in this scenario because many rabbis see a woman's mental health as an extension of her physical health. Risk to a woman's life is widely considered an acceptable reason for abortion. Shira, the social worker and mother of five children whom I discussed in chapter 3, explained regarding abortions that "there are many rabbis that will deliver a legal judgment from the position of *shalom bayit* [a peaceful home] or for health [of the mother]."[17] Though she lowered her voice for this part of our conversation, indicating that there might be something illicit in what she was saying, Shira assured me that there is an abundance of guidance on these matters for the Haredi community. Shira's reference to shalom bayit and a mother's health as reasons for permitting abortion have been understood broadly to include a mother's mental health and the emotional and physical toll of having a disabled child. According to the women I spoke to, they know which rabbis will give permission for an abortion if the child born will threaten the stability of a marriage or any individual therein.

Abortions in the case of fetal diagnosis reveals that Haredi women understand these abortions as a preventative measure for their own mental health as well as their future reproductive potential.[18] When I asked about that hypothetical scenario, each woman spoke about how horrible it would be to wait nine months, expecting a healthy baby, only to find out that it would not survive. An abortion at any stage prior to full-term gestation is better than the alternative, according to these women. This is because a woman who gives birth to a baby with severe challenges will need to provide it with extra care and therefore likely will not have many more children. Alternatively, a woman whose baby dies soon after birth might be too traumatized to get pregnant soon after. When I asked women why abortions after fetal diagnosis were considered issues of shalom bayit, these were the types of explanations they provided. Although their answers reflected a vague understanding of the types of disabilities and how much extra help they might require, they feared most of all that a disabled child would disrupt their future reproductive lives.[19]

Concerns over the quality of Israeli Jewish children have proliferated in broader Israeli discourse alongside the pronatalist argument. Israeli reproductive medicine has been focused on diagnosing fetal anomalies in order to prevent the birth of disabled children that will impede their full participation in Israeli society. These concerns are often framed in the argument that Israel wants to build the army with strong, capable soldiers.[20] However, this does not apply to the Haredi community where the majority of individuals do not serve in the Israeli army. Instead, government rhetoric about the quality of Haredi children reflects a fear that poverty-stricken families have unrestrained fertility and become a drain on the Israeli economy. Larissa Remennick, who has written about the prominence of prenatal testing in Israel, explains, "The general message potential parents are receiving from this prevailing social milieu is: if you have a disabled or sick child, you will face all the consequences yourself, your child will be isolated and ostracized, will be a burden on you and on society."[21]

EFRAT unites the demographic concern with rhetoric about strengthening the Jewish population. EFRAT views each abortion it prevents as a contribution to the survival of Jews in Israel. This is because it sees each baby as not just one person but as representative of all the children that person will have and all the progeny that will come. In the late 1970s, Dr. Schussheim was working as a general physician when a woman came to him with her nine-year-old son, who needed stitches. Although Schussheim did not remember her, she thanked him for convincing her to maintain a pregnancy that other doctors told her to terminate. A decade prior, this woman had an X-ray while she was pregnant, and her doctors told her that the baby would be born with severe disabilities as a result. Schussheim, however, told her that latest studies show that diagnostic X-rays will not harm the fetus. Tidhar explained to me, "She had the baby and he was perfectly healthy, and that baby must be in his late thirties or early forties, a person with a big family. He [Schussheim] was shocked that by giving very simple medical information he was able to save this whole person. You know, not just a broken leg, but save a person. A whole person. And all of his generations to come. He was very moved by that." Decades ago, if Schussheim, like the other doctors, was convinced that this fetus would have been born with severe disabilities, he would not have convinced her to maintain the pregnancy. If that had been the case, then the baby would not have the demographic potential that they see in all healthy Jewish babies.

This can also be seen in the way that EFRAT pairs its donors with women thinking about abortion.[22] Although women never find out the name of the donor who "sponsored" their child, EFRAT believes that by assigning each baby to a donor, the donors can feel more connected to the process. Donations of at least $1,200 merit this pairing. When EFRAT sends the donor his or her first thank-you note during a woman's pregnancy, the donor is told of a woman's due date. After she gives birth and the baby has been named, the donors receive letters saying, "Mazal tov! I am pleased to inform you of the birth of 'your' child." Although "your" is in quotation marks, indicating that these children do not really belong to the donor, the letters reinforce the idea that without the donor, the baby would not exist. The letters continue, "Through your generous donations to EFRAT, Jewish children were given the gifts of existence and the privilege to see the light of day. You can see no greater return on your investment than the lives you saved, no greater dividend than the generations to come . . . These children will both increase the population of Israel and contribute to the survival of our Jewish nation." The letters promote the idea that this baby is not alone but considered part of the collective Jewish people and that this donation has helped increase the Jewish population in Israel. It is important to note, moreover, that as the letter references the increase in Jewish population and the "survival of the Jewish nation," it is referring to the fact the babies born should be healthy enough to serve in the army and then have children. This is because the Jewish nation refers to not just the Jewish people but also the state of Israel.

The process of cultivating a donor for EFRAT also emphasizes the pronatalist aspect of its work. In an English pamphlet designed for potential American donors, EFRAT lists eight reasons to become a donor. The first is "You are actually saving a life." Because EFRAT only aims to prevent abortions among women who need financial and social support, a monetary donation can go straight to providing women what they need. The second reason is that a donor is "making a demographic difference for Israel." The pamphlet explains, "You are helping Israel in its demographic struggle for survival as a Jewish State. EFRAT creates its own wave of 'Inner Aliya' by saving the lives of over 3,000 Jewish children each year." Inner aliyah (*aliyah pnimit*) usually refers to the pronatalist policies for Jews, which increase the Jewish population internally through reproduction. This is contrasted with policies known for encouraging the immigration of Jews

Figure 5.1. Brochure from the EFRAT organization for English-speaking donors: eight reasons to support EFRAT. Published with permission of the EFRAT organization.

to Israel, otherwise known as aliyah. EFRAT claims that its work of preventing the abortion of Jewish babies is a form of internal aliyah.

The staff of EFRAT feels strongly that each baby they "save" contributes to Israel as a state with a majority Jewish population. For example, EFRAT stays in touch with women whose children were born with EFRAT's help. During her child's birthday month, a woman receives a letter from EFRAT congratulating her on her child's birthday. I helped Rachel, one of EFRAT's employees, stuff these letters one day. Rachel commented that these letters are very "exciting" because it helps her think that the work they do at EFRAT actually helps create more Jewish lives. Ruti, more methodical in her intentions, maintains that these letters help to keep EFRAT on women's minds. She hopes that if they hear of a friend or relative who is considering abortion they will recommend EFRAT. Each month EFRAT sends out approximately eight hundred letters to a collection of women who gave birth during that month since 1997 (this is when it began a computer registry). The letters request that women send EFRAT a current picture of their child, which the organization then displays prominently on a wall in its offices. At the monthly staff meetings, EFRAT employees and volunteers look through these pictures on a slide presentation. Children are often photographed with various markers of Jewish identity, such as wearing costumes during the Jewish month of Adar to celebrate Purim or standing next to a hanukkiah (candelabra) as they celebrate Hanukkah. EFRAT employees love looking at these photos and seeing how their work has directly contributed to the growth of the Jewish people. They are proud of the work that they do, and at each meeting, they comment on the impact that they have. Ruti remembers many of the women and their unique stories, and at the staff meetings, she often adds personal details about a woman's struggles.

Schussheim discusses details of the stories he hears as well. At these staff meetings, he often shares letters he received during the month. For example, at one staff meeting I attended, Schussheim read a letter he received from a woman who had an abortion ten years prior. Although she thought that having an abortion would bring an end to her struggles, she realizes now that she has been trapped by her fears and her regret. Schussheim shared this letter as a reminder to his employees that the work they are doing is indeed helping women come to terms with the reality of abortion and offering them support, no matter what decision they make. At another monthly meeting, he shared a letter from one of EFRAT's volunteers that emphasizes the dire need for the work that they do. This volunteer shared that she met with a woman who is seven months pregnant and just found out she is carrying twins. In the letter, she wrote, "The woman told her doctor that she is not able to provide financial support for twins, and the doctor answered her saying that she should come the following week to an advanced ultrasound, and she will write that they found problems with the fetus. This way the [abortion] committee will permit the abortion." As he read the letter, the staff gasped and shook their heads, clearly disturbed by this doctor's proposal to lie to the committee. Although Schussheim acknowledges that he would support an abortion after a fetal diagnosis, he and the staff at EFRAT are opposed to the doctor's willingness to lie about a diagnosis when the real reason is financial. Schussheim frequently meets with couples in his office and offers them medical advice. They provide him with information about a fetal diagnosis that they received from the doctor, and he interprets the information and talks with them about what life would be like with a baby who has that diagnosis. Sometimes, he instructs them to get a second medical opinion because he is not convinced of the results of the test. Schussheim also understands, though, that there are circumstances where abortions would be necessary—namely, those where a mother's life is at risk or in cases of severe disability. These pictures and letters are intended to help EFRAT's employees and volunteers remember that the work they are doing—even if far removed from the women they serve—is helping increase the Jewish people through the birth of healthy Jewish babies.

EFRAT delicately balances the tension between pronatalism on the one hand and abortion for fetal disability or a mother's health on the other by understanding these abortions to be part of a larger goal of creating a physically strong Israeli army that can defend Israel. Furthermore, to ensure the reproduction of future generations, EFRAT's pronatalist rhetoric reflects an interest in the reproductive potential of all children. One of the rabbinic phrases EFRAT uses frequently on its advertisements, brochures, and letterhead is "Saving a life is equal to saving the world." This phrase reflects its interest in preventing abortion for the sake of the potential future generations. Haredi women acknowledge the pronatalist ethic but express this concern not in terms of what is good for the state but rather what is good for them and their families. Women consider how a disabled child might disrupt the rest of her family, her ability to work, and importantly, her ability to have more children. Inasmuch as a disabled child might interrupt her reproductive potential, Haredi women see those fetal diagnoses as threatening the existence of their own future children.

ABORTIONS FOR FINANCIAL NEED

While EFRAT considers abortions after a fetal diagnosis or that risk a woman's health "necessary" abortions because of the demographic challenge they pose,

Figure 5.2. Brochure from EFRAT. The phrase at the top refers to EFRAT as the largest life-saving organization in the world. The phrase in Hebrew at the bottom reads, "A lack of money is no reason to end a life." The child in the center is holding a globe, meant to refer to another one of the organization's slogans, "Saving a life is equal to saving the entire world." The speech bubble coming out of the child's mouth reads, "Aren't I worth NIS 4,500?!" The implication is that for NIS 4,500, a donor could save the whole world. Published with permission of the EFRAT organization.

it views abortions for financial need as "unnecessary abortions." On its website, EFRAT explains that its name derives from a biblical midrash of Yocheved and Miriam saving Israelite babies after the pharaoh's decree to kill all Israelite male babies. Shortly thereafter, Miriam received the name Efrat, which has some of the same letters as the Hebrew words *pru ur'voo* (be fruitful and multiply). The organization explains, "Miriam personally intervened, endangering her own life to save Jewish children from certain death. In addition, she provided the children's families with all their needs. As a result of her bravery, the Jews continued to multiply and the Jewish nation survived. We at EFRAT aspire to emulate Efrat's accomplishments and save the lives of unborn Jewish children."[23] EFRAT's antiabortion concern, then, is focused on women who cannot afford to have another child and seek abortion as a remedy.

In the way it decorates its office, advertises itself, and motivates its staff, EFRAT emphasizes what it views as the tragedy of a woman's financial situation determining her reproductive choices. One of its most famous slogans, plastered on billboards, bus stops, and promotional materials, is "We don't end a life because of money." The walls of EFRAT's small office in Jerusalem are covered with pictures of babies they have "saved" and newspaper articles that highlight the problem it is trying to address. Donors frequently visit the office to meet the staff, speak to Schussheim, and see the warehouse of gifts given to women who choose not to terminate their pregnancies. When a donor enters the cramped and busy offices, Schussheim takes them into his office and shows off the bulletin board of articles about EFRAT. The bulletin board fills an entire wall of his office, and it is overflowing with articles. Schussheim makes sure that each visitor sees one article in particular. It is from November 7, 2002, and was featured in the newspaper *Yediot Achronot*. The story is about a woman who had an abortion because she could not pay the debt she had accrued. The article discusses her various debts, and the woman says that she simply could not afford to have the baby. Schussheim and Tidhar explained to me and many other visitors that this story is typical in Israel and is precisely the problem they are trying to solve.

EFRAT does not provide financial support to just any woman who needs it. A woman needs to prove—during her pregnancy—that she will get an abortion if she does not receive EFRAT's financial help. First, a woman considering an abortion must call EFRAT or one of its three thousand volunteers all over the country. The volunteer assigned to her case develops a relationship with her and becomes a supportive friend. A woman then must submit documentation to EFRAT. She must show proof of her pregnancy, a note from her doctor, and a copy of the application to the abortion approvals committee in the hospital, if she has already applied. Most women reach out to EFRAT after receiving permission from a hospital's abortion committee. Ruti explained that she would rather reach women earlier because "it's hard to convince a person who is already on a runway." A woman must also submit information about her salary, debts she owes, where she lives, and how much rent she pays. The volunteer will also gather information about the involvement of a partner and whether he is pressuring her to have an abortion, as well as the woman's religious affiliation (secular, traditional, religious, or Haredi), information on her other living children, whether the applicant has procured an abortion in the past, and whether someone recommended that she abort this current pregnancy. Together with a woman's application form, this information helps EFRAT's committee understand how likely it is that this woman will get an abortion and therefore how deserving she is of EFRAT's financial help.

Shortly after a woman sends in her application, she receives a letter with the committee's decision. The committee, composed of external reviewers who consult Schussheim and Tidhar, divides applicants into three categories: those who are not considering abortion, those who are considering abortion but have not decided, and those who EFRAT has convinced not to have an abortion.

According to the committee, if not for EFRAT, this last group of women would have had an abortion. The first group receives a note explaining that EFRAT prefers to support women who are thinking about abortion and thus EFRAT cannot offer them any financial support. They are encouraged, however, to appeal to the committee if their financial status should change. These women have until twenty-five days after the birth to provide EFRAT with a birth certificate. The applicants who have not decided whether to have an abortion have fifteen days after the birth to fax the details of the birth to EFRAT's office. Once they receive this information, EFRAT sends them baby clothing. If a woman still needs EFRAT's help, she has another ten days to fax the birth certificate; at this point she can choose to receive a crib or a stroller and either diapers and food or a larger portion of diapers. The last group, those who have been convinced not to have an abortion, receive the most help from EFRAT because they are considered "saves." Like the other women, they must send in the birth certificate in a timely manner to prove that they did, in fact, give birth to the baby. EFRAT allows them to choose from a variety of baby items: a crib, stroller, or bath and food and diapers or just diapers for an entire year.

EFRAT describes the money and materials it provides women after the birth as the tools it uses to convince women not to abort. In a video sent to prospective donors, social workers, and even women considering abortion, Schussheim states that when a woman becomes a client, EFRAT promises her it will follow up with her and take upon itself all the monetary responsibilities of pregnancy and the new baby. He explains, "And these are the ways in which we convince a woman that she cannot have an abortion and cannot end the life." EFRAT's dual mission—supporting women and increasing the Jewish population—is accomplished by responding to the economic problems facing many Jewish families in Israel.

Frequently, women call into EFRAT after they have already given birth, hoping that EFRAT can help them with a gift of a stroller or a crib. Each time Ruti receives one of these calls, she apologizes but makes very clear that they do not help women who did not fill out an application during the pregnancy. This is because EFRAT is committed to preventing abortions through financial support. A woman who has already given birth is not going to terminate her pregnancy, so she cannot be considered a "save." Although this is the case for most women, EFRAT has a different approach to Haredi women who appeal to them after they have already given birth. On an otherwise quiet day volunteering, the staff at EFRAT argued passionately about a Haredi woman who called in that day asking for help. She has nine children and a baby who is eleven months old. One of her children needed to go to the hospital, and she called EFRAT to ask for a new stroller for the baby. The staff member who answered the phone did not know what to do, and Ruti was not in the office. As the staff, mostly religious women in their twenties, discussed this case, they debated about whether EFRAT is a *gemach*, a Jewish free loan fund that often carries supplies that can be loaned out to members of the Jewish community, or whether it should really only function to prevent abortions. Although Ruti was not there to resolve the dispute, she shared with me that these are common requests from Haredi families, and they try to provide help when the request arrives. This response differs significantly from the way Ruti responded to non-Haredi families in a similar scenario, and it speaks to both the unique relationship that EFRAT shares with the Haredi community and the fact that financial problems are particularly dire among Haredim.

Despite the fact that Israeli Haredi women work outside the home in a variety of professions, the Haredi population is suffering from extreme poverty. In 2010, the National Insurance Institute of Israel released a report indicating that one in four Israelis live below the poverty line. The report explains that most of the poor families are either Arab or ultra-Orthodox. Another report, this one released the same year by the Industry, Trade, and Labor Ministry, found that over half of the country's ultra-Orthodox citizens live below the poverty line.[24] This is much greater than the rate of poverty in the general population (19 percent). Sixty-seven percent of Haredi children are defined as poor.[25] Though Haredim only account for 10 percent of the population in Israel, they make up 20 percent of the country's poor citizens.[26] The average Haredi household has a gross monthly income that lags behind their non-Haredi peers.[27] Haredi men aged twenty-five to sixty-four earn on average approximately NIS 7,600 ($2,103) per month, while non-Haredi Jewish men earn almost NIS 12,800 ($3,542) each month. Women's monthly incomes lag much farther behind men overall, but Haredi and non-Haredi Jewish women's salaries are closer together. Haredi women earn NIS 5,900 ($1,633) while their non-Haredi counterparts earn NIS 8,500 ($2,352) each month.[28]

Earned income is so low because Haredi men's labor force participation differs significantly from their secular counterparts. Fifty-four percent of Haredi men participate in the workforce, meaning they are either actively employed or looking for work, as opposed to 91 percent of non-Haredi Jewish men. Haredi women's labor force participation, though, is almost equivalent to non-Haredi Jewish women.[29] However, their work hours, occupations, and, therefore, salaries differ significantly from the secular workforce. Fifty-nine percent of Haredi women work fewer than thirty-five hours per week, while only 24 percent of non-Haredi Jewish women work similar hours. Haredi women most frequently cite childcare responsibilities as reasons for their part-time work.[30] Additionally, a majority of Haredi women (53 percent) work in education, which carries a lower salary than other professions that are more popular in the non-Haredi workforce.[31] These figures might begin to shift in the coming decades, as the percentage of Haredi women engaged in academic study has been climbing. Now, 23 percent of Haredi women are pursuing or have pursued an academic degree, compared with 15 percent of Haredi men.[32] Lacking basic computer literacy, many Haredi men and women are severely limited in their job choices. Only 38 percent of Haredim use a computer, compared with 76 percent of secular individuals.[33] Recent research indicates that a higher percentage (50 percent) of Haredi women use the internet, primarily through their workplaces.[34]

Even though more Haredi men are entering the workforce, Haredi society in Israel maintains a culture of glorifying poverty in order to remain distinct from the surrounding non-Orthodox society.[35] This social structure encourages women, but not men, to work and earn an income for the family. In her research on poverty and mate preference among Haredim in Israel, Nechumi Yaffe explains, "This has produced a rare social structure in which men achieve status in the community, not through wealth accumulation, but through their religious devotion and achievements." In the matchmaking process, women look for mates who are respected as religious scholars. Once married, he often remains in a kollel as she enters the workforce. A married man in a kollel generally receives about NIS 1,500 (roughly $400) per month from the yeshiva, an amount that is subsidized by the Israeli government. Haredi men remain in a kollel despite their poverty because studying in a yeshiva signals a commitment to the group and its values of religious devotion and poverty.[36] The family's modest social security stipend increases with each child they have, but not enough to support a growing family.[37]

Recently, subsidies for families with many children have decreased dramatically, leading to a reduction in support for Haredi families in particular. The total fertility rates of ultra-Orthodox Jews climbed from 6.49 children per woman in the 1980s to 7.61 in the 1990s.[38] This increase in fertility followed an expansion of government support to the ultra-Orthodox community.[39] In 2003, however, government financial support decreased for these families. Prior to 2003, a family with 10 children received about NIS 6,000 each month. Now, however, that same family might receive only NIS 2,000 to NIS 3,000.[40] Total fertility rates have continued to drop, to around 6 children per woman, in the Haredi community, following the decrease in government stipends for these families. There are other ways that Haredi families receive government support. Married men receive stipends for remaining in a kollel, and Haredi families pay reduced tuition rates in preschool, elementary, and boarding schools. They pay reduced property taxes and health insurance premiums, and they benefit from the expansion of child allowances.[41] Because of the fact that these subsidies and other incentives enter the community through different sources, it is difficult to determine precisely how much government support the Haredi community receives.[42]

Since the 1960s, the Israeli government has struggled to figure out how to support large families in order to minimize the socioeconomic gap in Israeli society without disincentivizing work or leading to a drop in the birth rate.[43] Even during the British Mandate period, Yishuv leaders attempted to balance the tension between encouraging Jewish fertility and limiting the cost of social welfare programs.[44] This has been especially difficult given the fact that Jewish groups with the highest fertility rates have often been those requiring the most governmental aid. In response to Mizrahi advocacy groups, like the Israeli Black Panthers, the Israeli government reformed a program in 1975 to provide monthly child allowance grants that would offset the cost of raising large families. This program offered families subsidies for each child under the age of eighteen. In the tax reform of 1975, the government increased allowances significantly for higher birth-order children. The fourth child in a family, therefore, received a much higher allowance than the second child.[45] Although the program did little to reduce the rates of child poverty, after the tax reform of 1975, ultra-Orthodox women's fertility climbed significantly in response to the grants, doubling that of non-Orthodox Jewish women.[46]

High rates of poverty that accompany—and in some ways are a result of—high fertility rates and limited government support mean that financial concerns are often motivations of family size. Specifically, economic concerns are behind Haredi women's use of birth control.[47] Although Haredi women use different forms of birth control, from hormonal pills to IUDs and diaphragms, depending on preferences, there is also another way that women can avoid pregnancy. Women who do not use these forms of birth control because they do not want to ask their rabbi or because they do not think he will permit it, especially if their reasoning is financial, can make monthly visits to a clinic in Meah Shearim that will tell them if they are ovulating. For NIS 40 (US$11), they can walk into this clinic and get an ultrasound. If they find out that they are ovulating, women who do not want to get pregnant will avoid intercourse. This might not be a long-term solution, but it is relatively affordable and can be done with minimal medical or rabbinic involvement.

Sometimes, though, women do get pregnant, even when they do not expect it, and cannot afford another baby. In these cases, it is unlikely that a rabbi would approve of an early first trimester abortion for a woman and fetus who are otherwise healthy. Many women, however, do consider financial difficulties to be a sufficient reason for abortion. As the primary breadwinners and the primary caretakers in the Haredi community, Haredi women are more acutely aware of the financial stress a new baby would add to their family. In her forties with eleven children, Elisheva remembers a time when the Israeli government supported Haredi families more significantly, making it easier to raise large families. Although her youngest children are still at home, she is trying to buy an apartment for her oldest child and his wife, just as her own parents did for her, and she is struggling. For most Haredi individuals, the situation is more severe, and as a result, she sees a reduction in the Haredi community. Elisheva's description of the trend toward smaller family sizes included her feeling that this was not just a reduction in number but a lessening of Haredi values.

Although most women who appeal to EFRAT for financial or material support must show proof that they are considering abortion or that it is likely that they will terminate their pregnancies, Haredi women are not expected to provide EFRAT with that documentation because EFRAT is particularly interested in helping Haredi women maintain their high birth rates. Even if a Haredi woman is not seriously considering an abortion, EFRAT will provide these families with financial support. The staff are sympathetic to the high rates of poverty among Haredim, and they recognize Haredi women as significant contributors to Jewish demographic growth in Israel.

Ruti shared with me a few stories about Haredi women who received financial support despite not really seeking an abortion. A thirty-six-year-old Haredi woman reached out to EFRAT after her twins were born prematurely. The family has one other child at home and requested some financial help. The mother has lupus and the father studies in a kollel, so they do not have the means to support themselves. Ruti explained that this is representative of 90 percent of the Haredi women who reach out to EFRAT. These are women who have no intention of aborting. Some, like the thirty-six-year-old described, do not even apply until after the birth. Nonetheless, they need some help, and EFRAT functions as a kind of social welfare organization for them. Ruti says the help they offer is "symbolic": a month's supply of diapers, pacifiers, food, and bottles, worth about $400.

Ruti estimates that 10 percent of Haredi applicants, though, are considered "saves" in the true sense of the term. These are women who are contemplating abortion and have applied to the pregnancy termination committee at their hospital. When I was in the office, Ruti received an application from a Haredi woman who was pregnant with twins who would be her eighth and ninth children. She is divorced, though, and a different man is the father of the twins. Although he told her they would get married, he left her while she was pregnant. EFRAT had to promise her a great deal of financial support (some from other partner organizations) to convince her to continue the pregnancy, but it succeeded. Another woman applied to EFRAT because she was pregnant with her sixth child in five years. Her letter was filled with anguish over having to decide between having another child and supporting her other children. EFRAT also provided her with its largest package of support.

The concern that Haredi women would terminate pregnancies because they cannot afford to raise their children has occupied abortion discourse for decades. Although initially legislators focused on closing the social gap caused by the poverty among large Sephardi and Mizrahi families, the debate over legalizing abortion in the 1970s brought the plight of large Haredi families into greater focus. During the Knesset debates at that time, one of the most contested issues was the "fifth clause," otherwise known as the "socioeconomic clause." This stipulation would have allowed for abortion "when there is a possibility of disruption of the woman's life or the family's life (as with large families)."[48] The inclusion of this clause was motivated by the advocacy of Mizrahi organizations like the Israeli Black Panthers, who are previously mentioned, and likely directed at closing the social gap by helping these large and poor families limit their family size. However, religious members of Knesset (MKs) thought the clause was directed at Haredi women. This clause would have made it easy for a poor Haredi woman to procure an abortion, and the religious MKs wanted to avoid any possibility that poverty or family size should drive reproductive decisions among Haredi women.[49] In late 1979, the coalition government with Agudat Israel repealed the clause.[50] Although the abortion law does not officially permit abortion for financial reasons, the law still leaves room for women to terminate their pregnancies if they are unable to afford another child.[51] Haredi women in particular know that when they are in that position, they can either proceed with an abortion or turn to EFRAT for the financial support they need to care for another child.

EFRAT understands its role in this equation to be religiously sanctioned. In a promotional video for EFRAT, one scene features Dr. Schussheim holding a baby boy at the baby's circumcision. Schussheim delivers a small speech to accompany the event: "The rabbis say that there are three partners in the creation of a baby—Mom, Dad, and God. This creation that I'm holding in my hands has an additional partner: EFRAT."[52] Schussheim gives EFRAT credit because about six months earlier, the organization convinced this baby's mother not to end her pregnancy by offering her material support for the first year of the baby's life. Schussheim sees the financial support that EFRAT provided as equivalent to the contributions of the mother, the father, and God in the creation of this human being. This is because EFRAT maintains that to cultivate a higher birth rate among Jews in Israel, families require more financial support. By offering this financial support to women seeking abortions, EFRAT has created its own solution to the struggle between fertility and finances in Israel.

CONCLUSION: ABORTION, FERTILITY, AND FINANCES

Haredi women understand their reproductive authority to support many prenatal decisions, including prenatal testing, ultrasounds, and where to give birth. Women cannot make autonomous decisions about pregnancy termination, however, because abortion seems to challenge the shared goal that underlies women's reproductive authority: the reproduction of Haredi life. Certain types of abortions can be seen as consistent with this shared pronatalist goal, however. Specifically, Haredi women maintain that pregnancy termination following a poor fetal diagnosis, or when faced with a risk of injury or death to a woman, is not only understandable but also expected and rabbinically supported. There are two reasons for the support. One reason is that the continuation of these pregnancies would threaten a woman's reproductive future and her ability to create more children. Another reason, however, is that when women decide to terminate a pregnancy after a fetal diagnosis, they are thinking of the children already in existence, whom they are obligated to care for and support financially. If their time and energy is occupied with a child who has severe needs, it will threaten the health of their entire family. This is also the case for a pregnancy that threatens a woman's life. If she dies, the entire structure of her family must change. In this way, Haredi women's pronatalism is not just pro-birth but pro-family.

It is not as clear how an abortion for financial reasons could be supported by Haredi norms. Even Haredi women themselves deny that financial concerns drive their reproductive decisions. This is because Haredi society glorifies poverty. In order for Haredi society to support full-time yeshiva study for men, despite the high rates of poverty, they must believe that this life of financial instability has value. Terminating a pregnancy for financial reasons would be an affront to the glorification of poverty. In this case, poverty would become an obstacle to Haredi survival. If poverty became an acceptable reason to terminate pregnancies, rates of termination would skyrocket, or men would leave the kollel to get jobs. EFRAT's financial and material support of Haredi families reflects an awareness of the severe financial need that motivates reproductive decisions in the Haredi community.

The current Haredi economic structure, however, wherein women are achieving higher rates of education and employment, almost on par with their non-Haredi counterparts, is leading to a situation where financial concerns are challenging high rates of reproduction. Despite Haredi women's insistence that abortion for financial need runs counter to the goals and norms of the Haredi community, financial need is surely driving reproductive decisions. Haredi women are required to work in order to sustain Haredi men's full-time yeshiva study, and the birth of a child that prevents a woman's ability to support the family ultimately will prevent her husband's continued learning. In this way, abortions due to financial need allow these Haredi educational and economic norms to persist. These abortions, therefore, are not as rebellious as Haredi women seem to think. As Haredi women come to limit their family size due to financial considerations, they complicate the pronatalist discourse in Haredi communities. In addition to fetal health and future reproductive ability, then, financial considerations also function as a limit on pronatalism.

NOTES

1. Peters, *Trust Women*, 172.

2. For more on anencephaly, see Centers for Disease Control and Prevention, "Birth Defects."

3. See Taragin-Zeller, "Conceiving God's Children," for another example of this.

4. EFRAT has been accused of selling babies to ultra-Orthodox Jews in America. I did not encounter this in my research, though this is further evidence of the special relationship between EFRAT and Haredi Jews. See Shternbach and Weiss, "Baby Sellers."

5. Remennick, "Quest for the Perfect Baby"; Weiss, *Conditional Love*.

6. For more on disability studies and selective abortion, see Asch, "Prenatal Diagnosis and Selective Abortion"; Steinbock, "Disability, Prenatal Testing, and Selective Abortion"; and Parens and Asch, *Prenatal Testing and Disability Rights.*

7. For decades, this clause referred to women under the age of seventeen and over the age of forty. In 2014, the Ministry of Health expanded abortion coverage to include women under twenty and over thirty-three. Therefore, the rest of the clauses only apply to women between the ages of thirty-three and forty.

8. Amir and Benjamin, "Abortion Approval as a Ritual of Symbolic Control," 16.

9. Ibid., 20.

10. Steinfeld, "War of the Wombs."

11. Steinfeld, "War of the Wombs"; Central Bureau of Statistics, *Sociodemographic Characteristics of Women*.

12. Central Bureau of Statistics, *Sociodemographic Characteristics of Women*.

13. This was before the expanded coverage of abortion for women under thirty-three and over forty. This statistic applies to women who were under the age of twenty and over forty.

14. Israeli Ministry of Health, "Pregnancy Termination."

15. Rosenberg-Friedman, *Birthrate Politics in Zion*.

16. Steinfeld, "Wars of the Wombs," 10.

17. "Shalom bayit" is considered a more lenient reason, and "health of the mother" is also lenient since it is often stretched to account for her psychological health.

18. See Landsman, *Reconstructing Motherhood and Disability in the Age of "Perfect" Babies*," for more on this topic.

19. In *Testing Women, Testing the Fetus*, Rayna Rapp also finds that women do not receive sufficient information about what types of disabilities a baby might face after a fetal diagnosis. See also Imhoff, "Why Disability Studies Needs to Take Religion Seriously," for more on the vagueness within Jewish studies regarding different disabilities.

20. M. Weiss, *Chosen Body*.

21. Remennick, "Quest for the Perfect Baby," 26.

22. EFRAT does not receive any governmental support. It is supported entirely by donors.

23. See CRIB-EFRAT, "About Us."

24. Weiler-Polak, "Report: One in Four Israelis Live under Poverty Line."

25. *Statistical Report on Ultra-Orthodox Society in Israel*, 16.

26. Weiler-Polak, "Report: One in Four Israelis Live under Poverty Line"; Zrahiya, "More Than Half of Israel's Ultra-Orthodox Living in Poverty."

27. Weiler-Polak, "Report: One in Four Israelis Live under Poverty Line"; Zrahiya, "More Than Half of Israel's Ultra-Orthodox Living in Poverty."

28. *Statistical Report on Ultra-Orthodox Society in Israel*, 22.

29. Ibid., 19.

30. Ibid., 20.

31. Ibid., 20.

32. Ibid., 12.

33. Weiler-Polak, "Report: One in Four Israelis Live under Poverty Line"; Zrahiya, "More Than Half of Israel's Ultra-Orthodox Living in Poverty."

34. Neriya-Ben Shahar, "Negotiating Agency."

35. Yaffe et al., "Poor Is Pious." This is likely why the Haredi community reports satisfaction with its socioeconomic status despite high rates of poverty. See *Statistical Report on Ultra-Orthodox Society in Israel*, 16.

36. Berman, "Sect, Subsidy, and Sacrifice." For more on the kollel movement, see Schiffman and Finkelman, "Kollel Movement in the State of Israel."

37. All Israeli families receive subsidies for each child they have, and with their higher birth rates, Haredi families receive more in child subsidies. Families who are extremely poor also receive welfare money. Noah Efron, in *Real Jews*, found that these social welfare measures, combined with the fact that most Haredim do not serve in the army or pay taxes, give secular society the impression that Haredim are "parasites" on the Israeli public.

38. Fargues, "Protracted National Conflict and Fertility Change," 451.

39. For more on the correlation between fertility and subsidies, see Berman, "Subsidized Sacrifice"; Manski and Mayshar, "Private Incentives and Social Interactions."

40. Lidman, "As Ultra-Orthodox Women Bring Home the Bacon, Don't say the F-Word."

41. Berman, "Sect, Subsidy, and Sacrifice," 912.

42. N. Efron, *Real Jews*, 87–98. In fact, recent research reveals that some of the assumptions about the connection between Haredi political power and funding for education are mistaken. Despite increased political power, funding for Haredi pupils is decreasing. See Lipshits, "Budgeting for Ultra-Orthodox Education."

43. Schiff, "Politics of Fertility Policy in Israel."

44. Rosenberg-Friedman, *Birthrate Politics in Zion*.

45. Manski and Mayshar, "Private Incentives and Social Interactions," 187. Charles Manski and Joram Mayshar do not use total fertility rates because these are "a synthetic-cohort construct that may not adequately represent the childbearing decisions of actual women." Instead, they have used special data from the Central Bureau of Statistics that followed families from 1983 to 1995 (191).

46. Ibid., 194–95. Eli Berman, in "Sect, Subsidy and Sacrifice," argues that subsidies such as these had a significant influence on the rise in fertility among Haredi women, but Manski and Mayshar do not make that same causal connection, maintaining instead that there were many influences on women's fertility during this time.

47. Taragin-Zeller, "Conceiving God's Children"; Taragin-Zeller, "Towards an Anthropology of Doubt."

48. Yishai, "Abortion in Israel."

49. Raucher, "Cultural and Legal Reproduction of Poverty."

50. Portugese, *Fertility Policy in Israel*.

51. Raucher, "Cultural and Legal Reproduction of Poverty."

52. The original phrase comes from the Talmud, BT Kiddushim 30b.

—ⲱ—

CONCLUSION

Haredi Women's Bodies and Beyond

THIS BOOK HAS TOLD THE story of how Haredi women cultivate reproductive agency through their embodiment of pregnancy. This process engenders their religious authority. Doctors, rabbis, and the Israeli government attempt to control Haredi women's reproduction, and although Haredi women turn to their rabbis for most instruction in their lives, they reject any incursion into their reproductive authority. In this conclusion, I return to the main elements of my argument to emphasize how this research challenges prevailing methods and claims in two main bodies of scholarship: Jewish studies and religious ethics. Studying Haredi women's embodied religious experiences forces a reevaluation of what religious authority looks like and the sources from which it develops. Consequently, this book reexamines one of the fundamental tensions in religious studies—namely, the question of what defines a religion: people, scripture, or something else? The way we answer this question determines how we study religion, what we know about religious authority and the embodiment of authority figures, and how we construct religious ethics.

Scholarship in Jewish studies leans heavily toward the study of rabbinic texts, with some notable exceptions that have focused on the bodies of those who authored these rabbinic texts.[1] This is problematic because scholarship about Judaism excludes women when it focuses on literature to which women were not given access (as readers or authors) until recently. Moreover, Jewish studies scholarship that focuses on rabbinic texts to the tacit exclusion of other sources perpetuates the falsehood that texts, discourse, and rabbinic elites (both historical and contemporary) alone define Judaism. This book adds to a growing field of scholarship about Judaism that rejects this single definition of religious identity and religious authority.[2] I have turned to Haredi Judaism to see if, in fact, religious identity and authority are found through the knowledge of and adherence to rabbinic and scriptural texts. Haredi Judaism is where one would expect to find the strictest adherence to religious laws and thus the elevation of rabbinic authority above all else. What I discovered, however, is that when we listen to different voices—literally, the voices of Haredi women—we find that religious identity and religious authority also come from bodies.

Scholars of Haredi Judaism have continued to emphasize books over bodies as sources of religious authority. Research centers almost exclusively on Haredi men and on yeshiva learning, the epitome of the prioritization of book knowledge. It is not unusual to find that scholarship that purports to be about Haredi Jews is actually just about Haredi men—and even then, mostly about those men who study in yeshiva. See, for example, the recent eight-hundred-page book *Hasidism: A History*, which was written exclusively by men and consequently focuses almost entirely on Hasidic men.[3] The book claims to offer a comprehensive history of Hasidic Judaism, but Hasidic women are overlooked. Haredi women are taken up in sections of these larger texts or by a few noteworthy scholars, such as Ada Rapoport-Albert, Shayna Weiss, Kimmy Caplan, Lea Taragin-Zeller, Tsipy Ivry, and Tamar El Or.[4] However, the broad assumption is that Haredi Judaism is synonymous with Haredi men and, even more so, with the study of religious texts. This focus reinforces a male-oriented Haredi ideology about the role of books in the construction of authority. Most scholars have overlooked embodiment and the way it conveys, constructs, and threatens authority in Haredi life.

One possible reason for this is that the Haredi body in Israel is in tension with the ideal Israeli body. The imagined Zionist male body—muscular and tan, ready to fight in the army or work in the fields—was meant to construct a new secular Judaism. This image was intentionally contrasted with the religious bodies of Haredi men, pale and fragile, who are hunched over texts.[5] Gideon Aran writes, "Owing to the centrality of the body in Israeli discourse, disabled people, among others, are treated like second-class citizens. Similar reasons play a part in making the Haredim a marginal group with dubious status. A widespread perception among Israelis identifies the Haredi body as 'other' and also defective, grotesque and contemptible."[6] As Israelis came to view the Haredi body as grotesque, scholars focused instead on Haredi men, whose noncorporeal functions are supreme, leading to the concentration on yeshiva life. This approach, however, overlooks two important considerations: (1) Haredi men are also embodied, and (2) large segments of the Haredi population do not study in the yeshiva. It is not just Haredi women but also a growing percentage of Haredi men whose families cannot sustain this lifestyle. Scholarship, however, has reinforced the norm that to embody religious authority is to neglect one's body entirely, focusing instead on one's intellectual qualities.

Attention to Haredi bodies is usually reserved for studies of Haredi women; however, this scholarship has argued that women's bodies are subservient to the texts, conforming to religious norms at every turn.[7] Women's embodiment is at best subversive and at worst a handicap because of the way that bodies—particularly leaky ones—need to be controlled by the laws in the books. This scholarship assumes that women's bodies place them in a secondary position to men's noncorporeal identities. Owing to their access to the books, men can control their bodies in accordance with rabbinic instruction. Women's bodies, however, keep them from the books. Menstruation and childrearing responsibilities restrict women's access to rabbinic texts. In a circular fashion, women's lack of direct access to the texts results in their inability to control their own bodies. Therefore, the scholarship on women's bodies implies that women need men's book knowledge to help them control their bodies. In this vein, women's bodies are necessary (because they reproduce) but constantly under someone else's authority. Women hold an important but secondary status in Haredi Judaism because of their embodiment, which results in their bodies constantly being regulated by the books.

One might think that Haredi women's fertility rates would earn them an honorable status in the scholarship on reproduction in Israel. This scholarship surrounds the state's pronatalist agenda and the way that women have fought to satisfy the state's reproductive goals in quantity and quality of offspring. Many scholars have assumed that Haredi women embrace their childbearing role without question, merely following religious ideas of pronatalism. However, until very recently, nobody actually asked these women.[8] Scholarship on reproduction among Haredim in Israel seems to operate under the assumption that they have so many children because they are ignorant or passive. However, as Rhoda Kanaaneh demonstrated among Palestinian women in the Galilee, reproductive choices are expressions of national and ethnic identity.[9] For Haredi women, reproduction reflects their religious identity, but that does not mean it is performed in strict adherence to religious norms. By failing to investigate Haredi women's reproductive lives, scholars of reproduction in Israel have assumed, like scholars of Haredi Jews, that Haredi women performed reproductive tasks in obedience to religious norms—that their bodies were controlled by the books.

WOMEN AS EMBODIED RELIGIOUS AUTHORITIES

This ethnography of Haredi women demonstrates that embodiment is a source of authority among women. We are then forced to question the received understanding that books dictate, define, and control Haredi life.

On the one hand, the Haredi world understands that books, or the religious laws contained therein, offer instructions for controlling women's bodies. Women must wear clothing that conceals all bare skin and covers their hair. Their regular menstrual cycles are subject to complex religious laws that dictate when they can touch or even serve food to their husbands. Furthermore, their bodies, even when covered, are considered so sexually distracting to men that they are physically separated during prayer times and at many other times as well. From the perspective of Haredi men, women's bodies are not sources of authority but rather sources of shame and objects that must be controlled. In fact, women's bodies threaten men's ability to exercise their religious authority.

In this book, I have shown that bodily experience is much more important than books in women's reproductive agency. For Haredi women, their pregnant bodies are sources of authority. In this way, they challenge the established way of knowing in the Haredi world. Even if Haredi women use pregnancy advice books or rabbinic instruction received through friends or relatives, as they recounted in their conversations with me, Haredi women do not prioritize this knowledge. They claim that book knowledge and rabbinic instruction are misguided or naive when it comes to reproduction. Instead, they ascribe their knowledge and therefore their authority to their embodied experiences. This book has provided many examples of this kind of prioritization, but one more succinctly demonstrates this. I accompanied Ilana to an ultrasound late in her sixth pregnancy. Although she spoke confidently to me earlier in the pregnancy about how her body provided her all the information she needed, rejecting rabbinic and medical authority, Ilana confessed that she is always a little nervous going into the ultrasounds. As I sat in the room while she had her ultrasound, I noticed Ilana calm down considerably and smile while watching the image of an almost full-term fetus on the screen. The technician gave her a few photos to take home. Ilana held the photos in her hand, looking at them as we left the clinic. Suddenly, she shoved them into her purse, creasing them in a way that surprised me, given how thrilled she had been to see the pictures just a moment earlier. I asked her why she did that, and she said she saw her rebbetzin across the street. Ilana's rabbi does not approve of women getting ultrasounds because he is afraid they will get additional testing, or even an abortion, if they see something they do not like. Ilana explained, "I know he does not want me to get ultrasounds, but it makes me feel better to see the baby on the screen." Ilana could have prioritized her rabbi's instruction. He likely opposes ultrasounds and abortions based on his reading of rabbinic texts. Ilana, however, prioritized her own desire to get an ultrasound. After five pregnancies, she knows that the ultrasound will help her remain calm about the health of the fetus growing inside her. While on the one hand she is aware that her embodied experiences are valuable sources of authority, Ilana also knows that not everyone feels this way. Therefore, she hid the proof of her ultrasound before her rabbi's wife could see what she had done and report back to her husband.

Women's agency over reproductive decisions is based on this embodied authority, which they understand to be a source of religious authority. Bolstered by their intimate knowledge of the financial limitations of their families, the separation they maintain from their husbands, and the theological assertion that a pregnant woman embodies God's authority over creation, Haredi women draw on their pregnancy experiences as they make decisions in a way that contradicts normative religious doctrine yet is fully in line with Haredi theology and cultural ideology. Women make reproductive decisions based on their embodied authority, not on whether their actions will conform to rabbinic norms.

Haredi Judaism looks drastically different when we consider women's embodied experiences to be sources of authority and knowledge. For instance, as I explained in chapter 3, pregnancy is generally shrouded in silence and taboo, as Haredi Jews fear that discussing or celebrating a pregnancy will yield unwanted results or put the pregnancy in danger. Some, like Ronit in chapter 4, were fearful of the ways those around them could influence the developing fetus, but for the most part, Haredi women experienced pregnancy as an opportunity for authority. In fact, Haredi women's agency is possible because of these communal taboos. The silence gives them space to act without the interference of male authority figures. Instead of hiding a pregnancy or not wanting to discuss it, Haredi women claimed each pregnancy as a point of pride. They knew that each pregnancy conveyed more authority, and they harnessed that authority to escape the patriarchal forces surrounding them, including husbands, rabbis, and doctors. When we look at pregnancy from the point of view of Haredi women, we see that it is not merely a time of anxiety, waiting, or expecting. Instead, pregnancy is a time of learning, growing, and challenging the accepted knowledge in the community. Pregnancy is not a period of ten months between events with male participation—conception and birth. For Haredi women, pregnancy is a time of their religious authority.

Importantly, what becomes clear from this book is that pregnancy is a religious event. It is women's religious participation in Haredi Judaism. Pregnancy is how women connect to God, exercise religious authority, contribute to the future of Haredi Judaism, and hasten the coming of the Messiah. Repeated pregnancies provide women the opportunity to demonstrate their devotion to Haredi religious and communal ideals. Men demonstrate their devotion and participation in Haredi life through their book knowledge and their commitment to yeshiva learning. In many ways, the yeshiva is a locus for the reproduction of Haredi Jewish life. Along similar lines, pregnancy is a locus for the literal reproduction of Haredi life as well as the development of Haredi women's religious life. Pregnancy provides them with knowledge, just as yeshivas provide men with knowledge. Pregnancy generates the interpretation of key theological concepts in Haredi life—hishtadlut and bitachon. Pregnancy facilitates Haredi women's individual relationships with God. Reproduction is not merely a medical event to be regulated by the rabbis or doctors. Instead, it is a foundational time in Haredi women's religious development. In this way, pregnancy is a religious experience, and women's reproductive authority defines Haredi life, as much as the yeshiva and rabbinic authority define another part of Haredi life.

MEN ARE EMBODIED AUTHORITIES TOO

As I argue throughout the book that Haredi women prioritize their embodied authority, it is not the case that women alone draw on their embodied authority. Haredi men are also embodied, and their embodiment is inseparable from their authority. This book's focus on Haredi women's embodiment opens up new avenues of inquiry into the study of religious bodies as loci for authority.

Men's bodies carry significant cultural meaning, though they have not yet been recognized as signifiers or creators of authority. Within studies of Haredi Judaism, a few recent works have looked at Haredi men as corporeal beings, and not just those of intellectual and spiritual identity. For instance, Yehuda Goodman's article on ultra-Orthodox men at a mental health rehabilitation center explores the connection between mental illness and bodily action in the Haredi world. Although Goodman recognizes that Haredi men are embodied, he nonetheless insists that health and authority come when one is able to prioritize the texts and ensure bodily conformity to normative authorities.[10] Gideon Aran's ethnography of Haredi bodies is noteworthy and focuses almost exclusively on men's bodies.[11] And Lynn Davidman's work highlights Haredi men and women's embodiment.[12] These recent works, among others, recognize that to have a body is to be embodied—to have that body constructed and understood—within a particular historical, religious, and cultural context.[13]

Haredi men's embodiment is central to the construction of laws and norms that oppose viewing even their own naked bodies.[14] Different parts of their bodies are also ascribed different moral values. The penis, for instance, is understood to be "the essence of physicality and the sources of impurity," according to Aran.[15] Feet also hold special significance as the lowest part of one's body and therefore susceptible to exposure from demons or impurities on the ground. Haredi men, therefore, will always cover their feet with shoes or socks, even at night or when outside in warm weather.[16] Men's bodies, similar to women's bodies, are subject to the rabbinic laws that aim to mitigate exposure to impurity because of the potential for defilement or distraction.

Rabbinic laws and Haredi rabbis oppose the influence of embodiment in the construction of authority. During prayer and study, Haredi men often wear a belt (*gartel* in yiddish) that separates their upper body from their lower body.[17] The area above the belt represents the person, his spiritual center, his thoughts, heart, and holiness. The lower region is that which should be kept separate due to the possibility that it might corrupt one's identity. Haredi men see their lower bodies as the core of their physicality, and it is rejected as that which is potentially dangerous. This understanding implies that one's authority in rabbinic laws is due to one's ability to limit the influence of his body. Embodiment is therefore not only unnecessary but seen as an impediment toward the construction of religious authority.

While Haredi men deny the role of embodiment in constructing authority, their bodies nevertheless convey authority. Look simply at the way Haredi men's clothing choices align them with particular rabbinic leaders. Short pants or long coats, square hats or round ones, are public demonstrations of one's allegiances to the authorities they believe to be correctly interpreting the ancient laws. Haircuts also perform a similar function. The length of a man's *peyot* (sidelocks) or beard indicates a specific adherence to religious laws that he has deemed to be correct interpretations. Walking down the street of a Haredi neighborhood, one might see a variety of clothing choices and haircuts, each socially recognized as conveying one's commitment to particular rabbinic authorities. Haredi men also claim that wearing eyeglasses is an embodied sign of one's erudition. Aran found that they frequently state, "While the secular children are playing football, our children are reading the Torah, and that's why they are short-sighted."[18] Despite the fact that Haredi men use their bodies to convey this authority, discursively, they prioritize a hierarchy where book knowledge takes precedence. In an effort to dismiss embodiment as a critical source of knowledge and authority, they insist that one's body is only a reflection of the knowledge one has gained from learning Torah, as seen in the quote about eyeglasses.

In their reflection of book knowledge, though, their bodies are constructing an image of what authority looks like. The length of their hair, the type of clothing they wear, and the areas they enter or do not enter become externally recognized measures of their authority. Men's bodies, therefore, convey the authority they have gained through book learning, in much the same way that women's pregnant bodies convey the authority they have gained through the process of reproduction. Their bodies convey this authority because the community understands these symbols to refer to the attainment of particular goals of moral value to that community: yeshiva scholarship for men and motherhood for women. In other communities, their bodies do not convey authority but perhaps something else. This is what it means to live an embodied life: our bodily movements, the clothing we wear, and how we use our bodies to communicate with others is all shaped by our cultural context and is understood and valued within a cultural context. The discursive insistence on book knowledge for religious authority belies the awareness that one's embodiment actually holds great potential for religious authority. One's body has the potential to overtake one's mind or what the rabbis perceive as his true identity. As such a powerful force, it is subject to many laws that limit its influence. When so much effort has been made to control the influence of one's body, one is tacitly recognizing the fact that embodiment can also be a source of authority.

As we saw with Haredi women whose authority is limited to reproductive issues—and even then, only begins when they are pregnant for the third time—authority means many different things at different times. Religious authority shifts and evolves as one's embodiment changes across time and space. This is because religion itself is lived differently in different bodies, and each of those types of bodies deserve our attention as scholars attempting to understand religion. Future research with Haredi men should appreciate the influence of embodiment in religious authority instead of glossing over it or suggesting that one's body has a secondary role to one's intellect. Scholars of Judaism should continue to turn their attention to the variety of Jewish bodies—not just cis men and women, but also trans, gender nonconforming, disabled, young, old, racial minority, fat, and thin bodies. Scholarship on religious leaders and movements should pay more attention to the embodied elements of religious life, not merely the writings of prominent leaders. This, too, is religious authority.

EMBODIED AUTHORITY IN RELIGIOUS ETHICS

My emphasis on the connection between embodiment and religious authority offers an important corrective to the field of religious ethics as well. In an attempt to create normative religious guidelines on ethical issues, scholars have turned to books as sources of authority. In contrast to those who see religious ethics coming solely from sacred texts or rabbinic interpretations and legal applications, my analysis focuses on the self-consciously embodied moral agent who constructs a reproductive ethic that is intricately woven into her bodily experience and the cultural understanding of that bodily experience. When we see that normative religious ethics hold a secondary status on the ground, we are forced to reevaluate our methods in the field of religious ethics. Ethics—and religious ethics in particular—must be viewed from the perspective of embodied moral agents so that our ethical discourse can better reflect the lived realities of ethics.

Moreover, following the work of Aana Vigen and Christian Scharen, I maintain that ethnography among marginal voices is especially required to offer a corrective to the text-based methodology prominent in religious ethics and thereby construct a more ethical discourse of ethics.[19] Because of its reliance on the interpretation of rabbinic texts, Jewish ethics has, intentionally or not, marginalized women's voices.[20] More than twenty years after Dena Davis called for more female voices in Jewish ethics because that would improve the conversation, particularly on issues related to women's bodies, there are still few women involved in the academic field of Jewish ethics.[21] And those of us who are part of the conversation (and I would include here rabbis, clergy, *yoatzot halakha*) are among the most educated and privileged of Jewish women. Making Jewish texts the sine qua non of Jewish ethics means that anyone who does not have access to those texts is not part of the conversation. On a daily basis, however, Haredi women determine the most ethical action based on a variety of external and embodied values. Even when they know what a text-based response would be, they do not think these responses are appropriate. Attention to women's experiences and their approaches to ethics highlights the fact that the engagement with texts yields only part of a Jewish ethics discourse. Women's experiences provide us with an alternative discourse of ethics. This ethnography drives home the point that embodied individuals construct ethics based on those embodied experiences. This is as true for Haredi women as it is for contemporary Jewish ethicists, reading and interpreting texts based on their own embodiment.

The final question here is how an ethnography such as this one, embedded in a particular context, can speak to the global context of ethical questions. Can this ethnography provide us with normative reproductive ethics rather than a description of how one particular group of women makes reproductive decisions? The question, so often posed as a critique of ethnography as ethics, is flawed. The text-reliant approach is itself particular, yet more easily framed in universal terms. Legal codes incorporate limited voices and speak to (and from) a particular subset of the population, despite claiming to be universal and normative. As a method of ethics, ethnography is more transparent in its contextual commitments. Furthermore, ethics should consider the unique moral worlds and inescapable context of moral deliberation.[22] Bioethics especially cannot remain, as feminist scholar Margrit Shildrick wrote, "out of touch with bodies themselves."[23] Many advocate for conducting empirical or ethnographic research to respond to these critiques of bioethics, and some have already incorporated social science methods into bioethics.[24] Tensions remain over how to, in Arthur Kleinman words, "reconcile the clearly immense differences in the social and personal realities of moral life with the need to apply a universal standard to those fragments of experience that can foster not only comparison and evaluation but also action."[25]

What I suggest here as a takeaway from this account of reproductive ethics among Haredi women is not systematic reproductive ethics drawn from ethnographic findings but rather a demonstration of how the ethnographic method augments the ethical discourse. An ethnographic approach to ethics demonstrates the wide chasm between normative ethics and lived ethics, highlighting the many values that practitioners hold and negotiate. Ethnography can help fill this gap in normative ethics through a greater understanding of lived ethics. Scholars of religion who take an anthropological approach have argued that religion must be understood from within the context and varieties of lived religious practice.[26] To appreciate the lived realities of religious practitioners' lives is to complicate our notion of religion and to contextualize religious norms. So, too, with ethics and religious ethics in particular. The ethnographic approach to the study of religion and reproductive ethics that I have taken in this book provides the "thick description"[27] necessary for comprehending how financial, religious, cultural, familial, and political factors affect an individual's reproductive practices and should therefore reformulate reproductive ethics. Moreover, it demonstrates the impact that embodied experience has on religious identity, religious authority, and therefore religious ethics. Importantly, ethnography features the perspectives of individuals on the margins, instead of the perspectives of those in positions of privilege.

As the discourse itself becomes more ethical through the incorporation of ethnography, it will cultivate a more ethical response. The global context, then, is ethics discourse itself.

NOTES

1. Clearly, rabbinics does not make up the entirety of Jewish Studies, but this has been a strong current in the field, and a few scholars are looking at this literature as composed of embodied individuals. See, for example, D. Boyarin, *Carnal Israel*; Balberg, *Purity, Body, and Self in Early Rabbinic Literature*; Wasserfall, *Women and Water*.

2. This field has been populated by scholarship from a variety of areas, including history, literature, anthropology, and sociology, to name a few. Some examples include Sered, *What Makes Women Sick*; Sered, *Women as Ritual Experts*; Weissler, *Voices of the Matriarchs*; Magnus, *A Woman's Life*; Kay, *Seyder Tkhines*; S. Levine, *Mystics, Mavericks, and Merrymakers*; Fader, *Mitzvah Girls*; Benjamin, *Obligated Self*; Imhoff, *Masculinity and the Making of American Judaism*.

3. Biale et al., *Hasidism: A History*. See also Susannah Heschel and Sarah Imhoff, "Where Are All the Women in Jewish Studies?"

4. See El-Or, *Educated and Ignorant*; Rapoport-Albert, *Hasidic Studies*; Rapoport-Albert, "Emergence of a Female Constituency"; Caplan, "Internal Popular Discourse of Israeli Haredi Women"; S. Weiss, "Beach of Their Own"; Taragin-Zeller, "Conceiving God's Children"; Ivry, Teman, and Frumkin, "God-Sent Ordeals and Their Discontents."

5. S. Weiss, "Beach of Their Own."

6. Aran, "Denial Does Not Make the Haredi Body Go Away," 78.

7. Fader, *Mitzvah Girls*; S. Levine, *Mystics, Mavericks, and Merrymakers*; Sered, *Women as Ritual Experts*; Davidman, *Tradition in a Rootless World*; Benor, *Becoming Frum*.

8. A few notable exceptions are Teman and Ivry, "Pregnancy as a Way of Life"; Ivry, Teman, and Frumkin, "God-Sent Ordeals and Their Discontents"; Taragin-Zeller, "Towards an Anthropology of Doubt," "Between Modesty and Beauty," and "Have Six, Have seven, Have Eight Children"; and Birenbaum-Carmeli, "Your Faith or Mine."

9. Kanaaneh, *Birthing the Nation*.

10. Goodman, "You Look, Thank God, Quite Good on the Outside."

11. Aran, "Denial Does Not Make the Haredi Body Go Away."

12. Davidman, *Tradition in a Rootless World*.

13. See also Hakak, *From the Yeshiva to the Army*; Stadler, "Playing with Sacred/Corporeal Identities"; Aran, Stadler, and Ben-Ari, "Fundamentalism and the Masculine Body."

14. Aran "Denial Does Not Make the Haredi Body Go Away."

15. Ibid., 86.

16. Ibid., 87–88.

17. Ibid., 86–87.

18. Ibid., 85–86.

19. Scharen and Vigen, *Ethnography as Christian Theology and Ethics.*

20. See more in Raucher, "Ethnography and Jewish Ethics."

21. Davis, "Abortion in Jewish Thought." See, for example, the work of Zoloth, "Reading Like a Girl"; Henning, "Jewish Bioethics"; Belser, "Privilege and Disaster"; Filler, "Classical Rabbinic Literature and the Making of Jewish Ethics"; and Levi, "Polyvocal Body."

22. Gammeltoft, "Between 'Science' and 'Superstition'"; Kaufert and O'Neil, "Biomedical Rituals and Informed Consent"; Anspach, *Deciding Who Lives*; Bosk, *All God's Mistakes*; Gorden and Paci, "Disclosure Practices and Cultural Narratives"; Kaufman, "Construction and Practice of Medical Responsibility"; Zussman, "Contribution of Sociology to Medical Ethics."

23. Shildrick, "Beyond the Body of Bioethics," 2.

24. See, for example, Hoffmaster, "Can Ethnography Save the Life of Medical Ethics?"; Fox and Swazey, "Examining American Bioethics"; Nelson, *Stories and Their Limits*; Kleinman, *Writing at the Margin* and "Moral Experience and Ethical Reflection"; Anspach, *Deciding Who Lives*; and Bosk, *Forgive and Remember* and *All God's Mistakes.*

25. Kleinman, "Moral Experience and Ethical Reflection," 70.

26. See, for example, Orsi, "Everyday Miracles."

27. Geertz, *Interpretation of Cultures.*

WORKS CITED

Abraham, Abraham S. *Medical Halacha for Everyone: A Comprehensive Guide to Jewish Medical Law in Sickness and Health.* Jerusalem: Feldheim, 1980.

Abu-Lughod, Lila. "A Tale of Two Pregnancies." In *Women Writing Culture,* edited by Rutgh Behar and Deborah A. Gordon, 339–49. Berkeley: University of California Press, 1995.

Agadjanian, Victor. "Women's Religious Authority in a Sub-Saharan Setting: Dialectics of Empowerment and Dependency." *Gender and Society* 29, no. 6 (2015): 982–1008.

Amir, Delila, and Orly Benjamin. "Abortion Approval as a Ritual of Symbolic Control." In *The Criminalization of a Woman's Body,* edited by Clarice Feinman, 5–26. New York: Haworth, 1992.

———. "Defining Encounters: Who Are the Women Entitled to Join the Israeli Collective?" *Women's Studies International Forum* 20, no. 5/6 (1997): 639–50.

Anspach, Renee R. *Deciding Who Lives: Fateful Choices in the Intensive-Care Nursery.* Berkeley: University of California Press, 1993.

Aran, Gideon. "Denial Does Not Make the Haredi Body Go Away: Ethnography of a Disappearing (?) Jewish Phenomenon." *Contemporary Jewry* 26 (2006): 75–113.

Aran, Gideon, Nurit Stadler, and Eyal Ben-Ari. "Fundamentalism and the Masculine Body: The Case of Jewish Ultra-Orthodox Men in Israel." *Religion* 38 (2008): 30.

Asch, Adrienne. "Prenatal Diagnosis and Selective Abortion: A Challenge to Practice and Policy." *American Journal of Public Health* 89, no. 11 (1999): 1649–57.

Avishai, Orit. "'Doing Religion' in a Secular World: Women in Conservative Religions and the Question of Agency." *Gender and Society* 22, no. 4 (August 2008): 409–33.

Avishai, Orit, Lynne Gerber, and Jennifer Randles. "The Feminist Ethnographer's Dilemma: Reconciling Progressive Research Agendas with Fieldwork Realities." *Journal of Contemporary Ethnography* 42, no. 4 (2012): 394–426.

Balberg, Mira. *Purity, Body, and Self in Early Rabbinic Literature*. Berkeley: University of California Press, 2014.

Bangstad, Sindre. "Saba Mahmood and Anthropological Feminism after Virtue." *Theory, Culture, and Society* 28, no. 3 (2011): 28–54.

Bano, Masooda, and Hilary Kalmbach, eds. *Women, Leadership, and Mosques: Changes in Contemporary Islamic Authority*. Leiden, Netherlands: Brill, 2011.

Barilan, Yechiel Michael. *Jewish Bioethics: Rabbinic Law and Theology in Their Social and Historical Contexts*. Cambridge: Cambridge University Press, 2014.

Baumel, Samuel. *Sacred Speakers: Language and Culture among the Haredim in Israel*. New York: Berghahn Books, 2006.

Becker, Gay. *The Elusive Embryo: How Women and Men Approach New Reproductive Technologies*. Berkeley: University of California Press, 2000.

Belcove-Shalin, Janet. "Becoming More of an Eskimo: Fieldwork among the Hasidim of Boro Park." In *Between Two Worlds: Ethnographic Essays on American Jewry*, edited by Jack Kugelmass, 77–104. Ithaca, NY: Cornell University Press, 1988.

Belser, Julia Watts. "Privilege and Disaster: Toward a Jewish Feminist Ethics of Climate Silence and Environmental Unknowing." *Journal of the Society of Christian Ethics* 34, no. 1 (Spring/Summer 2014): 83–101.

Benjamin, Mara. *The Obligated Self: Maternal Subjectivity and Jewish Thought*. Bloomington: Indiana University Press, 2018.

Benjamin, Orly, and Hilla Ha'elyon. "Rewriting Fertilization: Trust, Pain and Exit Points." *Women's Studies International Forum* 25, no. 6 (2002): 667–78.

Benor, Sarah Bunin. *Becoming Frum: How Newcomers Learn the Language of Orthodox Judaism*. New Brunswick, NJ: Rutgers University Press, 2012.

Ben Shitrit, Lihi. "Women, Freedom, and Agency in Religious Political Movements: Reflections from Women Activists in Shas and the Islamic Movement in Israel." *Journal of Middle East Women's Studies* 9, no. 3 (2013): 81–107.

Berkovitch, Nitza. "Motherhood as a National Mission: The Construction of Womanhood in the Legal Discourse in Israel." *Women's Studies International Forum* 20, no. 5/6 (1997): 605–19.

Berman, Eli. "Sect, Subsidy, and Sacrifice: An Economist's View of Ultra-Orthodox Jews." *Quarterly Journal of Economics* 115, no. 3 (2000): 905–53.

———. "Subsidized Sacrifice: State Support of Religion in Israel." *Contemporary Jewry* 20, no. 1 (1999): 167–200.

Berninson, Ilana. "Time of Labor—Time of Cancellation." [Hebrew.] In *Hachana Ruchanit L'Leida*, edited by Moshe and Dafna Hasdai, 51–52. N.p.: n.p.

Biale, David, David Assaf, Benjamin Brown, Uriel Gellman, Samuel Heilman, Moshe Rosman, Gadi Sagiv, and Marcin Wodzinski, eds. *Hasidism: A New History*. Princeton, NJ: Princeton University Press, 2018.

Bilu, Yoram. "From Milah (Circumcision) to Milah (Word): Male Identity and Rituals of Childhood in Jewish Ultra-Orthodox Communities." *Ethos* 30, no. 2 (2003): 172–203.

Birenbaum-Carmeli, Dafna. "Reproductive Policy in Context: Implications on the Rights of Jewish Women in Israel, 1945–2000." *Policy Studies* 24, no. 2 (2003): 101–14.

———. "Your Faith or Mine: A Pregnancy Spacing Intervention in an Ultra-Orthodox Jewish Community in Israel." *Reproductive Health Matters* 16, no. 32 (2008): 185–191.

Boas, Hagai, Yael Hashiloni-Dolev, Nadav Davidovitch, Dani Filc, and Shai J. Lavi, eds. *Bioethics and Biopolitics in Israel*. Cambridge: Cambridge University Press, 2018.

Bordo, Susan. "The Body and the Reproduction of Femininity." In *Writing on the Body: Female Embodiment and Feminist Theory*, edited by Katie Conboy, Nadia Medina, and Sarah Stanbury, 90–112. New York: Columbia University Press, 1997.

Bosk, Charles. *All God's Mistakes: Genetic Counseling in a Pediatric Hospital*. Chicago: University of Chicago Press, 1992.

———. *Forgive and Remember: Managing Medical Failure*. Chicago: University of Chicago Press, 1979.

Boyarin, Daniel. *Carnal Israel: Reading Sex in Talmudic Culture*. Berkeley: University of California Press, 1993.

Boyarin, Jonathan. "Waiting for a Jew: Marginal Redemption at the Eighth Street Shul." In *Between Two Worlds: Ethnographic Essays on American Jewry*, edited by Jack Kugelmass, 52–76. Ithaca, NY: Cornell University Press, 1988.

Bronner, Ethan, and Isabel Kershner. "Israelis Facing a Seismic Rift over Role of Women." *New York Times*, January 14, 2012. http://www.nytimes.com /2012/01/15/world/middleeast/israel-faces-crisis-over-role-of-ultra-orthodox -in-society.html?pagewanted=1&ref=opinion.

Brown, Tamara Mose, and Erynn Masi di Casanova. "Mothers in the Field: How Motherhood Shapes Fieldwork and Researcher-Subject Relations." *Women's Studies Quarterly* 37, no. 3/4 (2009): 42–57.

Browner, Carole H., and Nancy Press. "The Normalization of Prenatal Diagnostic Screening." In *Conceiving the New World Order*, edited by Faye D. Ginsburg and Rayna Rapp, 307–22. Berkeley: University of California Press, 1995.

Brusa, Margherita, and Yechiel Michael Barilan. "Childbirth in Israel: Home Birth and Newborn Screening." In *Bioethics and Biopolitics in Israel: Socio-Legal, Political, and Empirical Analysis*, edited by Hagai Boas, Yael Hashiloni-Dolev,

Nadav Davidovitch, Dani Filc, and Shai J. Lavi, 180–201. Cambridge: Cambridge University Press, 2018.

Bucar, Elizabeth M. *Creative Conformity: The Feminist Politics of U.S. Catholic and Iranian Shi'i Women*. Washington, DC: Georgetown University Press, 2001.

———. "Dianomy: Understanding Religious Women's Moral Agency as Creative Conformity." *Journal of the American Academy of Religion* 78, no. 2 (2010): 662–86.

Bynum, Carolyn Walker. *Holy Feast and Holy Fast: The Religious Significance of Food to Medieval Women*. Berkeley: University of California Press, 1987.

Campbell, Heidi. "Religious Engagement with the Internet within Israeli Orthodox Groups." *Israel Affairs* 17, no. 3 (2007): 364–83.

———. "'What Hath God Wrought': Considering How Religious Communities Culture (or Kosher) the Cell Phone." *Continuum: Journal of Media and Cultural Studies* 21, no. 2 (2007): 191–203.

Caplan, Kimmy. "God's Voice: Audiotaped Sermons in the Haredi World." *Modern Judaism* 17, no. 3 (1997): 253–79.

———. "The Internal Popular Discourse of Israeli Haredi Women." *Archives de sciences sociales des religions* 48, no. 123 (July/September 2003): 77–101.

———. "The Media in Haredi Society in Israel." [Hebrew.] *Kesher* 30 (2001): 18–30.

Centers for Disease Control and Prevention. "Birth Defects: Facts about Anencephaly." December 5, 2019. https://www.cdc.gov/ncbddd/birthdefects/anencephaly.html.

Central Bureau of Statistics. "Families, by Type of Family, Religious Lifestyle of Persons Residing in the Dwelling, Size of Family, and Population Group 2017." Jerusalem: Central Bureau of Statistics, 2018.

———. "Fertility Rates, by Age and Religion." Vital Statistics—Statistical Abstract of Israel 2018—No. 69. Subject 3, table 13. September 20, 2018. https://www.cbs.gov.il/en/publications/Pages/2018/Vital-Statistics-Statistical-Abstract-of-Israel-2018-No-69.aspx.

———. *Sociodemographic Characteristics of Women Applying for Pregnancy Terminations in Israel 2003*. Publication No. 1324 (May 2008). Jerusalem: Central Bureau of Statistics, 2008.

Chajut, Aya. "Shlomo Artzi Denounces Ban on Women Artists at Benefit Concert." *Haaretz*, October 31, 2019. https://www.haaretz.com/israel-news/.premium-shlomo-artzi-denounces-ban-on-women-artists-at-benefit-concert-1.8059768.

Chaves, Mark. *Ordaining Women: Culture and Conflict in Religious Organizations*. Boston: Harvard University Press, 1997.

Clare, Stephanie. "Agency, Signification, and Temporality." *Hypatia* 24, no. 4 (2009): 50–62.

Cohen, Yoel. *God, Jews and the Media*. London: Routledge, 2012.

CRIB-EFRAT. "About Us: Why the Name 'Efrat'?" Accessed January 22, 2020. http://www.efrat.org.il/english/about/?id=66.

Csordas, Thomas. "Embodiment as a Paradigm for Anthropology." *Ethos* 18, no. 1 (1990): 5–47.

Czarnecki, Danielle. "Moral Women, Immoral Technologies: How Devout Women Negotiate Gender, Religion, and Assisted Reproductive Technologies." *Gender and Society* 29, no. 5 (2015): 716–42.

Dahari, Sylvia, and Tami Perlman. "Labor—Next to God in Prayer." [Hebrew.] In *Hachana Ruchanit L'Leida*, edited by Moshe and Dafna Hasdai, 34–35. N.p.: n.p.

Das, Veena. *Life and Words: Violence and the Descent into the Ordinary.* Berkeley: University of California Press, 2006.

Davidman, Lynn R. *Becoming Un-Orthodox: Stories of Ex-Hasidic Jews.* Oxford: Oxford University Press, 2015.

———. *Tradition in a Rootless World: Women Turn to Orthodox Judaism.* Berkeley: University of California Press, 1991.

———. "Truth, Subjectivity, and Ethnographic Research" In *Personal Knowledge and Beyond: Reshaping the Ethnography of Religion*, edited by James V. Spickard, J. Shawn Landres, and Meredith B. McGuire, 17–26. New York: NYU Press, 2002.

Davis, Dena S. "Abortion in Jewish Thought: A Study in Casuistry." *Journal of the American Academy of Religion* 60, no. 2 (Summer 1992): 313–24.

———. "Beyond Rabbi Hiyya's Wife: Women's Voices in Jewish Bioethics." *Second Opinion* 16 (March 1991): 10–30.

———. "Method in Jewish Bioethics." In *Theology and Medicine: Religious Methods and Resources in Bioethics*, edited by Paul F. Camenisch, 109–26. Dordrecht, Netherlands: Kluwer Academic Publishers, 1994.

Davis-Floyd, Robbie E. *Birth as an American Rite of Passage.* Berkeley: University of California Press, 1992.

Davis-Floyd, Robbie E., and Elizabeth Davis. "Intuition as Authoritative Knowledge in Midwifery and Home Birth." In *Childbirth and Authoritative Knowledge: Cross-Cultural Perspectives*, edited by Robbie E. Davis-Floyd and Carolyn F. Sargent, 315–49. Berkeley: University of California Press, 1996.

Diprose, Rosalyn. *The Bodies of Women: Ethics, Embodiment and Sexual Difference.* London: Routledge, 1994.

Doorn-Harder, Pieternella van. *Women Shaping Islam: Reading the Qur'an in Indonesia.* Urbana: University of Illinois Press, 2006.

Dorff, Elliot. *Matters of Life and Death: A Jewish Approach to Modern Medical Ethics.* Philadelphia: Jewish Publication Society, 1998.

Duncan, Ann W. "Sacred Pregnancy in the Age of the 'Nones.'" *Journal of the American Academy of Religion* 85, no. 4 (December 2017): 1089–115.

Efron, John M. *Medicine and the German Jews: A History.* New Haven: Yale University Press, 2001.

Efron, Noah. *Real Jews: Secular vs. Ultra-Orthodox and the Struggle for Jewish Identity in Israel*. New York: Basic Books, 2003.

Eilberg-Schwartz, Howard. *People of the Body: Jews and Judaism from an Embodied Perspective*. Albany: State University of New York Press, 1992.

El-Or, Tamar. *Educated and Ignorant: Ultraorthodox Jewish Women and Their World*. Boulder: Lynne Rienner Publishers, 1994.

Ellenson, David H. "How to Draw Guidance from a Heritage: Jewish Approaches to Mortal Choices." In *Contemporary Jewish Ethics and Morality*, edited by Elliot N. Dorff and Louis E. Newman, 129–39. New York: Oxford University Press, 1995.

Fader, Ayala. *Mitzvah Girls: Bringing up the Next Generation of Hassidic Jews in Brooklyn*. Princeton, NJ: Princeton University Press, 2009.

———. "Nonliberal Jewish Women's Audiocassette Lectures in Brooklyn: A Crisis of Faith and the Morality of Media." *American Anthropologist* 115, no. 1 (2013): 72–84.

———. "Reflections on Queen Esther: The Politics of Jewish Ethnography." *Contemporary Jewry* 27, no. 1 (2007): 112–36.

———. "Ultra-Orthodox Jewish Interiority, the Internet, and the Crisis of Faith." *HAU: Journal of Ethnographic Theory* 7, no. 1 (2017): 185–206.

Fagenblat, Michael. *A Covenant of Creatures: Levinas' Philosophy of Judaism*. Stanford: Stanford University Press, 2010.

Fargues, Philippe. "Protracted National Conflict and Fertility Change: Palestinians and Israelis in the Twentieth Century." *Population and Development Review* 26, no. 3 (2000): 441–82.

Fassin, Didier, ed. *A Companion to Moral Anthropology*. Chichester, UK: Wiley-Blackwell, 2012.

Filler, Emily. "Classical Rabbinic Literature and the Making of Jewish Ethics: A Formal Argument." Paper presented at the Annual Meeting of the Society for Jewish Ethics, January 9–12, 2014, Seattle, Washington.

Finkelman, Yoel. "The Ambivalent Haredi Jew." *Israel Studies* 19, no. 2 (2014): 264–93.

Finkelstein, Michal, and Baruch Finkelstein. *B'Shaah Tovah: Madrich Refui Hilchati Lherayon v'Leida*. Jerusalem: Feldheim, 2002. Published in English as *Nine Wonderful Months: B'Sha'ah Tovah; The Jewish Woman's Clinical and Halachic Guide to Pregnancy and Childbirth*. Jerusalem: Feldheim, 2001.

Firer, Elimelech. "Lots of Ways to Help Heal." [Hebrew.] Accessed January 14, 2020. https://www.ezra-lemarpe.org/articleoffirer.

Fobersky, Dov. "Bikur Cholim Belongs to the Haredi Community." [Hebrew.] *B'Hadrei Haredim*, September 14, 2009. https://www.bhol.co.il/news/109358. Originally accessed September 2010; content of the page has since been updated.

Foucault, Michel. *Power/Knowledge: Selected Interviews and Other Writings 1972–1977*. Edited by Colin Gordon. Brighton: Harvester Press, 1980.

———. "The Subject and Power." In *Michel Foucault: Beyond Structuralism and Hermeneutics*, edited by Hubert L. Dreyfus and Paul Rabinow, 208–28. Brighton, UK: Harvester Press, 1982.

Fox, Renee C. "Observations and Reflections of a Perpetual Fieldworker." *Annals of the American Academy of Political and Social Science* 595 (2004): 309–326.

Fox, Renee, and Judith Swazey. "Examining American Bioethics: Its Problems and Prospects." *Cambridge Quarterly of Healthcare Ethics* 14, no. 4 (October 2005): 361–73.

Franklin, Sarah. "Postmodern Procreation: A Cultural Account of Assisted Reproduction." In *Conceiving the New World Order*, edited by Faye D. Ginsburg and Rayna Rapp, 323–45. Berkeley: University of California Press, 1995.

Friedman, Menachem. "Back to Grandmother: The New Ultra-Orthodox Woman." *Israel Studies* 1, no. 1 (1988): 21–26.

———. "The Haredim and the Israeli Society." In *Whither Israel? The Domestic Challenges*, edited by Keith Kyle and Joel Peters, 177–201. London: I. B. Taurus, 1994.

———. "The Haredi Society." [Hebrew.] Jerusalem: Jerusalem Institute for Israel Studies, 1991.

———. "Life Tradition and Book Tradition in the Development of Ultraorthodox Judaism." In *Israeli Judaism*, edited by Shlomo Deshen, Charles Seymour Liebman, and Moshe Shokeid, 127–48. New Brunswick: Transaction Publishers, 1995.

Fuchs, Theresa Sophie. "'This Time I Was a Person': Orthodox Jewish Home Birthers' Conceptualizations of (Home)Birth in Israel." MA thesis, Free University of Berlin, 2016.

Gammeltoft, Tine. "Between 'Science' and 'Superstition': Moral Perceptions of Induced Abortion among Young Adults in Vietnam." *Culture, Medicine, and Psychiatry* 26, no. 3 (October 2001): 313–38.

Galahar, Ari. "Haredi Matchmaking Rates Skyrocketing." *Ynet News*, May 31, 2009. http://www.ynetnews.com/articles/0,7340,L-3723775,00.html.

Gantz, Michal. "Childbirth and Women's Strength in the Haredi Community in Israel." [Hebrew.] MA thesis, Hebrew University, 2003.

Gaster, Theodor H. *Customs and Folkways of Jewish Life*. New York: William Sloane, 1966.

Geertz, Clifford. *The Interpretation of Cultures: Selected Essays*. New York: Basic Books, 1973.

Geiger, Brenda, and Dorit Alt. "Haredi/Chabad Women's Acculturation Experience in a Non-Haredi Institute of Higher Education in Northern Galilee." *Women in Judaism: A Multidisciplinary Journal* 11, no. 1 (2014): 1–25.

Georges, Eugenia. "Fetal Ultrasound Imaging and the Production of Authoritative Knowledge in Greece." *Medical Anthropology Quarterly*, n.s., 10, no. 2 (1996): 157–75.

Ghosh, Nandini. "Doing Feminist Ethnography: Exploring the Lives of Disabled Women." *Indian Anthropologist* 42, no. 1 (2012): 11–26.

Gil, Tami. "To Give Birth at Bikur Cholim." [Hebrew.] *B'Hadrei Haredim*, March 6, 2011. https://www.bhol.co.il/news/79702.

Gilson, Erinn. *The Ethics of Vulnerability: A Feminist Analysis of Social Life and Practice.* New York: Routledge, 2014.

Ginsburg, Faye D., and Rayna Rapp. *Conceiving the New World Order.* Berkeley: University of California Press, 1995.

Goldin, Sigal. "Technologies of Happiness: Fertility Management in a Pro-Natal Context." In *Citizenship Gaps: Migration, Fertility, and Identity,* edited by Adriana Kemp and Yonah Yona, 265–302. Jerusalem: Van Leer, 2008.

Goodman, Yehuda. "'You Look, Thank God, Quite Good on the Outside': Imitating the Ideal Self in a Jewish Ultra-Orthodox Rehabilitation Site." *Medical Anthropological Quarterly* 23, no. 2 (2009): 122–41.

Goodman, Yehuda, and Eliezer Witztum. "Cross-Cultural Encounters between Careproviders: Rabbis Referral Letters to a Psychiatric Clinic in Israel." *Social Science and Medicine* 55, no. 8 (2002): 1309–23.

Gorden, Deborah, and Eugenio Paci. "Disclosure Practices and Cultural Narratives: Understanding Concealment and Silence around Cancer in Tuscany, Italy." *Social Science and Medicine* 44, no. 10 (June 1997): 1433–52.

Gordis, Daniel H. "Wanted—The Ethical in Jewish Bio-Ethics." *Judaism* 38, no. 1 (1989): 28–40.

Goshen-Gottstein, Esther R. *Growing Up in Geula: Mental Health Implications of Living in an Ultra-Orthodox Jewish Group.* Ramat Gan, Israel: Bar Ilan University, School of Education, 1980.

Glazer, Nurit. "Spiritual Preparation for Labor." [Hebrew.] In *Hachana Ruchanit L'Leida,* edited by Moshe and Dafna Hasdai, 12–33. N.p.: n.p.

Gribetz, Sarit Kattan. "Pregnant with Meaning: Women's Bodies as Metaphors for Time in Biblical, Second Temple, and Rabbinic Literature." In *The Construction of Time in Antiquity: Ritual, Art and Identity,* edited by Jonathan Ben-Dov and Lutz Doering, 173–204. Cambridge: Cambridge University Press, 2017.

Griffith, R. Marie. *God's Daughters: Evangelical Women and the Power of Submission.* Berkeley: University of California Press, 2001.

Haelyon, Hilla. "'Longing for a Child': Perceptions of Motherhood among Israeli-Jewish Women Undergoing In Vitro Fertilization Treatments." *Nashim: A Journal of Jewish Women's Studies and Gender Issues* 12 (Fall 2006): 177–202.

Hakak, Yohai. *From the Yeshiva to the Army.* [Hebrew]. Jerusalem: Floersheimer Institute for Policy Studies, 2003.

Halbertal, Moshe. "On Belief and Believers." [Hebrew.] In *On Faith: Studies in the Concept of Faith and Its History in Jewish Tradition,* edited by Moshe Halbertal, David Kurtsvail and Avi Sagi, 11–38. Jerusalem: Keter Press, 2005.

Han, Sallie. *Pregnancy in Practice: Expectation and Experience in the Contemporary US*. New York: Berghahn Books, 2013.

Harris, Gillian, Linda Connor, Andrew Bisits and Nick Higginbotham. "Seeing the Baby: Pleasures and Dilemmas of Ultrasound Technologies for Primiparous Australian Women." *Medical Anthropology Quarterly* 18, no. 1 (2004): 23–47.

Harwood, Karey. *The Infertility Treadmill: Feminist Ethics, Personal Choice, and the Use of Reproductive Technologies*. Chapel Hill: University of North Carolina Press, 2007.

Hashiloni-Dolev, Yael. "The Effect of Jewish-Israeli Family Ideology on Policy Regarding Reproductive Technologies." In *Bioethics and Biopolitics in Israel: Socio-Legal, Political, and Empirical Analysis*, edited by Hagai Boas, Yael Hashiloni-Dolev, Nadav Davidovitch, Dani Filc, and Shai J. Lavi, 119–38. Cambridge: Cambridge University Press, 2018.

Heilman, Samuel. *Defenders of the Faith: Inside Ultra-Orthodox Jewry*. Berkeley: University of California Press, 1992.

Heilman, Samuel, and Menachem Friedman. "Religious Fundamentalism and Religious Jews: The Case of the Haredim." In *Fundamentalisms Observed*, edited by Martin E. Marty and R. Scott Appleby, 197–264. Chicago: University of Chicago Press, 1991.

Henning, Alyssa. "Jewish Bioethics: Tracing Its Past, Mapping Its Present and Shaping Its Future." Paper presented at the Annual Meeting of the Society of Jewish Ethics, January 4, 2013, in Chicago, Illinois.

Heschel, Susannah, and Sarah Imhoff. "Where Are All the Women in Jewish Studies?" *Forward*, July 3, 2018. https://forward.com/culture/404416/where-are-all-the-women-in-jewish-studies/.

Hoffmaster, Barry. "Can Ethnography Save the Life of Medical Ethics?" *Social Science and Medicine* 35, no. 12 (December 1992): 1421–32.

Imhoff, Sarah. *Masculinity and the Making of American Judaism*. Indiana: Indiana University Press, 2017.

———. "Why Disability Studies Needs to Take Religion Seriously." *Religions* 8, no. 9 (2017): 186. https://doi.org/10.3390/rel8090186.

Inbari, Motti. "The Modesty Campaigns of Rabbi Amram Blau and the Neturei Karta Movement, 1938–1974." *Israel Studies* 17, no. 1 (2012): 105–29.

Inhorn, Marcia C. *Local Babies, Global Science: Gender, Religion, and In Vitro Fertilization in Egypt*. New York: Routledge, 2003.

Irshai, Ronit. *Fertility and Jewish Law: Feminist Perspectives on Orthodox Response Literature*. Waltham, MA: Brandeis University Press, 2012.

Isak, Dorit. "Morbidity Characteristics for Breast Cancer Regarding Population Groups of Different Religious Levels." [Hebrew.] MA thesis, Hebrew University, 2001.

Israeli Ministry of Health. *Pregnancy Termination According to the Law, 1990–2007*. [Hebrew.] Israeli Ministry of Health: Jerusalem, 2008.

Ivry, Tsipy. *Embodying Culture: Pregnancy in Japan and Israel.* New Brunswick, NJ:
    Rutgers University Press, 2010.
———. "Kosher Medicine and Medicalized Halacha: An Exploration of Triadic
    Relations among Israeli Rabbis, Doctors, and Infertility Patients." *American
    Ethnologist* 37, no. 4 (2010): 662–80.
Ivry, Tsipy, Elly Teman, and Barbara A. Bernhardt. "Pregnancy as a Proclamation
    of Faith: Ultra-Orthodox Jewish Women Navigating the Uncertainty of
    Pregnancy and Prenatal Diagnosis." *American Journal of Medical Genetics* 155,
    Part A (2011): 69–80.
Ivry, Tsipy, Elly Teman, and Ayala Frumkin. "God-Sent Ordeals and Their
    Discontents: Ultra-Orthodox Jewish Women Negotiate Prenatal Testing." *Social
    Science and Medicine* 72, no. 9 (2011): 1527–33.
Jakobovits, Immanuel. *Jewish Medical Ethics: A Comparative and Historical Study
    of the Jewish Religious Attitude to Medicine and Its Practice.* New York: Bloch
    Publishing, 1975.
Jeffay, Nathan. "In Israel, Haredi and Muslim Women Are Having Fewer
    Children." *Forward,* July 15, 2011. http://forward.com/articles/139391
    /in-israel-haredi-and-muslim-women-are-having-fewer/.
Jordan, Brigitte. "Authoritative Knowledge and Its Construction." In *Childbirth and
    Authoritative Knowledge: Cross-Cultural Perspectives,* edited by Robbie Davis-Floyd
    and Carolyn F. Sargent, 55–79. Berkeley: University of California Press, 1997.
———. "Cosmopolitan Obstetrics: Some Insights from the Training of
    Traditional Midwives." *Social Science and Medicine* 28, no. 9 (1989): 925–44.
Kahn, Susan Martha. "Making Technology Familiar: Orthodox Jews and
    Infertility Support, Advice, and Inspiration." *Culture, Medicine and Psychiatry* 30
    (2006): 467–80.
———. "Rabbis and Reproduction: The Uses of New Reproductive Technologies
    among Ultra-Orthodox Jews in Israel." In *Infertility around the Globe,* edited
    by Marcia C. Inhorn and Frank Van Balen, 283–97. Berkeley: University of
    California Press, 2002.
———. *Reproducing Jews: A Cultural Account of Assisted Conception in Israel.*
    Durham, NC: Duke University Press, 2000.
Kanaaneh, Rhoda Ann. *Birthing the Nation: Strategies of Palestinian Women in
    Israel.* Berkeley: University of California Press, 2002.
katzeyefilms. "Bishvilaych—The Evelyne Barnett Women's Comprehensive
    Medical Center." August 19, 2010. YouTube video, 6:06. https://www.youtube
    .com/watch?v=zYoYouH-P_U.
Kaufert, Joseph M., and John D. O'Neil. "Biomedical Rituals and Informed
    Consent: Native Canadians and the Negotiation of Clinical Trust." In *Social
    Science Perspectives on Medical Ethics: Culture, Illness and Healing,* vol. 16, edited
    by George Weisz, 41–64. Dordrecht, Netherlands: Springer, 1990.

Kaufman, Sharon R. "Construction and Practice of Medical Responsibility: Dilemmas and Narratives from Geriatrics." *Culture, Medicine and Psychiatry* 21, no. 1 (March 1997): 1–26.

Kaul-Seidman, Lisa R. "Fieldwork among the Ultra-Orthodox: The Insider-Outsider Paradigm Revisited." *Jewish Journal of Sociology* 44 (2002): 30–55.

Kay, Devra. *Seyder Tkhines: The Forgotten Book of Common Prayer for Jewish Women*. Philadelphia: Jewish Publication Society, 2004.

Kelly, Kimberly. "In the Name of the Mother: Renegotiating Conservative Women's Authority in the Crisis Pregnancy Center Movement." *Signs: Journal of Women in Culture and Society* 38, no. 1 (2012): 203–30.

Keshet, Yael, and Ido Liberman. "Coping with Illness and Threat: Why Non-religious Jews Choose to Consult Rabbis on Healthcare Issues." *Religion and Health* 53 (2014): 1146–60.

Klassen, Pamela E. *Blessed Events: Religion and Home Birth in America*. Princeton, NJ: Princeton University Press, 2002.

———. "The Scandal of Pain in Childbirth." In *Suffering Religion*, edited by Elliot R. Wolfson and Robert Gibbs, 73–93. New York: Routledge, 2002.

Kleinman, Arthur. "Moral Experience and Ethical Reflection: Can Ethnography Reconcile Them? A Quandary for 'The New Bioethics.'" *Daedalus* 128, no. 4 (1999): 69–97.

———. *Writing at the Margin: Discourse between Anthropology and Medicine*. Berkeley: University of California Press, 1995.

Korteweg, Anna. "The Sharia Debate in Ontario: Gender, Islam, and Representations of Muslim Women's Agency." *Gender and Society* 22, no. 4 (2008): 434–54.

Landsman, Gail. *Reconstructing Motherhood and Disability in the Age of "Perfect" Babies*. New York: Routledge, 2009.

Lave, Jean, and Etienne Wenger. *Situated Learning: Legitimate Peripheral Participation*. New York: Cambridge University Press, 1991.

Lazarus, Ellen. "What Do Women Want? Issues of Choice, Control, and Class in Pregnancy and Childbirth." *Medical Anthropology Quarterly* 8, no. 1 (1994): 25–46.

Lehmann, David, and Batia Siebzehner. "Holy Pirates: Media, Ethnicity and Religious Renewal in Israel." In *Religion, Media, and the Public Sphere*, edited by Birgit Meyer and Annelies Moors, 91–111. Bloomington: Indiana University Press, 2006.

———. "Power Boundaries and Institutions: Marriage in Ultra-Orthodox Judaism." *Archives of European Sociology* 50, no. 2 (2009): 273–307.

Leon, Nissim. "The Political Use of the Teshuva Cassette Culture in Israel." *Contemporary Jewry* 31 (2011): 91–106.

Levi, Rebecca J. E. "A Polyvocal Body: Mutually Corrective Discourses in Feminist and Jewish Bodily Ethics." *Journal of Religious Ethics* 43, no. 2 (June 2015): 244–67.

Levine, Stephanie W. *Mystics, Mavericks, and Merrymakers: An Intimate Journey among Hasidic Girls*. New York: New York University Press, 2003.

Lidman, Melanie. "As Ultra-Orthodox Women Bring Home the Bacon, Don't Say the F-Word." *Times of Israel*, January 1, 2016. https://www.timesofisrael.com /as-ultra-orthodox-women-bring-home-the-bacon-dont-say-the-f-word/.

Lipshits, Hadar. "Budgeting for Ultra-Orthodox Education—The Failure of Ultra-Orthodox Politics, 1996–2006." *Israel Studies* 20, no. 2 (2015): 135–62.

Mackler, Aaron. *Introduction to Jewish and Catholic Bioethics: A Comparative Analysis*. Washington, DC: Georgetown University Press, 2003.

Maffi, Irene. *Women, Health and the State in the Middle East: The Politics and Culture of Childbirth in Jordan*. London: I. B. Tauris, 2013.

Magnus, Shulamit. *A Woman's Life: Pauline Wengeroff and Memoirs of a Grandmother*. Portland, OR: Littman Library of Jewish Civilization, 2016.

Mahmood, Saba. "Feminist Theory, Embodiment, and the Docile Agent: Some Reflections on the Egyptian Islamic Revival." *Cultural Anthropology* 6, no. 2 (2001): 202–36.

———. *Politics of Piety: The Islamic Revival and the Feminist Subject*. Princeton, NJ: Princeton University Press, 2012.

Manski, Charles F., and Joram Mayshar. "Private Incentives and Social Interactions: Fertility Puzzles in Israel." *Journal of the European Economic Association* 1, no. 1 (2003): 181–211.

Markowitz, Fran. "Blood, Soul, Race, and Suffering: Full Bodied Ethnography and Expressions of Jewish Belonging." *Anthropology and Humanism* 31, no. 1 (2006): 41–56.

Martin, Emily. *The Woman in the Body*. Boston: Beacon Press, 1987.

Mattingly, Cheryl, and Jason Throop. "The Anthropology of Ethics and Morality." *Annual Review of Anthropology* 47 (2018): 475–92.

Merom, Nava. "Spiritual Treatment." [Hebrew.] In *Hachana Ruchanit L'Leida*, edited by Moshe and Dafna Hasdai, 60–66. N.p.: n.p.

Miller, Richard. "On Making a Cultural Turn in Religious Ethics." *Journal of Religious Ethics* 33, no. 3 (September 2005): 409–43.

Mitchell, William. "A Goy in the Ghetto: Gentile-Jewish Communication in Fieldwork Research." In Between Two Worlds: Ethnographic Essays on American Jewry, edited by Jack Kugelmass, 225–39. Ithaca, NY: Cornell University Press, 1988.

Morgan, Lynn M. "Magic and a Little Bit of Science: Technoscience, Ethnoscience, and the Social Construction of the Fetus." In *Bodies of Technology: Women's Involvement in Reproductive Medicine*, edited by Ann R. Saetnan, Nelly Oudshoorn, and Marta Kirejczyk, 355–67. Columbus: Ohio State University, 2000.

National Insurance Institute of Israel. "Covering the Mother's Hospitalization Expenses." Accessed January 2020. https://www.btl.gov.il/English%20Home page/Benefits/Maternity%20Insurance/Pages/Hospitalizationgrant.aspx.

Nehushtan, Hilla. "The Impurities of Experience: Researching Prostitution in Israel." In *Ethnographic Encounters in Israel: Poetics and Ethics of Fieldwork*, edited by Fran Markowitz, 187–200. Indiana: Indiana University Press, 2013.

Nelson, Hilde Lindemann, ed. *Stories and Their Limits: Narrative Approaches to Bioethics*. New York: Routledge, 1997.

Neriya-Ben Shahar, Rivka. "'For We Ascend in Holiness and Do Not Descend': Jewiish Ultra-Orthodox Women's Agency through Their Discourse about Media." *Journal of Modern Jewish Studies* 18, no. 2 (2019): 212–26.

———. "Negotiating Agency: Amish and Ultra-Orthodox Women's Responses to the Internet." *New Media and Society* 19, no. 1 (2017): 81–95.

Newman, Louis. "What Are We Doing When We Do Jewish Ethics? Halakha, Aggadah, and Contemporary Jewish Ethical Discourse." Paper presented at the Annual Meeting of the Society of Jewish Ethics, January 9–12, 2014, Seattle, Washington.

Orsi, Robert. "Everyday Miracles: The Study of Lived Religion." In *Lived Religion in America: Toward a History of Practice*, edited by David Hall, 3–21. Princeton, NJ: Princeton University Press, 1997.

Parens, Eric, and Adrienne Asch. *Prenatal Testing and Disability Rights*. Washington, DC: Georgetown University Press, 2000.

Peshkova, Svetlana. "Leading against Odds: Muslim Women Leaders and Teachers in Uzbekistan." *Journal of Feminist Studies in Religion* 31, no. 1 (2015): 23–44.

Peters, Rebecca Todd. *Trust Women: A Progressive Christian Argument for Reproductive Justice*. Boston, MA: Beacon Press, 2018.

Portugese, Jacqueline. *Fertility Policy in Israel: The Politics of Religion, Gender, and Nation*. Westport, CT: Praeger, 1998.

Porush, Tova. "A Study of Pre-marital Education Predominantly within the Haredi Community." MA thesis, Touro College, 1993.

Rapoport-Albert, Ada. "The Emergence of a Female Constituency in Twentieth Century HaBaD." In *"Let the Old Make Way for the New": Studies on Hasidism and Its Opponents, Haskalah and the Musar Movement*, edited by Ada Rapoport-Albert, David Assaf, Israel Bartal, Shmuel Feiner. Jerusalem: Zalman Shazar Center for Jewish History, 2009.

———. *Hasidic Studies: Essays in History and Gender*. Liverpool, UK: Littman Library of Jewish Civilization, 2018.

Rapp, Rayna. "Refusing Prenatal Diagnosis: The Meanings of Bioscience in a Multicultural World." *Science, Technology and Human Values* 23, no. 1 (1998): 45–70.

———. *Testing Women, Testing the Fetus: The Social Impact of Amniocentesis in America*. New York: Routledge, 2000.

Rashi, Tsuriel. "The Kosher Cell Phone in Ultra-Orthodox Society: A Technological Ghetto within the Global Village?" In *Digital Religion: Understanding Religious*

Practice in New Media Worlds, edited by Heidi A. Campbell, 173–82. London: Routledge, 2013.

Raucher, Michal. "Be Fruitful and Multiply. . . Except. . . ." In *The Oxford Handbook on Religious Perspectives on Reproductive Ethics*, edited by Dena Davis. Oxford: Oxford University Press, forthcoming 2020.

———. "The Cultural and Legal Reproduction of Poverty: Abortion Legislation in Israel." *Journal of Feminist Studies in Religion* 30, no. 1 (2014): 147–56.

———."Ethnography and Jewish Ethics: Lessons from a Case Study in Reproductive Ethics." *Journal of Religious Ethics* 44, no. 4 (2016): 636–58.

———. "Feminist Ethnography Inside and Outside the Field." Feminist Studies in Religion. May 18, 2018. http://www.fsrinc.org/feminist-ethnography-parenting/.

———. "Whose Womb and Whose Ethics? Surrogacy in Israel and in Jewish Ethics." *Journal of Jewish Ethics* 3, no. 1 (2017): 68–91.

Ravitsky, Vardit, and Michael Gross. "Israel: Bioethics in a Jewish-Democratic State." *Cambridge Quarterly of Healthcare Ethics* 12, no. 3 (2003): 247–55.

Raz, A. E., and Vizner, Y. "Carrier Matching and Collective Socialization in Community Genetics: Dor Yeshorim and the Reinforcement of Stigma." *Social Science and Medicine* 67, no. 9 (2008): 1361–69.

Remennick, Larissa. "Childless in the Land of Imperative Motherhood: Stigma and Coping among Infertile Israeli Women." *Sex Roles* 43, no. 11–12 (2000): 821–41.

———. *Fertility Regulation Problem: The Israeli Scene in the International Context.* Jerusalem: Israel Women's Network, 1996.

Remennick, Larissa, and Amir Hetsroni. "The Quest for the Perfect Baby: Why Do Israeli Women Seek Prenatal Genetic Testing?" *Sociology of Health and Illness* 28, no. 1 (2006): 21–53.

Rinaldo, Rachel. "Pious and Critical: Muslim Women Activists and the Question of Agency." *Gender and Society* 28, no. 6 (2014): 824–46.

Robbins, Joel. "Between Reproduction and Freedom: Morality, Value, and Radical Cultural Change." *Ethnos* 72, no. 3 (2007): 293–314.

Roberts, Elizabeth. *God's Laboratory: Assisted Reproduction in the Andes.* Berkeley: University of California Press, 2012.

Rock-Singer, Cara. *Prophetesses of the Body: American Jewish Women and the Politics of Embodied Knowledge.* Submitted in partial fulfillment of the requirements for the degree of doctor of philosophy in the Graduate School of Arts and Sciences, Columbia University, 2018.

Rosenberg-Friedman, Lilach. *Birthrate Politics in Zion: Judaism, Nationalism, and Modernity under the British Mandate.* Bloomington: Indiana University Press, 2017.

Rosner, Fred. "Autopsy in Jewish Law and the Israeli Autopsy Controversy." In *Jewish Bioethics*, edited by J. David Bleich and Fred Rosner, 331–48. New York: Hebrew Publishing Company, 1979.

Rosner, Fred, and J. David Bleich, eds. *Jewish Bioethics*. Hoboken: KTAV Publishing, 2000.

Rothman, Barbara K. *The Tentative Pregnancy: Prenatal Diagnosis and the Future of Motherhood*. New York: Viking Penguin, 1987.

Saetnan, Ann R. "Thirteen Women's Narratives of Pregnancy, Ultrasound, and Self." In *Bodies of Technology: Women's Involvement in Reproductive Medicine*, edited by Ann R. Saetnan, Nelly Oudshoorn, and Marta Kirejczyk, 331–54. Columbus: Ohio State University, 2000.

Sandelowski, Margarete. "Compelled to Try: The Never-Enough Quality of Conceptive Technology." *Medical Anthropology Quarterly*, n.s., 5, no. 1 (1991): 29–47.

Scharen, Christian, and Aana Vigen. *Ethnography as Christian Theology and Ethics*. New York: Continuum, 2011.

Schiff, Gary. "The Politics of Fertility Policy in Israel." In *Modern Jewish Fertility, Studies in Judaism and Modern Times*, vol. 1, edited by Paul Ritterband, 225–78. Leiden, Netherlands: Brill, 1981.

Schiffman, Daniel, and Yoel Fikelman. "The Kollel Movement in the State of Israel: A Pedagogical and Ideological Typology." *Israel Studies Review* 29, no. 1 (2014): 106–28.

Schneider, Carl J., and Dorothy Schneider. *In Their Own Right: The History of American Clergywomen*. New York: Crossroad, 1997.

Schwartz, Shuly. *The Rabbi's Wife: The Rebbetzin in American Jewish Life*. New York: NYU Press, 2007.

Seeman, Don. "Ethnography, Exegesis, and Jewish Ethical Reflections: The New Reproductive Technologies in Israel." In *Kin, Gene, Community: Reproductive Technologies among Jewish Israelis*, edited by Daphna Birenbaum-Carmeli and Yoram S. Carmeli, 340–62. New York: Berghahn Books, 2010.

Seidman, Naomi. *Sarah Schenirer and the Bais Yaakov Movement: A Revolution in the Name of Tradition*. Liverpool: Liverpool University Press, 2019.

Sered, Susan Starr. "Food and Holiness: Cooking as a Sacred Act among Middle-Eastern Jewish Women." *Anthropological Quarterly* 61, no. 3 (1988): 129–39.

———. "Healing as Resistance: Reflections upon New Forms of American Jewish Healing." In *Religion and Healing in America*, edited by Linda L. Barnes and Susan S. Sered, 231–52. New York: Oxford, 2005.

———. "Rachel's Tomb: Societal Liminality and the Revitalization of a Shrine." *Religion* 19, no. 1:27–40.

———. "Religious Rituals and Secular Rituals: Interpenetrating Models of Childbirth in a Modern, Israeli Context." *Sociology of Religion* 54, no. 1 (1993): 101–14.

———. *What Makes Women Sick? Maternity, Modesty and Militarism in Israeli Society*. Hanover: University Press of New England, 2000.

————. *Women as Ritual Experts: The Religious Lives of Elderly Jewish Women in Jerusalem.* Oxford: Oxford University Press, 1992.

Shalev, Carmel, and Sigal Goldin. "The Uses and Misuses of In Vitro Fertilization in Israel: Some Sociological and Ethical Considerations." *Nashim: A Journal of Jewish Women's Studies and Gender Issues* 12, no. 1 (2006): 151–76.

Shapira, Amos. "In Israel, Law, Religious Orthodoxy and Reproductive Technologies." *Hastings Center Report* 17, no. 3 (1987): 12–14.

Shaw, Rhonda. "Performing Breastfeeding: Embodiment, Ethics and the Maternal Subject." *Feminist Review* 78, no. 1 (2004): 99–116.

Shildrick, Margrit. "Beyond the Body of Bioethics: Challenging the Conventions." In *Ethics of the Body: Postconventional Challenges,* edited by Margrit Shildrick and Roxanne Mykitiuk, 1–28. Cambridge: Massachusetts Institute of Technology Press, 2005.

Shternbach, Ariella, and Arik Weiss. "Baby Sellers: The Women Who Were Forced to Sell Their Babies to Haredi Families." [Hebrew.] *Hadashot 13.* September 14, 2019. https://13news.co.il/item/news/domestic/articles/baby-sellers-358215/?fbclid=IwARopHoYZHdJ8SVkkJm6yRhUZ63MvAftpPrRyafwTmA2PJ66-MMKBisutX6o.

Shvarts, Shifra. *Health and Zionism: The Israeli Health Care System, 1948–1960.* New York: University of Rochester Press, 2008.

Siegal, Gil, ed. *Bioethics Blue and White: Bioethics and Medical Law in Israel.* [Hebrew.] Jerusalem: Bialik Publishing, 2015.

Sinclair, Daniel B. *Jewish Biomedical Law: Legal and Extra-Legal Dimensions.* Oxford: Oxford University Press, 2003.

Soloveitchik, Haym. "Rupture and Reconstruction: The Transformation of Contemporary Orthodoxy." *Tradition* 28, no. 4 (1994): 64–130.

Stacey, Judith. "Can There Be a Feminist Ethnography?" *Women's Studies International Forum* 11, no. 1 (1988): 21–27.

Stadler, Nicolas, and Lea Taragin-Zeller. "Like a Snake in Paradise: Fundamentalism, Gender, and Taboos in the Haredi Community." *Archives de sciences sociales des religions,* 2017/1, no. 177:133–56.

Stadler, Nurit. "Is Profane Work an Obstacle to Salvation? The Case of Ultra-Orthodox (Haredi) Jews in Contemporary Israel." *Sociology of Religion* 63, no. 4 (2002): 455–74.

————. "Playing with Sacred/Corporeal Identities: Yeshiva Students' Fantasies of Military Participation." *Jewish Social Studies* 13, no. 2 (2007): 155–78.

————. *A Well-Worn Tallis for a New Ceremony: Trends in Israeli Haredi Culture.* Boston: Academic Studies Press, 2012.

————. *Yeshiva Fundamentalism: Piety, Gender, and Resistance in the Ultra-Orthodox World.* New York: New York University Press, 2009.

Statistical Report on Ultra-Orthodox Society in Israel. Abstract. Jerusalem Institute for Israel Studies, Israel Democracy Institute, 2016.

Steinberg, Avraham. *Encyclopedia of Jewish Medical Ethics.* Vol. 1. Jerusalem: Feldheim, 1998.

Steinbock, Bonnie. "Disability, Prenatal Testing, and Selective Abortion." In *Prenatal Testing and Disability Rights,* edited by Eric Parens and Adrienne Asch, 108–23. Washington, DC: Georgetown University Press, 2000.

Steinfeld, Rebecca. "Wars of the Wombs: Struggles over Abortion Policies in Israel." *Israel Studies* 20, no. 2 (2015): 1–26.

Stoler-Liss, Sachlav. "'Mothers Birth the Nation': The Social Construction of Zionist Motherhood in Wartime in Israeli Parents' Manuals." *Nashim: A Journal of Jewish Women's Studies and Gender Issues* 6 (2003): 104–18.

Strathern, Marilyn. "Displacing Knowledge: Technology and the Consequences for Kinship." In *Conceiving the New World Order: The Global Politics of Reproduction,* edited by Faye D. Ginsburg and Rayna Rapp, 346–63. Berkeley: University of California Press, 1995.

Tappan, Robert. "More Than Fatwas: Ethical Decision Making in Iranian Fertility Clinics." In *Islam and Assisted Reproductive Technologies: Sunni and Shia Perspectives,* edited by Marcia C. Inhorn and Soraya Tremayne, 103–29. New York: Berghan Books, 2012.

Taragin-Zeller, Lea. "Between Modesty and Beauty: Reinterpreting Female Piety in the Israeli Haredi Community." In *Love, Marriage, and Jewish Families Today: Paradoxes of the Gender Revolution,* edited by Sylvia Fishman Barack, 308–26. Waltham: Brandeis University Press, 2015.

———. "'Conceiving God's Children': Toward a Flexible Model of Reproductive Decision-Making." *Medical Anthropology: Cross Cultural Studies in Health and Illness* 38, no. 4 (2019): 370–83.

———. "Have Six, Have Seven, Have Eight Children: Daily Interactions between Rabbinic Authority and Free Will." [Hebrew.] *Judaism, Sovereignty, and Human Rights* 3 (2017): 113–38.

———. "Towards an Anthropology of Doubt: The Case of Religious Reproduction in Orthodox Judaism." *Modern Jewish Studies* 18, no. 1 (2019): 1–20.

Tavory, Iddo. *Summoned: Identification and Religious Life in a Jewish Neighborhood.* Chicago: University of Chicago Press, 2016.

Taylor-Guthartz, Lindsey. "Overlapping Worlds: The Religious Lives of Orthodox Jewish Women in London." PhD thesis, University College London, 2016.

Teman, Elly. *Birthing a Mother: The Surrogate Body and the Pregnant Self.* Berkeley: University of California Press, 2010.

Teman, Elly, and Tsipy Ivry. "Pregnancy as a Way of Life among Ultra-Orthodox Jewish Women." Paper presented at the Eighty-First Annual Meeting of the Eastern Sociological Society, February 24–27, 2011, in Philadelphia, Pennsylvania.

Thompson, Charis. *Making Parents: The Ontological Choreography of Reproductive Technologies.* Cambridge: Massachusetts Institute of Technology Press, 2005.

Toverdovitch, Bracha. "Towards Spiritual Motherhood." [Hebrew.] In *Hachana Ruchanit L'Leida,* edited by Moshe and Dafna Hasdai, 36–42. N.p.: n.p.

Traina, Christina, Eugenia Georges, Marcia C. Inhorn, Susan Martha Kahn, and Maura A. Ryan. "Compatible Contradictions: Religion and the Naturalization of Assisted Reproduction." In *Altering Nature,* vol. 2, *Religion, Biotechnology, and Public Policy, Philosophy and Medicine,* edited by Andrew Lustig, Baruch A. Brody and Gerald P. McKenny, 15–85. Dordrecht: Springer, 2008.

Tsarfaty, Orly, and Dotan Blais. "Between 'Cultural Enclave' and 'Virtual Enclave': Ultra-Orthodox Society and the Digital Media." [Hebrew.] *Kesher* 32 (2002): 47–55.

Tylor, Edward B. "On a Method of Investigating the Development of Institutions: Applied to Laws of Marriage and Descent." *Journal of the Anthropological Institute of Great Britain and Ireland* 18 (1889): 245–72.

Washofsky, Mark. "On the Absence of Method in Jewish Bioethics: Rabbi Yehezkel Landau on Autopsy." *Jewish Law Association Studies,* 17 (2007): 254–78.

Wasserfall, Rahel, ed. *Women and Water: Menstruation in Jewish Life and Law.* Waltham, MA: Brandeis University Press, 2015.

Weiler-Polak, Dana. "Report: One in Four Israelis Live Under Poverty Line." *Haaretz,* November 9, 2010. http://www.haaretz.com/print-edition/news /report-one-in-four-israelis-live-under-poverty-line-1.323692.

Weingarten, Michael, and Eliezer Kitai. "Consultations with Rabbis." *Journal of Religion and Health* 34, no. 2 (1995): 135–40.

Weinreb, Alex, Dov Chernichovsky, and Aviv Brill. "Israel's Exceptional Fertility." In *State of the Nation Report 2018.* Jerusalem: Taub Center for Israel Studies, December 2018.

Weir, Allison. "Feminism and the Islamic Revival: Freedom as a Practice of Belonging." *Hypatia* 28, no. 2 (2013): 323–40.

Weiss, Meira. *The Chosen Body: The Politics of the Body in Israeli Society.* Stanford: Stanford University Press, 2002.

———. *Conditional Love: Parents' Attitudes toward Handicapped Children.* Westport, CT: Bergin and Garvey, 1994.

Weiss, Shayna. "A Beach of Their Own: The Creation of the Gender-Segregated Beach in Tel Aviv." *Journal of Israeli History* 35, no. 1 (2016): 1–18.

Weissler, Chava. *Voices of the Matriarchs: Listening to the Prayers of Early Modern Jewish Women.* Boston: Beacon Press, 1998.

Weissman, Deborah. "Bais Yaakov as an Innovation in Jewish Women's Education: A Contribution to the Study of Education and Social Change." *Studies in Jewish Education* 7 (1995): 278–99.

Wenger, Etienne. "Toward a Theory of Cultural Transparency: Elements of a Social Discourse of the Visible and Invisible." PhD diss., University of California, Irvine, 1990.

Yafeh, Orit. "The Time in the Body: Cultural Construction of Femininity in Ultraorthodox Kindergartens for Girls." *Ethos* 35, no. 4 (2007): 516–53.

Yaffe, Nechumi Malovicki, Nevin Solak, Eran Halperin, and Tamar Saguy. "'Poor Is Pious': Distinctiveness Threat Increases Glorification of Poverty among the Poor." *European Journal of Social Psychology* 48, no. 4 (2018): 460–71.

Yishai, Yael. "Abortion in Israel: Social Demand and Political Responses." In *Women in Israel: Studies of Israeli Society*, vol. 6, edited by Yael Azmon and Dafna N. Israeli, 287–308. New Brunswick: Transaction Publishers, 1993.

Young, Iris. *On Female Body Experience: "Throwing Like a Girl" and Other Essays.* Oxford: Oxford University Press, 2005.

———. "Pregnant Embodiment: Subjectivity and Alienation." *Journal of Medicine and Philosophy* 9, no. 1 (1984): 45–62.

Yuval-Davis, Nira. "National Reproduction and 'the Demographic Race' in Israel." In *Woman, Nation, State*, edited by Nira Yuval-Davis and Floya Anthias, 92–109. London: Macmillan, 1989.

Zikmund, Barbara, Adair Lummis and Patricia Mei Yin Chang. *Clergy Women: An Uphill Calling.* Louisville, KY: Westminster John Knox Press, 1998.

Ziv, Hadas. "A Cognitive Dissonant Health System: Can we Combat Racism without Admitting It Exists?" In *Bioethics and Biopolitics in Israel: Socio-Legal, Political, and Empirical Analysis*, edited by Hagai Boas, Yael Hashiloni-Dolev, Nadav Davidovitch, Dani Filc, and Shai J. Lavi, 76–96. Cambridge: Cambridge University Press, 2018.

Zoloth, Laurie. "Reading Like a Girl: Gender and Text in Jewish Bioethics." *Judaism* 48, no. 2 (1999): 165–74.

Zrahiya, Zvi. "More Than Half of Israel's Ultra-Orthodox Living in Poverty." *Haaretz*, November 7, 2010. http://www.haaretz.com/themarker/more-than -half-of-israel-s-ultra-orthodox-living-in-poverty-1.323309.

Zu'bi, Himmat. "Palestinian Fertility in the Israeli Sphere: Palestinian Women in Israel Undergoing IVF Treatments." In *Bioethics and Biopolitics in Israel: Socio-Legal, Political, and Empirical Analysis*, edited by Hagai Boas, Yael Hashiloni-Dolev, Nadav Davidovitch, Dani Filc, and Shai J. Lavi, 160–179. Cambridge: Cambridge University Press, 2018.

Zussman, Robert. "The Contribution of Sociology to Medical Ethics." *Hastings Center Report* 30, no. 1 (January/February 2000): 7–11.

INDEX

ability (*yecholet*), 11

abortion, 3, 5; antiabortion organizations in Israel (*see* Bead Chaim; EFRAT; Nefesh Achat b'Yisrael); in British Palestine, 6; and fetal abnormality, 3, 145–48, 150–56, 160, 169; financial difficulty, 33, 146–50, 153–63, 168–70; and *halakhic* law (see *halakha*); illegal abortions, 151; in Israel, 24, 150–52, 150n7, 152n13; and maternal health, 146, 151–53, 155, 160, 169; and prenatal testing, 130, 139, 176–77; rabbinic permission for, 147–50, 155, 166–67, 169; as sensitive topic among Haredi women, 145; and Zionism, 6

achot bodeket (nurse who checks), 60–61

Arabs, Israeli, 6

Ark of the Covenant, 117

ART (assisted reproductive technologies), 6–8, 28

askanim (male rabbinic assistants), 51–52

Association for the Encouragement of the Increase in the Birth Rate among the Jewish People, 153

Auerbach, Shmuel (Rabbi), 63

authority (*samchut*), 11

ba'alot tshuvah (those who have "returned" to Judaism), 26n106

Bead Chaim, 24n104, 154

Beit Yaakov, 97–98

Ben Gurion, David, 6

Bikur Cholim, 42, 56–57, 66, 81, 104

bioethics: and ethnography, 182; Islamic, 8–9; Israeli, 19, 66–67; Jewish, 4–5, 16, 18, 20, 67; rabbinic interpretive sources of, 5; sacred textual sources of, 5

biological reproduction (and Haredi women): as constant, 5; as defining feature of life, 1; enabling a future for Haredim, 75–76, 84, 90, 178; as way of life, 4; as a woman's duty, 10, 111

Bishvilaych, 61, 63, 66

bitachon (faith), 33, 85, 126–29, 132–41, 178

body. *See* embodied authority; female body

British Palestine, 6

B'Shaah Tovah: Madrich Refui Hilchati Lherayon v'Leida, 77, 80–86, 88

caesarean section (c-section): desire to avoid, 72, 93–94, 135–36; medically recommended, 42, 60; planned, 2, 137

challah, 59

chevel leida (the rope of birth), 120

chevlei mashiach (birth pangs of the Messiah), 120

chevrusa (learning in pairs), 74

childbirth: classes (*see* prenatal classes); as couvade, 73n3; c-section (*see* caesarian section); and doulas (*see* doulas); God's involvement in, 133–35, 137–38; *halakhic* sources (see *halakha*); home birth, 134–35; labor, 21, 72–73, 82–83, 86–87, 123; as